An Overview Series Publication

Embedded Programming for the 80x51

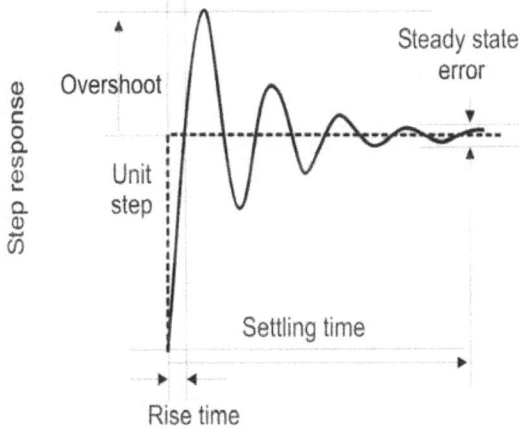

```
# include <reg51.h>
# include <stdio.h>
void main(void)
{
int x,y,z; //declare variables
z = x % y;   /* simple modulo (remainder) */
z = 12*x + y/2 - x*y*2/(x*z + y*2);
z = z/4+13*(x + y)/3 - x*y + 2*x*x;
x = y = z = 50;   /* multiple assignment
```

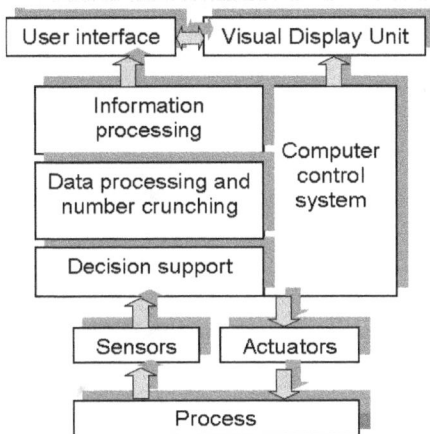

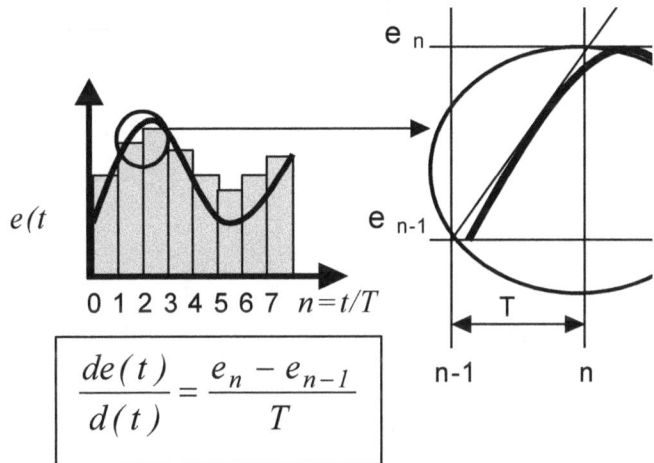

$$\frac{de(t)}{d(t)} = \frac{e_n - e_{n-1}}{T}$$

Dr. Goran I Bezanov PhD

published by MIG Consulting Ltd

This page is intentionally left blank

EMBEDDED PROGRAMMING

FOR THE 80x51

AN OVERVIEW SERIES PUBLICATION

By Goran Bezanov PhD

MIG Consulting Ltd

31 Vicarage Road, London SW14 8RZ

British Library Cataloguing in Publication Data

A catalogue record for this book is available from the British Library

International Standard Book Number: 978-0-9558153-1-7

To my Sons
Ognen and Milos

This page is intentionally left blank

PREFACE

This text provides an overview of embedded systems with particular emphasis on C programming for the 80x51 family of microcontrollers (MCUs). My aim was to write a textbook that can be read and understood by readers who are not very familiar with digital control systems. It was my intention that, from this text, they could gain sufficient understanding in order to know where to look for further direction. The scope of this text is to present embedded systems according to the diagram shown in Figure 1.

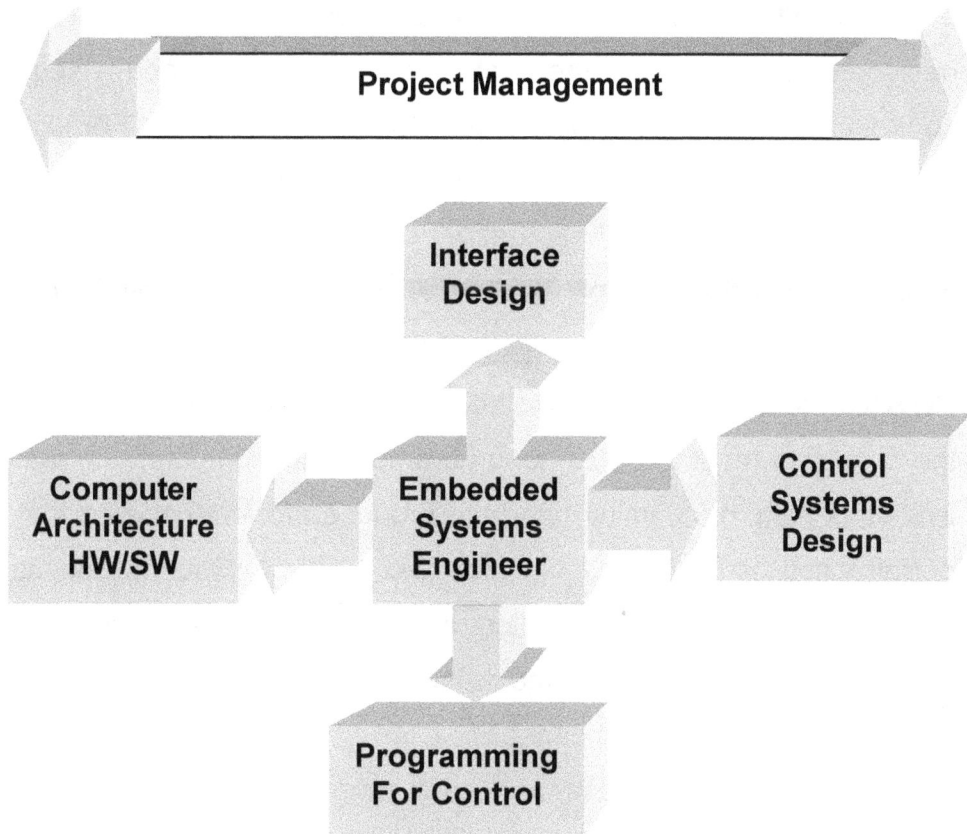

Figure 1. Context diagram

Here the embedded systems engineer needs to become familiar with four, relatively distinct engineering disciplines namely,

- **The controller hardware and software architecture:** The engineer must know how the internal ports and interfaces are configured and how they can be interfaced. At the same time the engineer must be familiar with the programming model of the device. How are the internal registers arranged? What programming languages can be used? How the special functions such as interrupt, timers, ports, etc, can be programmed?

- **Interfacing**: In many embedded applications a physical interface is required between the computer controller and the outside world. An engineer must become familiar with the physical requirements of any interface. Many electronic devices exist that provide standard interfaces to computers, but there are times where the engineer may need to complement these by introducing additional circuits.

- **Digital control**: In an embedded computer control system the engineer must understand the principle of operation of the controller that is being designed. In some cases the controller will be simple, and a sequence control algorithm can be implemented efficiently and simply. For example, a controller to implement the sequence of operations of a microwave could be produced relatively easily. On the other hand, a computer control system that controls the behaviour of a robotic mechanism will require extensive control analysis and design to ensure correct operation.

- **Programme design**: In order to be able to implement a control algorithm the engineer must be able to programme the computer. In real-time systems, this programming needs to produce efficient code so that time performance is optimised. In complex control systems, concurrent processes need to be controlled and so the software must support multitasking, multithreading and is some cases the hardware will also include parallel processing capabilities.

Thus it is seen that the embedded systems engineer needs to have a variety of skills, not to mention project management skills that are needed in all systems analysis and development work.

The aim of this text is to prepare the reader to work in the embedded systems area. The topics covered in this text are along the lines presented in the context diagram of Figure 1. The first chapter introduces the general application areas of embedded computer control systems in order to make the reader aware of the scope.

Chapter 2 deals with the general microprocessor architecture as well as the architecture of the 8051 microcontroller. This controller has been selected as a suitable device for many real-time and embedded applications.

Chapter 3 introduces a typical software development environment. The KEIL Integrated Development Environment (IDE) supports many processors, including the 8051 and it was selected as an example development system. A relatively dated version of this software is described in Chapter 3, but the principles of use and configuration of the IDE should be readily adaptable to newer versions of the software.

Chapters 4 and 5 deal with programming. Chapter 4 introduces assembly programming for the 8051 and Chapter 5 deals with C programming. Both chapters include exercises that can be implemented within the KEIL IDE without needing any additional software or hardware. The KEIL IDE provides a debug feature that allows the software to be debugged during run-time and it also provides access to all the peripherals such as Input/Output (I/O) ports, registers memory etc. This means that complete solutions can be simulated before being programmed into the system PROM.

Chapters 6 and 7 deal with control in discrete time domain. Chapter 6 introduces discrete modelling and also discusses how the process and the controller combine to complete a control system. Closed-loop or feedback control is also introduced here and a closed-loop transfer function in discrete form is derived. Models of controller and the process are done using difference equations and only the very simplest first order systems are considered. The aim is to show how discrete models can be used to describe control systems.

Chapter 7 introduces the basic concept of computer control and provides an example of the three-term (PID) controller in discrete form. Within these two chapters, as far as possible, I avoid methods of frequency domain analysis because these are very broad and their treatment is beyond the scope of this text.

In chapter 8, I provide a brief treatment of interfacing and cover some common devices such as DAC and ADCs. Chapter 9 briefly covers transducers and provides a few examples of the products available.

Overall this text is aimed to give an overview rather than provide detailed analysis of the subject matter and for this reason it is published as an Overview Series Publication. This is my first draft and I shall revise and correct the errors in the next.

Suggestions are welcome to: mig@consultant.com.

Thank you

Goran Bezanov (February 2010, London)

CONTENTS

CHAPTER 1 EMBEDDED AND REAL-TIME SYSTEMS

1.1. Introduction

The term embedded is very intuitive when applied to computer systems. It generally refers to a computer system, which is incorporated within another, main system so that it can perform a dedicated task or service for that system. As a direct result of this, many embedded systems have timing constraints that they must meet in order for the main system to have the required service. For this reason, many embedded systems are also considered to be real-time systems.

A feature of an embedded system or application is that it does not need to be visible to the end user. It may be hardware or software system or indeed a combination of the two, but as far as the main system is concerned, the embedded part simply provides a service. Another feature is that when an upgrade is required, it is not necessary to replace the main system, and it may be possible to perform the upgrade by simply replacing the embedded component. Figure 1.1 shows how the embedded system software and hardware interacts with the main system. In a very general sense, the embedded part will have a set of inputs and outputs.

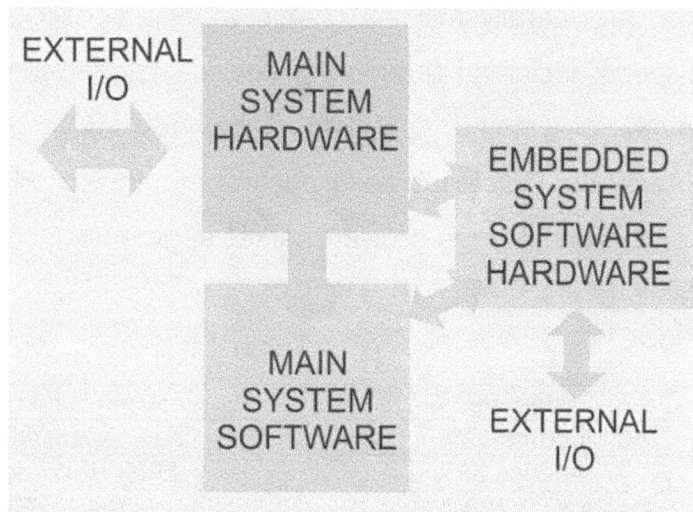

EXTERNAL I/O   MAIN SYSTEM HARDWARE   EMBEDDED SYSTEM SOFTWARE HARDWARE

MAIN SYSTEM SOFTWARE   EXTERNAL I/O

Figure 1.1 General components of an embedded system

Many, if not all of these will be related to the main system, which the embedded system is designed to support. However, the embedded system can also have direct external input/output (I/O). Generally, real-time and embedded systems operate in constrained environments in which computer memory and processing power are limited. Additionally, they need to provide services within strict time constraints. It is these memory, speed and timing constraints that dictate the use of real-time operating systems in embedded software. Much of modern equipment used in our daily life, relies on an embedded processing unit to control its operation. Applications vary in complexity and some examples include the following,

- Robotics and flexible manufacture systems (FMS), military, and space exploration equipment.
- Controllers for operating household appliances such as microwave ovens, dish washers, washing machines.
- Vehicle control systems, electronic control unit (ECU), trip computer.
- Electric motor-generator controllers.
- Mobile communication equipment.
- Computer systems for: Data processing, Networks management, Digital signal processing (DSP), Printing etc.

There are literally millions of microcontroller (MCU) based products around the world, including broadband devices, digital cameras, Digital TVs and entertainment systems, DVD recordable devices, digital set-top boxes, network routers from Cisco and laser printers etc. In fact, MCUs are used in a number of high-volume, high-growth market segments. [1] Some of these are shown in Table 1.0.

Table 1.0

Cable Modems 95%	Internet Backbone 40%
DSL Modems 52%	VoIP Applications 72%
WLAN Access 55%	DVD Recorders 70%
Cable STB 76%	Satellite STB 30%
Digital TV 59%	Colour Laser Printer 62%
Commercial Colour Copiers 73%	

1.2. General characteristics of embedded systems

As mentioned earlier, embedded systems are concerned with performing a specific service. These are typically, well-defined tasks such as for example the processing of sensor signals and converting these to a manageable format (input task). Having read the inputs, usually it is required to perform some calculations on these (process task). The output of the process will generally result is some action by the actuators (output task). This is seen in Figure 1.2 where sensors and actuators are shown in relation to the input, output and process tasks.

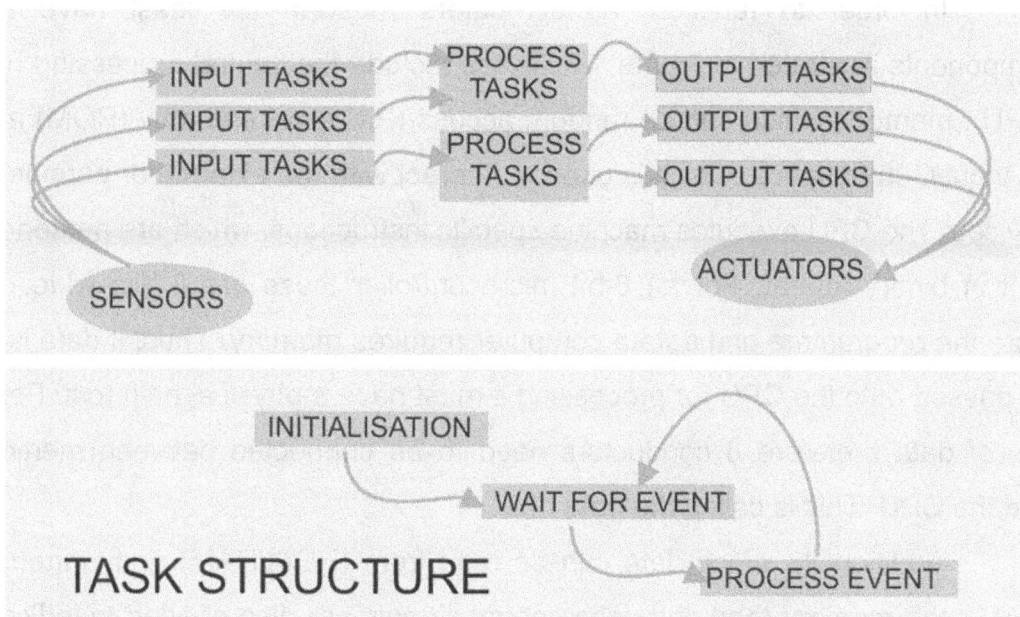

Figure 1.2. Task structure in embedded systems

Each of the tasks is made up of a number of stages. It begins with initialisation, which is really a set-up phase, and following this, it will enter a wait loop where it will wait for an event to occur that will trigger a process. There are many variants of embedded applications but the general characteristics of embedded systems can be described as follows,

- End user does not interact with the system as a computer but as a tool. In other words, the user does not need to know the details of the embedded system.

- Often SELF CONTAINED needing only an ON /OFF switch

- Typically DEDICATED to particular tasks within another system. i.e. ONLY perform the functions they are designed for.
- Almost ALWAYS operate WITH REAL-TIME CONSTRAINTS, i.e. they must meet deadlines and are therefore often classified as real-time systems (RTS).

In order to perform these tasks a microcontroller is equipped with hardware and software components. We generally describe this using the term architecture.

1.3.   Computer hardware architecture

In order to function, all computers must in the least have the components illustrated in Figure 1.3. These include the central processing unit (CPU), memory, which can be random access (RAM) or read only (ROM) and an Input/Output space, which is used to interact with the external or peripheral devices. The CPU executes machine specific instructions, which are presented to it in binary format. For an 8-bit microcontroller these are 8 bits wide. To store the programme and data a computer requires memory. Thus, if data is to be passed onto the CPU for processing it must have a physical path to it. For 8 bits of data therefore 8 conductors need to be connected between memory and the CPU. This is called the data bus.

Additionally, since data can be read from (ROM/RAM) and written to (RAM), the memory read and write control signals are also needed to indicate the direction of data flow. These signals form the basis of a control bus. A control bus is therefore used by the CPUs for communicating with other devices. The address bus is used to identify which device the CPU is communicating with and the data bus provides the actual data. The CPU and the device that it needs to access use the control bus to send commands from the CPU and return status signals from these devices. Thus as indicated in Figure 1.3, if for example the data is being read or written to the device the appropriate line (read or write) will be active (logic 0) or inactive (logic 1) as the case may be.

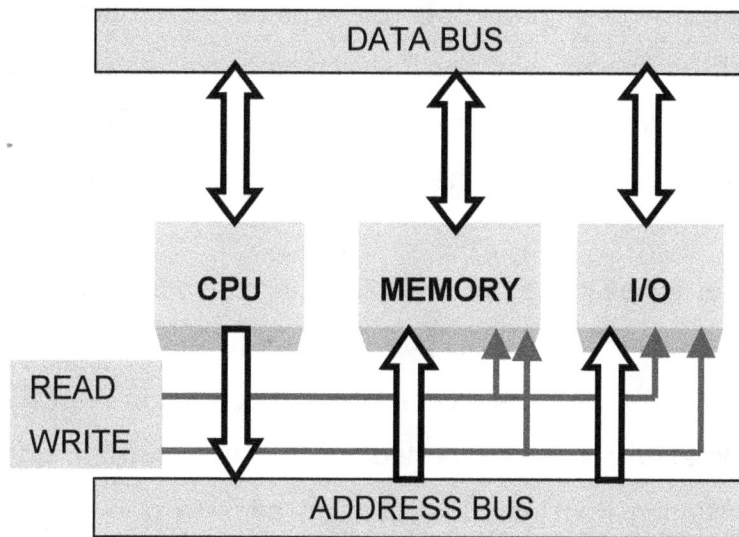

Figure 1.3. Typical computer architecture

In order to interact with the outside world the computer uses Input/Output (I/O) ports. These ports also need to be connected to the data bus. Now that two separate devices are seen to communicate with the CPU we must ensure that we do not confuse them. For this reason an address bus is included which enables every device to be given a unique address. Thus, by examining the value present on the address bus at the time of access. The CPU will determine which chip to access. More information about memory/IO read and write cycles can be obtained by referring to data sheets for a specific microprocessor, which include the relevant timing waveforms.

1.4. CISC and RISC Processors

The first computers that came into general use had very simple set of instructions including, add, subtract, increment, decrement, shift left and right etc. (i.e. Intel 8080). Later version such as the Intel 8088 had more instructions that could multiply, divide, decimal adjust etc. As the instruction set became more complex these computers became known as CISC (Complex Instruction Set Computers) and these were the first type of personal computers (PCs). Every CISC instruction given to the computer was decoded by the control unit and executed by the CPU.

At some stage in development, computer designers considered the idea of reducing the instruction set to a set of primitives and arranging a number of these to work in parallel. These were called Reduced Instruction Set Computers (RISC). In this way the instructions were made simple and they executed quickly. Provided that a large number of CPUs were available to execute instructions in parallel the result would provide fast computational speeds.

Consider for example the multiplication of two integers. i.e. $5 \times 4 = 20$. Assume that the instruction to ADD two numbers takes 10 CPU clock cycles to execute. If the multiplication instruction is not supported in the CPU instruction set, any multiplication can be performed by repetitive addition. For example to multiply 5×4 starting from result=0, perform addition of 5 to the result, four times. Each addition takes 10 clocks and so after four of these the time taken to execute the sum is 40 clocks. This is shown in Table 1.1.

Table 1.1

Clocks	0	10	10	10	10
Instruction	-	ADD 5	ADD 5	ADD 5	ADD 5
Result	0	5	10	15	20

Thus, ignoring any time lost to for example, jumps in a software loop, the multiplication takes 40 clock cycles to complete. If on the other hand four separate processors were used in parallel to execute the same arithmetic, then each would perform the addition in 10 clocks. Consequently, and assuming that data dependencies are neglected the multiplication instruction could complete in approximately 10 clock cycles, which is four times faster. (See Figure 1.4).

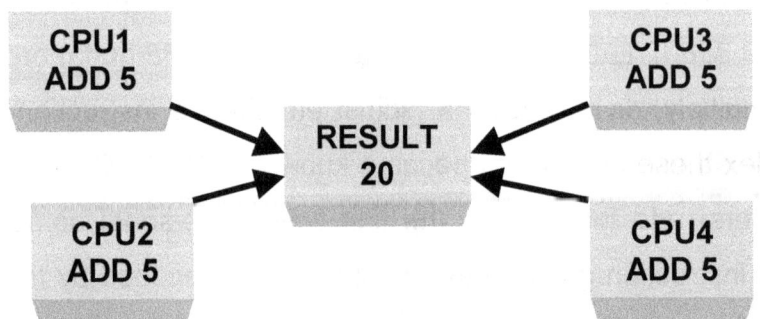

Figure 1.4. RISC execution by parallel processors

Embedded CISC

Perhaps the most common microcontroller on the market today is some variant of the Intel 8051. This is Harvard architecture, single chip microcontroller that was first introduced by Intel in 1980 for use in embedded systems. The Harvard architecture uses separate memory buses for instructions and data, allowing accesses to take place concurrently. Therefore, where Harvard architecture is used, instruction words for the processor may be a different bit size than the length of internal memory and registers; for example, 12-bit instructions used with 8-bit data registers.

At the time of writing a vast range of enhanced devices are available with 8051-compatible processor cores that are manufactured by a variety of independent manufacturers including Atmel, Infineon Technologies, Maxim Integrated Products (via its Dallas Semiconductor subsidiary), NXP (formerly Philips Semiconductor), Winbond, ST Microelectronics, Silicon Laboratories (formerly Cygnal), Texas Instruments and Cypress Semiconductor. Intel's official designation for the 8051 family of microcontrollers is MCS 51. [2]

It must be said that as far as applications are concerned there is no contest between the microcontroller and the microprocessor. In fact the two have very different areas of application, which rarely overlap.

Consider for example a relatively complex embedded systems, such as the landing gear control system on an aircraft, it is very likely that an 8-bit microcontroller will not be able to cope with the processing requirement and that consequently an embedded system which is based on a microprocessor will need to be designed.

Embedded RISC

As computers evolved, changes were in the favour of RISC. These included the following improvements,

- Caches to speed instruction fetches.
- Large increases in RAM memory chips and price reduction.
- Advanced optimising compilers.
- Improvements in power consumption

These are briefly explained next.

Cache RAM: Cache memory is RAM that a CPU can access more quickly than it can access regular RAM because it is located in the vicinity of the CPU and it also uses a high-speed data bus. As the CPU executes instructions, it searches through the cache memory first and if it finds the data, (from a previous reading of data), it does not have to do the more time-consuming reading of data from larger memory or secondary storage.

Cache memory is categorised according to the levels of accessibility to the CPU. A level one (L1) or primary cache is the closest to the CPU and in fact it is on the same chip as the microprocessor. For example, the PowerPC 601 processor has a 32-kilobyte level-1 cache built into its chip. [3] Note that this size of memory is considerably smaller than the typical size of a conventional RAM chip. The reason for this is the limited space that is available on the CPU chip. To help improve performance a secondary, level-two cache (L2) is usually added to work in conjunction with the L1 cache. This is a separate static RAM (SRAM) chip that works in conjunction with L1 cache. L2 Cache on computers can range from 64KB to 2MB in size. Some new processors are including L2 cache in the CPU architecture and in this case they provide a Level 3 (L3) cache, which is external to the CPU.

Main RAM: The main RAM is usually a dynamic RAM (DRAM) chip, which is cheaper and slower than SRAM. The pace of computer technology has resulted in cheaper production methods, falling component prices and increasing demand for RAM. Advanced RAM architectures have also increased the speed of RAM. For example, the Rambus XDR™ is new memory architecture and the manufacturer's claim that it achieves an order of magnitude performance improvement over today's standard memories. [4]

Optimising compliers: Recent trends in embedded applications have resorted to using RISC technology. The major concern with RISC is that in order to benefit from the technology, optimising compilers are required to maintain optimal instruction processing. Optimisation is a process of finding the most efficient way of executing a programme. Either by finding the quickest execution speed, or sometimes, optimising memory usage or other characteristics of a programme. [5] Example optimising options include the following,

Optimise the common cases: By identifying the common cases in code execution it is possible to identify unique properties that allow a fast path to be taken rather than the slow path. If the fast path is taken most often, then the result is an improvement in overall performance.

Avoid redundancy in computation: There are many instances where computational tasks are repeated. In these cases it may be possible to store results that are already computed and reuse them later, and so improving execution efficiency.

Less code: Reducing the number of active results stored during computation such as intermediate values implies less work for the CPU, cache, and memory is usually faster.

Code design: Writing code with fewer jumps offers more streamlined execution. Jumps are known to interfere with the pre-fetching of instructions, thus slowing down code.

Locality: Code and data that are accessed closely together in time should be placed close together in memory to increase spatial locality of reference.

Exploit the memory hierarchy: Accesses to memory are increasingly more expensive for each level of the memory hierarchy, so place the most commonly used items in registers first, then caches, then main memory, before going to disk.

Instruction parallelism: While designing the programme where possible the programmer should reorder operations to allow multiple computations to happen in parallel, either at the instruction, memory, or thread level. This is more easily done in object oriented programming languages where global control of threads is possible. In assembly programming threads can only be reasonably programmed in simple applications. For multithreading in larger systems, the programmer will find it difficult to organise thread execution and a programme development system that can do this is required.

Power consumption: Energy Consumption is becoming a critical concern that directly affects the mobility and lifetime of mobile and embedded systems. There are many embedded applications in which the processor idle time can be considerable. By monitoring activity it is possible to design power down features that will send the device into the low power consumption states during idle time, without significantly affecting overall performance of the device. For example, a study at HP has shown that by applying two techniques, the first a low power mode, and the other a full shut down mode, during idle times lasting 60 seconds, a 25% energy savings were achieved by running the system the low power mode while the savings reached 89% when the card was shutdown for the same duration. [6]

Other examples of power management chips include the Aurora PDA family of processors. [7] These processors use RISC technology with very low power consumption that feature an interconnection system that allows the board to be used either in a cable-less system, or as a standalone processor with conventional wiring. Another offering comes from Advantech who provide system-on-chip solutions as a highly integrated system design with superior performance and low power consumption. These include the ARM-based RISC system on modules (SOM), RISC single board computers, smart home control panels and Adam web I/O modules. [8]

A very interesting example of a complex embedded system for multimedia application is given in an IEEE publication [9] Here the authors report that they have developed a *200MHz* embedded RISC processor for multimedia applications. This processor has a dual super-scalar data path that consists of a 32-bit integer unit and a 64-bit single-instruction-multiple-data (SIMD) function unit. In this context super-scalar refers to a CPU architecture that supports parallelism. This processor also includes an on-chip concurrent Rambus DRAM controller that uses interleaved transactions to increase the memory bandwidth of the Rambus channel to 533 Mb/s. Transaction interleaving and instruction pre-fetching also reduces latency. A 64-bit, *200MHz* internal bus is used to transfer data between the CPU core, memory and the peripherals.

This level of performance is an example of using the best processor and bus technologies to put together a bespoke system to provide a specific function for a dedicated embedded application.

1.5. Types of operating systems

All computer systems are made up of digital hardware and use software to programme the way that the hardware behaves. Some computer systems are very simple and the programs that run on these are relatively straightforward input/output routines. On the other hand very sophisticated embedded processors are designed for high performance computing applications. For example, Intel blade-servers are used to deliver time-critical solutions in network IP packet processing. [10]

Therefore it can be said that in the area of embedded systems the operating system may range in complexity from the very simple to the very sophisticated. In a general sense, there are many types of operating systems, but the most common types can be classified into a number of categories.

- **Multi-user**- allows two or more users to run programs at the same time. Some operating systems permit hundreds or even thousands of concurrent users. (i.e. Linux, Windows, z/OS, Solaris).

- **Multiprocessing**- Supports the running of programs on more than one CPU. (i.e. Linux, Windows).

- **Multitasking**- allows more than one programme to run concurrently (at the same time) (i.e. Linux, Windows).

- **Multithreading**- allows different parts of a single programme to run concurrently. (i.e. Linux, Windows).

- **Network**- A network operating system performs the functions of a multi-user, multiprocessing and multitasking operating systems and additionally, implements protocol stacks as well as device drivers for networking hardware.

- **Real time** Responds to input within a specific time, which is determined by the so-called real-time constraints. (i.e. iRMX, INtime). Real-time kernel looks after task scheduling and other services.

1.6. Real-time Operating Systems (RTOS)

Many embedded systems are also time constrained and consequently these applications tend to fall into the real-time systems category. In the context of embedded computer applications real-time does not mean as fast as possible, instead it means that it operates in a timely fashion so that it can interact with its operating environment which demands a known, consistent, reliable and repeatable, timing performance. The distinctive feature of a RTOS is that it is typically implemented as a kernel. The kernel being a layer of abstraction between the hardware layer and the applications layer where the tasks are running.

The kernel in this context provides the services for the applications requiring access to hardware and also acts in such a way as to hide the activities between the two layers. While it is possible to implement an embedded programme without using a real-time kernel, a well established, proven kernel can save on development time. There are a large number of RTOS kernels on the market, and in general they all act as an interface between the application software and the system hardware. At the same time a RTOS kernel provides several categories of services to application software. These include: task management, dynamic memory allocation, and basic timer services.

The main distinction between a real-time O/S and a general purpose O/S is that their respective approach to timing for internal operations. In RTOS, the kernel timing is rigidly controlled. In this way, the operating system services consume established amounts of time. For example, in RTOS the expression of a timing constraint is as simple as: T *(display _value)* = *constant*. Thus, whatever the effects of other functions within the multitasking RTOS, the time to display a value will be constant. For this to happen the kernel in a RTOS has to be designed to cope with these constraints. The basic functional components of a RTOS kernel are shown in Figure 1.5. Here the central function is task management. In simple terms a task is an instance of execution of a programme, and when many tasks are running at the same time, that is to say concurrently, they have to be managed in such a way that they do not adversely affect each other.

Figure 1.5 shows that the central job of the RTOS kernel is task management. In a multi-tasking environment, more than one task ere executing and these may require access to resources such as memory and I/O. The task management must ensure that these resources are available. Common problems such as deadlock and mutual exclusion need to be prevented in the kernel. At the same time, a RTOS kernel must enforce timing constraints, for this reason timing control is essential and a timer strictly controls each kernel service. Synchronisation between tasks is also required, and quite often adjustment for communication delays need to be accounted for and compensated [11].

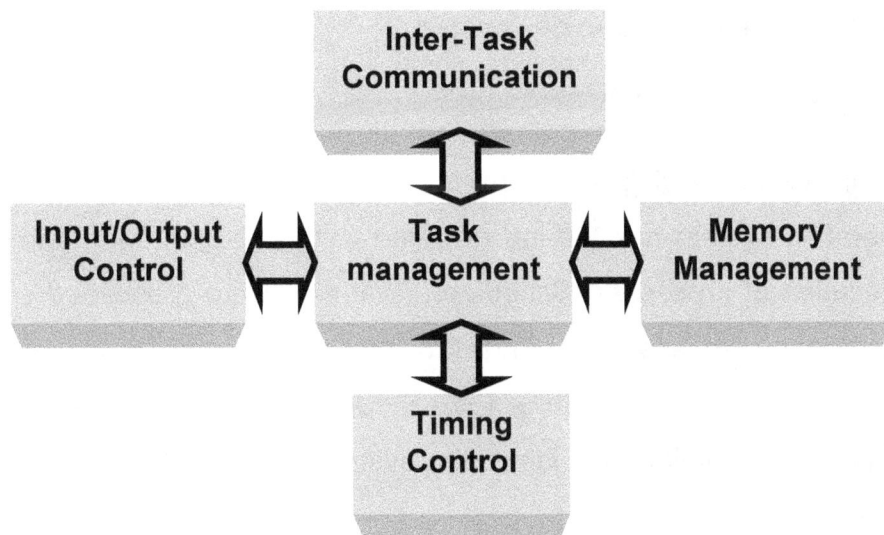

Figure 1.5 RTOS Kernel functions

Scheduling the execution of tasks is one of the major functions of any multi-tasking O/S, but in RTOS this is job is complicated by the real-time constraints. For this reason RTOS could never replace a general-purpose multitasking O/S and vice-versa. This is because the performance of a RTOS is geared towards satisfying the timing constraints, and this comes at the expense of flexibility that is offered by the general purpose O/S. In small, embedded applications, the RTOS may not need to manage many tasks, and therefore the scheduling of tasks is quite straightforward. However, modern embedded systems can be very complex, and the RTOS is required to perform complicated allocation of CPU, memory and other resources. It is therefore prudent to consider some general principles of scheduling.

RTSs are also divided into soft RTS and hard RTS depending on how important the timing constraints are in the application. In hard RTSs the timing constraints must be adhered to at all cost. In the event that they are not, the system fails and can potentially cause a hazard. In soft RTSs, if any timing constraint is not met, then the system continues to function, but with a diminished performance. However the system does not fail and is not hazardous while in operations. The kernel is responsible for task management and the way that this is done is by issuing dedicated scheduling algorithms. Some general aspects of scheduling are discussed next and specific reference to real-time systems will also be covered.

1.7. Scheduling

In a multi-tasking environment, whether real-time or general purpose, the operating system has the job of determining the sequence and timing of the execution of processes. Schedulers that adhere to prescribed scheduling policies do this. Process scheduling is divided into three levels,

- **High-Level** (or long term or job scheduling)- Deals with decisions as to whether to admit a new job to the system. All jobs enter the system into the READY queue.
- **Medium-Level**- decides whether to temporarily remove a process from the system or to re-introduce the process (to balance processor loading).
- **Low-Level** (short-term or processor scheduling)- Decides which ready process to assign to the CPU.

In order to maintain consistency schedulers work according to a prescribed policy, such as for example (First Come First Serve (FCFS), Shortest Job First (SJF) etc). Time slicing is often applied with scheduling policies in order to allocate a prescribed period of time to a task. For example, in a time-slicing environment the kernel may interrupt each process after a few milliseconds to switch control to another process. Schedulers that work at different levels have different tasks, but in a general sense, the objectives of scheduling are as follows,

- Provide maximum process throughput.
- Allocate jobs to the processor according to a policy. This way the processes are treated consistently.
- During busy periods, in order to prevent CPU over-load, it should avoid further loading (e.g. inhibit any new job new users) or reduce level of service (i.e. response time).

Scheduling levels

In order to better describe the various levels of scheduling it is necessary to introduce the three state and five state process models. These models describe the states that a process can take during execution. The assumption here is that there is a single processor that executes all the tasks. In a multitasking environment, where more than one task is being processed by a single CPU, it follows that tasks need to be in different states of execution. The three state diagram identifies the three states that a process can have as ready, running and blocked. The five state models allow the blocked and ready states to be suspended, and therefore these are added to the basic three states.

Three state diagram

In a multitasking environment each of the many processes can be in one of three distinct states. These are the ready, blocked and running states as shown in Figure 1.6. A process traverses between these states under the control of schedulers. With reference to Figure 1.6, it is seen that a process enters the system via the High Level Scheduler (HLS) and enters the READY state. There may be a queue of processes in this state and in this case they are maintained in a linked list of their respective Process Control Blocks (PCB).

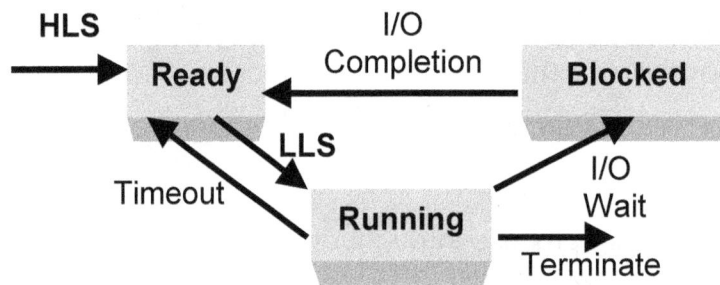

Figure 1.6 Three state Diagram

When the CPU is free to accept a process, it is the job of the Low Level Scheduler (LLS) to determine which of the processes that are in the READY queue, should be allocated to the CPU. The process that is in the running state can exit that state in one of three ways. Namely, it can terminate or the process can be timed out by the scheduler, in which case it is returned to the READY queue. It can also leave the running state if it enters an I/O wait and in this case the LLS sends the process into the BLOCKED state. If the process goes into a BLOCKED state then the LLS will place the next process in the READY queue into the RUNNING state. When the I/O wait for the BLOCKED process is complete, it is placed by the LLS into the READY state and its PCB joins the linked list queue.

Five state Diagram

The five-state model arises from the operations of the Medium Level Scheduler (MLS) where a process that is in READY or BLOCKED or RUNNING state can be SUSPENDED. This gives rise to two more states namely, the READY SUSPENDED and BLOCKED SUSPENDED states. This is shown in Figure 1.7. The reason to temporarily suspend a state can arise from a number of O/S related actions. For example, a Timer Interrupt would cause the CPU to suspend the currently executing process in order to pass control onto an interrupt service routine (ISR). When the ISR completes the process that was suspended can be resumed. However it has to be said that if the process was suspended form the running state, it cannot resume in that state and has to be returned to the READY queue. Therefore the transition from suspended state into running state is always through the ready state. This is because there is only one point of entry into the running state and this is from the ready queue. A more detailed description of the three levels of scheduling is given next.

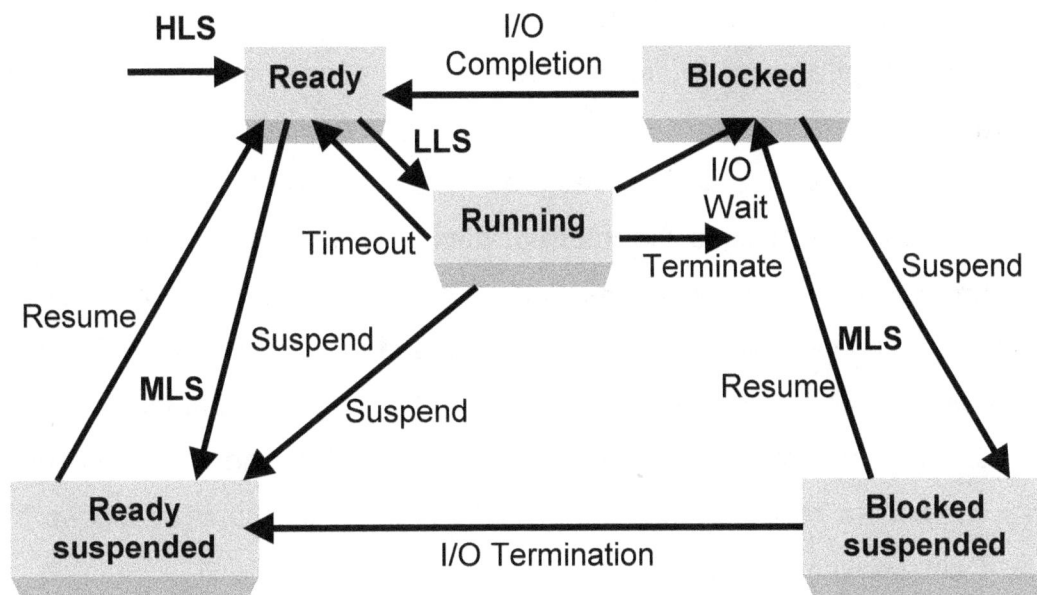

Figure 1.7 Five state Diagram

1.8. Scheduling policies

Scheduling policies are the rules according to which a decision is made as to whether a particular action is taken. In process terminology the actions refer to processes, and so can range from suspending, resuming, loading a process etc. These policies are therefore used to decide how to schedule the activities of the different tasks in a multitasking environment. Scheduling policies are divided in two major categories, namely pre-emptive and non-pre-emptive depending on whether the processes can be interrupted or not. Although the latter are more applicable to embedded and real-time systems, we will give a brief description of both categories.

Pre-emptive

In the pre-emptive scheme LLS may remove a process from the RUNNING state in order to allocate another process to the CPU. The cost of this in processing time is the added overhead of the context switching. Nevertheless, this may be justified in cases where a long process is in danger of monopolising the processor. Additionally, pre-emptive multitasking allows the computer system to more reliably guarantee each process a regular time-slice of CPU time. For this reason most RTOS kernels schedule tasks using a scheme called "priority-based pre-emptive scheduling." Here, each task is assigned a priority by the programmer, and while executing the task with a higher priority is allowed to pre-empt a task with a lower priority. Additionally, external I/O can also trigger a task to execute via an interrupt service routine (ISR). In this case the ISR is vectored to the interrupt and the hardware interrupt controller assigns the interrupt priority. For example, the Intel 8059 interrupt controller can support 8-levels of interrupts, and additionally can be cascaded to support 64 levels of hardware coded interrupts. In most RTOSs it is the kernel that controls the execution of an ISR. In the event that a number of interrupts occur at the same time, the kernel must decide which to execute first. The general response of the kernel following an interrupt is as follows,

- Complete the current instruction.
- Based on priority determine which task to allocate to the processor.
- Save the running conditions of the current state, this is normally done by a PUSH onto the STACK of the programme counter and the segment registers if these are used. In other words, the location where execution has stopped is pushed onto the STACK so that the programme can return to the same location.
- Run the ISR

Together, these 4 steps constitute a context switch. To give an order of magnitude, on an Intel 8086 a context switch takes a minimum of 50 µS.

The basic principle of priority-based interrupt is seen in Figure 1.8 where three tasks are being scheduled by the RTOS kernel.

Here it is shown that the lowest priority task is Task 1 and the highest priority task is Task 3. With reference to Figure 1.8, assuming that at time T0, the only task running is task 1. At time T1, task 2 with medium priority requires the CPU, and because it has a higher priority than task 1, it pre-empts it and takes over the CPU. Which is to say that task 2 is executing. At time T2, task 3 requires the CPU and because it is a higher priority, it pre-empts the currently running task, which is task 2. At T3 task 3 completes and releases the CPU.

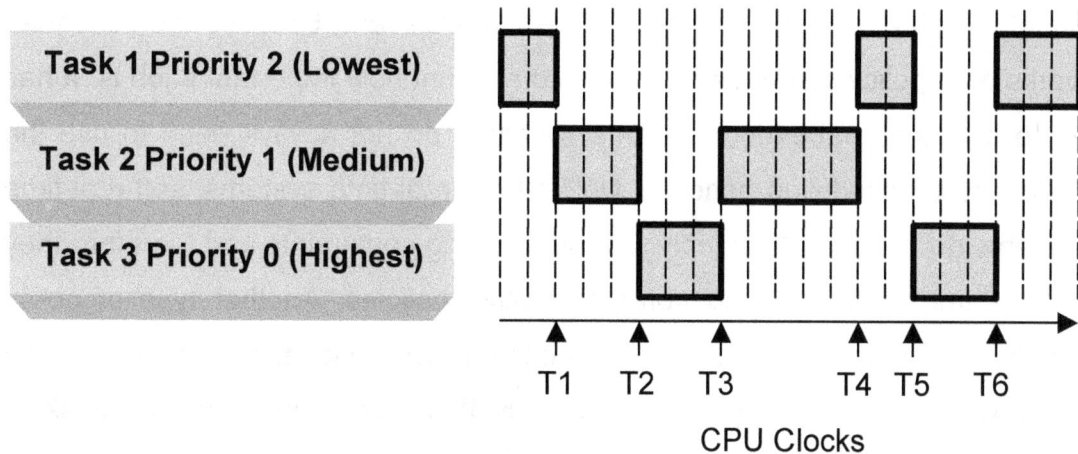

Figure 1.8: Timeline for Priority-based Pre-emptive Scheduling

At this time the scheduler has a choice to allocate either task 1 or task 2 to the CPU. Looking at their priorities, task 2 has a higher priority, and therefore gets the CPU.

When task 2 completes at T4, the CPU is allocated to task 1. At T5 task 3 decides to run again, and interrupts task 1 while it completes. At T6 task 3 completes and CPU is given to task 1. Thus, from this simplified example it can be seen that the principle of priority based scheduling is very straightforward. At any time that a task needs to run, the kernel checks to see if the task currently executing has a higher priority. If it does not then it can be pre-empted so that the higher priority task can run. The programmer of the system must ensure that each task is given the appropriate priority, which will typically be based on the functional requirements of the system.

Non-pre-emptive

In general purpose operating systems, where time constraints are not so critical, the allocation of tasks to the CPU can be scheduled according to a non pre-emptive principle. A scheduling discipline is non-pre-emptive if, once a process has been allocated to the CPU, the CPU cannot be taken away from that process. The only time the process will relinquish the CPU is when it terminates, or when it enters the BLOCKED state. Another, more drastic way to leave the READY state is when a non-maskable interrupt (NMI) occurs. (i.e. power loss). In non-pre-emptive systems, response times are more predictable because incoming jobs cannot displace waiting jobs, even if they have higher priority. In this case the priority of a task is irrelevant, because the scheduler works on a policy that does not take into account how important a job is. It has to be said that embedded real-time systems, do not always need to use the pre-emptive scheduling principle. Unlike hard real-time systems, soft real-time systems do not need to comply with strict timing constraints and therefore they can be implemented using non-pre-emptive policies. Another type of policy that is no longer very common is the cooperative policy that was used in the Windows 3.1 multitasking O/S. Effectively this was cooperative multitasking since each application when running would periodically relinquish control back to Windows scheduler so that another task can be scheduled. In some applications this principle is also referred to as fixed time task switching. The main disadvantage is in that if an error occurs and the application is unable to transfer control to the operating system, it may freeze the system.

As mentioned earlier, schedulers work according to a prescribed scheduling policy. There are 6 Low level scheduling policies that are most commonly applied to process scheduling, these are as follows,

- (SJF)   Shortest Job First.
- (FCFS)   First Come First Serve.
- (RR)   Round Robin.
- (SRT)   Shortest Remaining Time.
- (HRN)   Highest Response Ratio Next.
- (MFQ)   Multilevel feedback queue.

FCFS-First Come First Serve

This is a non-pre-emptive policy and consequently it favours long jobs over short jobs. This is because the waiting time to run time ratio is smaller for long jobs than for short jobs. Table 1.2 shows the typical ratios that can be expected with this policy. Here it is seen that the shortest job (P3) has the highest wait-to-run time ratio.

Table 1.2

Process	Estimated run-time (T_{ER})	Waiting time (T_W)	Ratio (T_W) /(T_{ER})
P1	10	0	0/10=0
P2	2	1	11/2=0.55
P3	1	13	13/1=13
P4	100	14	14/100=1.4

SJF – Shortest Job First

This is another non-pre-emptive policy and as the name implies it works on the principle that it schedules the shortest jobs first, leaving the longer jobs for later. The assumption here is that once the short jobs have been completed, and no more are left, the longer jobs can proceed. This avoids delaying the short jobs by waiting for long ones to finish. With SJF if there are a large number of shorter job there is a risk that the longer job suffers longer waits, and therefore may result in job starvation. For SJF an estimated run time must be available for each process and could be supplied by the job control language (JCL). Table 1.3 shows the typical ratios that can be expected with this policy. Here is seen that in comparison to the FCFS, all jobs have a lower wait-to-run-time ratio. However the highest ratio is for the longest job (P4).

Table 1.3

Process	Order SJF	Estimated run-time (T_{ER})	Waiting time (T_W)	Ratio (T_W) /(T_{ER})
P1	P3	1	0	0/1=0
P2	P2	2	1	1/2=0.5
P3	P1	10	3	3/10=0.3
P4	P4	100	13	13/100=1.3

SRT-Short Running Time

This is a pre-emptive variation of SJF that uses a timeout to context switch between jobs. It uses a time stamp to monitor the length of jobs and schedules these according to the principle of Shortest Remaining Time (SRT) policy. With this policy the job with the shortest time to completion is processed first. Each job runs for the duration of the timeout and then a new calculation is done to determine which of the remaining jobs are the shortest. Table 1.4 shows an example of the performance of this policy. Although this policy has the overhead of keeping a time-stamp, it is seen to be fair to all jobs, and more importantly, it guarantees that no jobs will be starved of CPU time.

Table 1.4 SRT

Process	Time	Order	Units of time elapsed FROM START						
	Unit	SJF	1	2	3	4	<--- >	10	11
P1	10	3	10	10	10	9			0
P2	2	2	2	1	0	-			-
P3	1	1	0	-	-	-			-
P4	100	4	100	100	100	100			39

Highest Response Next (HRN)

HRN is also a pre-emptive policy derived from SJF, which has been modified to allow the longer jobs to have a chance to complete. This is done by calculating a dynamic priority after each unit of execution time. It is based on the calculated priority value and the formula is as follows,

$$P = \frac{T_W + T_{RT}}{T_{RT}} \qquad (1.1)$$

where,

T_W - Wait time

T_{RT} - Run time

Looking at the equation 1.1 it is clear that P is never less than 1. For example, assume two processes P1 and P2 with run times of 5 and 10 units respectively have been waiting for 1 unit time. Their priority values can be calculated from (1.1) as follows,

$$P_1 = \frac{T_W + T_{RT}}{T_{RT}} = \frac{1+5}{5} = 1.2 \ and \ P_2 = \frac{T_W + T_{RT}}{T_{RT}} = \frac{1+10}{10} = 1.1$$

From the result it is seen that process P1 has a higher priority value and therefore takes precedence over P2.

Consider another example. Assume process P4 has a run time of 100 units and has been waiting for 12 units of time. At this time, another process P5, with a run time value of 10 units joins the queue. Another unit of time later, after P4 has waited for 13 units of time, P5 has been in the queue for 1 unit time and it has a running time of 10 units of time. The priority calculation for P4 and P5 would be,

$$P_4 = \frac{T_W + T_{ER}}{T_{ER}} = \frac{13+100}{100} = 1.13 \ and \ P_5 = \frac{T_W + T_{ER}}{T_{ER}} = \frac{1+10}{10} = 1.1$$

In this situation even though P4 is a long job the priority has moved up higher than P5, which has shorter running time but joins the queue later. Table 1.5 show the calculated priorities for a range of process lengths.

Table 1.5 HRN with the Priority calculated priority value

Process	Estimated run-time (T_{ER})	Waiting time (T_W)	Priority value ($T_W + T_{ER}$) /(T_{ER})
P1	10	0	10/10 =1
P2	2	10	12/2 =6
P3	1	12	13/1 =13
P4	100	13	113/100 =1.13

Round Robin

Round robin (RR) is a common scheduling scheme where processes are allocated the CPU in a rotating fashion with a timeout signalling the change form one process to the next. This is illustrated in Figure 1.9 where it is seen that a process is selected from ready queue in the FIFO sequence. In this case the FIFO schedule is P1, P2, P3 and P4 at the first pass and being closest to the CPU, P4 is executed first. Processes are assigned a quantum of time to run on processor, which must not be exceeded. As soon as the time quantum has been exceeded, an interrupt occurs and the executing process is placed at the back of the FIFO queue. Thus on the second pass the FIFO schedule is P4, P1, P2, P3 and at this point the CPU executes P3. A hardware timer that generates an interrupt at pre-set intervals usually provides the time quantum. This policy is pre-emptive which only occurs at expiry of the quantum time.

Perhaps the most significant feature of this policy is that it guarantees the completion of even the longest jobs. Since each process is allocated a quantum, and when this has expired, it moves to the back of the queue, every process remains in the queue until it has completed. Thus, for n processes in the queue and a fixed time quantum (Q) each process gets a proportion of CPU time given by,

$$P_{CPU} = Q = \frac{1}{n} \times T_{CPU}$$

Where,

P_{CPU} – proportion of CPU time given to a process

T_{CPU} – Total available CPU time

Thus CPU time is allocated to each process Q units at a time. It follows that no process waits longer than $T_W = (n-1) \times Q$ time units. Which is the length of time that the last process in the queue will have to wait before getting access to the CPU. This guarantee that every process will complete is the main advantage of the RR schedling scheme. The main disadvantage of this policy is the significant overheads because each quantum time generates a context switch.

The choice of time quantum is particularly important with the round robin scheduling policy. It should not be too short because this will increase the frequency of context switching. Every context switch takes a certain amount of CPU time and this can lead to a condition called 'thrashing', where the CPU spends all its time context switching and has no time to perform he processing.

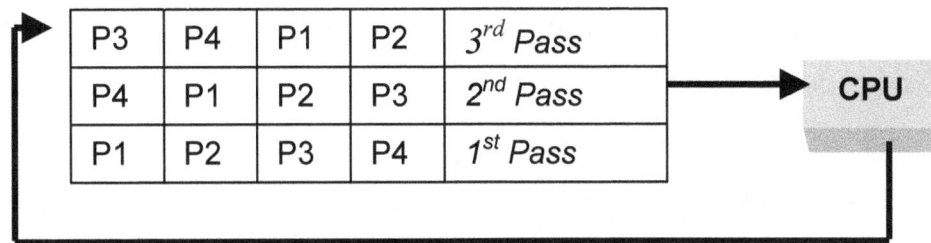

P3	P4	P1	P2	3rd *Pass*
P4	P1	P2	P3	2nd *Pass*
P1	P2	P3	P4	1st *Pass*

After a time slice "Quantum" the process
frees processor for next process

Figure 1.9 Round Robin Process Swapping

On the other hand if the time quantum is too long, that could introduce idle time, which happens when the process has terminated and the quantum has not elapsed. Typically quantum = *10-20 mS* but as mentioned earler it is decided according to the number of processes that are competing for the CPU.

Multi-level feedback queues (MFQ)

MFQs are a combination of first in first out (FIFO) queues arranged at different levels of hierarchy in accordance with the level of CPU usage. It combines several levels of FIFO queues with a time quantum applied in order to limit processor time given to each process. As the process runs, if it uses up its quantum and it does not complete, then it will return to the back of the queue at the next lower level. If the same process does not complete at this level, it will proceed to the back of the queue at the next lower level etc. The highest level is for processes with the shortest CPU time, and levels below this have progressively longer CPU time requirements. Transition from the higher level to the one below it is achieved by providing a timeout (quantum Q). This is seen in Figure 1.10 which shows that a new process enters at the highest level, and progresses down the levels after each Q has expired, for as long as it does not complete.

MFQs can be made adaptive by recording the level at which each process terminated when it was last in the queue. The next time that this process enters the queue, rather than placing it at the highest level, the sceduler will place the process at the level that it exited. In this manner the process will not waste time lingering in the higher levels where it is known from

25

past experience that it will not complete. This is an attempt to provide an adaptive policy which treats processes on the basis of their past behaviour.

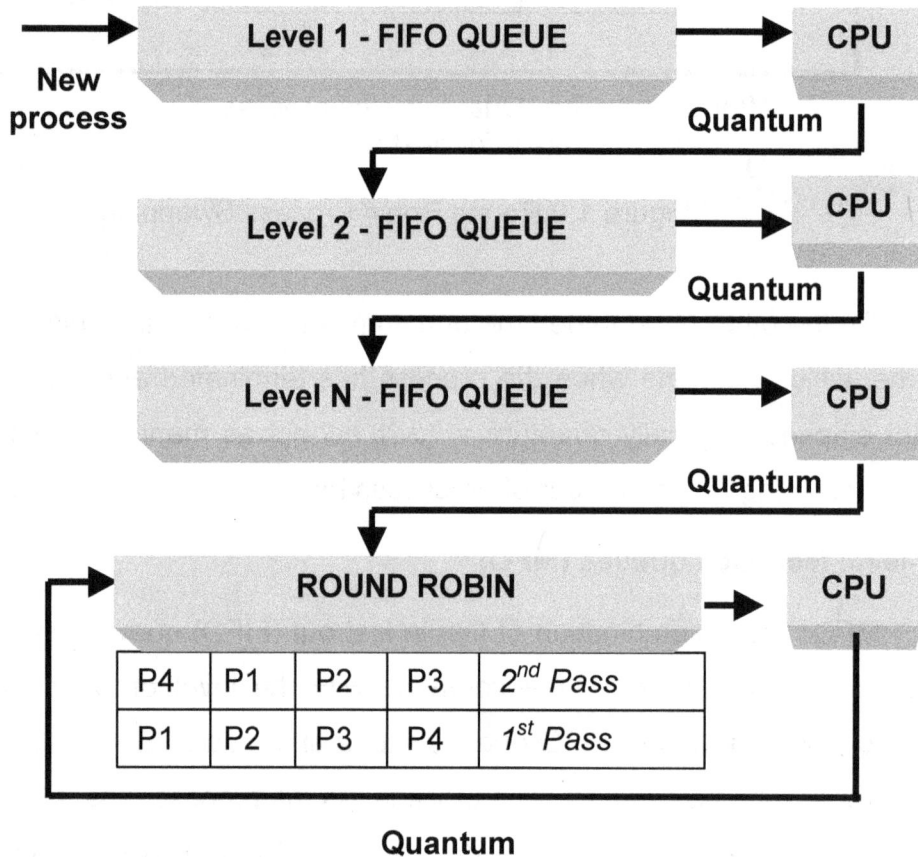

Figure 1.10 Multi-level feedback queues.

1.9.   Example RTOS

It was mentioned earlier that the timing determinism is the main aspect that distinguishes a RTOS from a general purpose O/S. This does not mean that all real-time systems will be quicker than their non real-time equivalents. It just means that the knowing the timing more precisely (i.e. more deterministic timing), allows the RTOS to guarantee timing performance. The issue of timing determinism features in many activities of operating system kernels, such as task scheduling, memory allocation and inter-task communication. On the other hand, general-purpose kernels in multi-tasking operating systems mostly offer non-deterministic services in these areas. A number of real-time operating systems implement these solutions in their compact high-performance kernels. [12]

There are a large number of RTOSs available, but for my part I have mostly been involved with the following, and therefore I shall be giving them as an example. They come from two separate sources KEIL [13] and TenAsys. [14] Some examples of the RTOS kernels provided by these are given next.

KEIL provides several real-time operating systems (or real-time kernels) that are fully integrated into their C language compilers. This means that a C programming compiler will compile C code according to the RTOS kernel timing and priority constraints that the programmer specifies. It may be obvious but I have to say that it is the programmer and how they have interpreted and applied the real-time constraints within their programme that determines the performance of every RTS application. The kernel is there simply to support the execution of this software application. The RTOS kernels provided by KEIL offer basic multitasking features needed in real-time applications and the basic variants are as follows,

RTX51: Real-Time Kernel is a complete real-time kernel for 8051-based applications with numerous tasks and many resources to manage. Controller Area Network (CAN) Bus support is provided for a number of 8051-based CAN microcontrollers as well as many external CAN controllers.

RTX51 Tiny: RTX51 Tiny Real-Time Kernel is a small real-time kernel (around 800 bytes) that supports 8051-based applications with reduced real-time requirements. RTX51 Tiny is perfect if you only need task switching or limited inter-task communications. It is included with the PK51 Professional Developer's Kit.

ARTX-166 Advanced RTOS: ARTX-166 Advanced RTOS is a complete real-time kernel for XC16x, C16x, and ST10 applications. These are 16-bit variants of the MCS-C251 family of processors. The AR166 lets you manage numerous tasks and resources. It includes a Flash file system and TCP/IP stack.

RTX166 Tiny: RTX166 Tiny Real-Time Kernel is a small real-time kernel that supports 166 and 167-based applications with reduced real-time requirements. Effectively, it is a scaled down version of the ARTX-166. It is perfect in applications that only need task switching or limited inter-task communications.

RL-ARM Real-Time Library: The RL-ARM Real-Time Library is a complete real-time kernel for ARM7, ARM9, and Cortex-M3 applications. These are applications that are designed to run on the 32-bit advanced RISC machines (ARM) architecture. The RL-ARM helps you manage numerous tasks and resources. It includes a Flash file system and TCP/IP networking suite.

Another provider of a RTOS that we have used quite extensively is the InTime RTOS from TenAsys. The InTime RTOS is designed and optimised specifically for the x86 architecture and Microsoft Windows software. The idea behind InTime appears to have been to utilise the existing processor and multitasking features of a general purpose O/S such as Windows, and to build a real-time kernel on top of this. In this way, InTime, takes advantage of all the benefits of Windows i.e. standard application programming interfaces (APIs), networking capabilities, user interface, and development environment, and builds on top of this a real-time kernel to handle time critical applications. InTime trial software can be downloaded from the TenAsys website. [14]

1.10. Computer software

Computer software provides a degree of flexibility that is not so easily provided by the hardware. By software programming, the hardware can be made to function in different ways. Figure 1.11 provides a simplified view of the computer programming hierarchy. Here the levels of programming are split into a number of categories at different levels of the hierarchy. The hierarchical decomposition is used to show that every level depends on the one below it for operation.

Software programming at high and low level includes system software, application software, programme loader, I/O control system etc. Here the low level programming languages such as assembly are used to provide very efficient code. High-level languages such as C and Java, are much more user friendly but the code that they produce is not as efficient as that produced by assembly programming. In all cases however the development tools that are used include, compilers, linkers, loaders and debugging tools.

Application programming usually requires a run-time library to enable portability. Operational and end users typically use scripting tools to write programs. Some visual programming tools include a GUI, to simplify the programming task (i.e. Visual Basic). With reference to Figure 1.11 a brief explanation of some software components is given as follows,

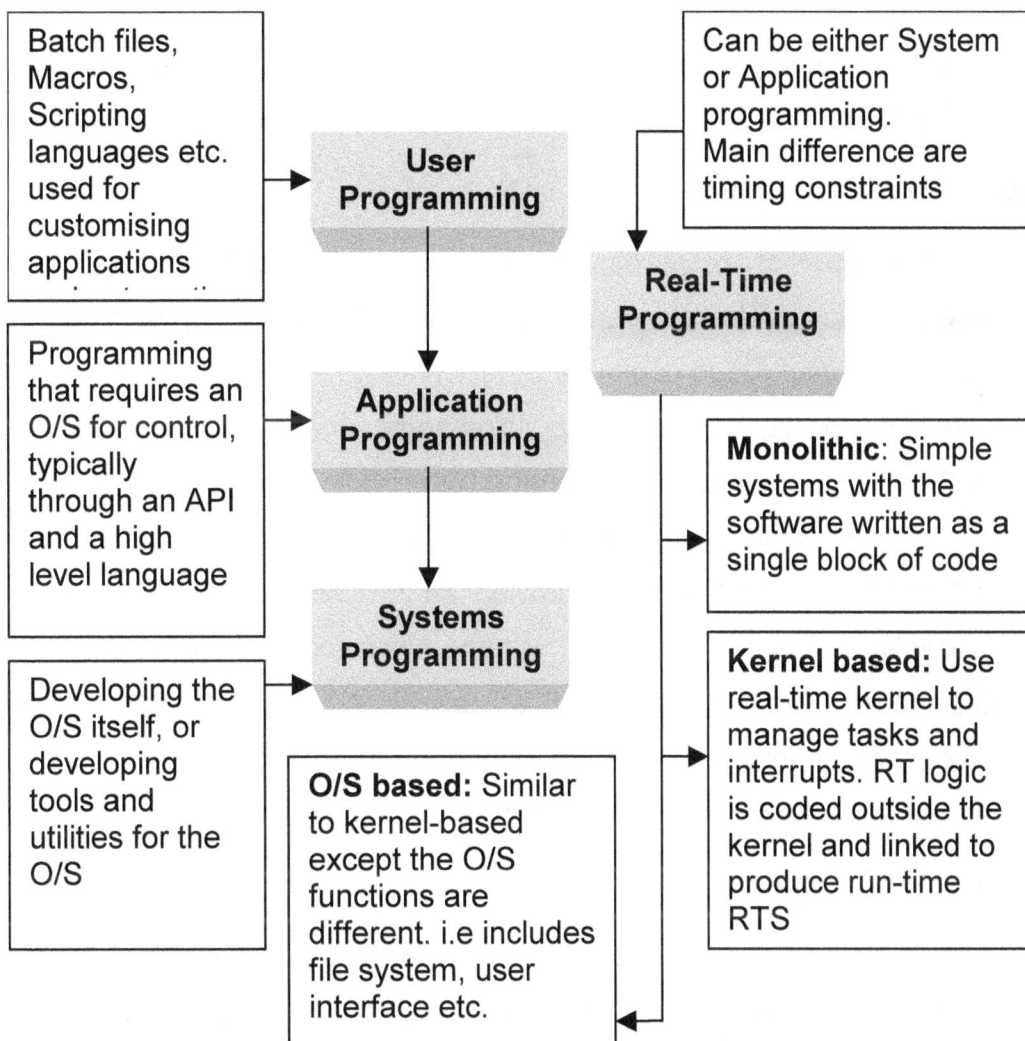

Batch files, Macros, Scripting languages etc. used for customising applications

User Programming

Can be either System or Application programming. Main difference are timing constraints

Programming that requires an O/S for control, typically through an API and a high level language

Application Programming

Real-Time Programming

Monolithic: Simple systems with the software written as a single block of code

Developing the O/S itself, or developing tools and utilities for the O/S

Systems Programming

Kernel based: Use real-time kernel to manage tasks and interrupts. RT logic is coded outside the kernel and linked to produce run-time RTS

O/S based: Similar to kernel-based except the O/S functions are different. i.e includes file system, user interface etc.

Figure 1.11. Computer programming hierarchy

User programming

This is used to describe programming by general users who have not been formally taught how to programme in a conventional programming language (i.e. assembly, C, C++, VBasic, Java etc). These are the languages that enable the users who need to change the actions and/or user interface of a system. For example, AutoCad has an embedded Lisp language for extensions, and Microsoft Office has an embedded Basic language. End user programmers also include, webmasters writing JavaScript; network administrators writing logon scripts and script to configure routers; as well as the experts in complex business automation tools like SAP (Systems, Applications, Products). [15]

Application Programming

This type of programming utilises an Application Programming Interface (API) to develop programs that run on the platform for which the API has been developed. [16] In computer programme development, APIs are a set of routines, protocols, and tools for building software applications. A good API makes it easier to develop a programme by providing all the building blocks, which can be easily put together by a programmer. Most operating environments, such as Windows, provide an API so that programmers can write applications that are consistent with the operating system. Although APIs are designed for programmers, they are also good for users because they guarantee that all programs using a common API will have similar interfaces. This makes it easier for users to learn new programs.

Systems programming

Systems programming produces software, which provides services to the computer hardware. Examples include implementing certain functions in the operating such as paging system (Virtual Memory) a disk defragmenter or a device driver for a network operating system. This level of programming requires a greater degree of hardware understanding by the programmer. More specifically, the programmer will utilise the properties of the hardware in order to write efficient code to perform systems functions. Originally systems programmers wrote in assembly language. With the growth of UNIX operating system, C language emerged as a viable and efficient systems programming language. (i.e. UNIX was written in C). An object-oriented variant of C namely C++, was used for O/S development such as the Windows NT and embedded C++ is used to write the I/O Kit drivers of Mac OS X. As an example of a typical architecture of a popular O/S, Figure 1.12 shows the Windows 2000 architecture. Here it is seen that the architecture is divided into two parts, the User mode and the Kernel mode. User mode refers to all the applications, services, system processes and the environment subsystem, all of which go through the dynamic link library in order to access the kernel mode. The kernel is part of the operating system that provides the very basic services for all other parts of the operating system.

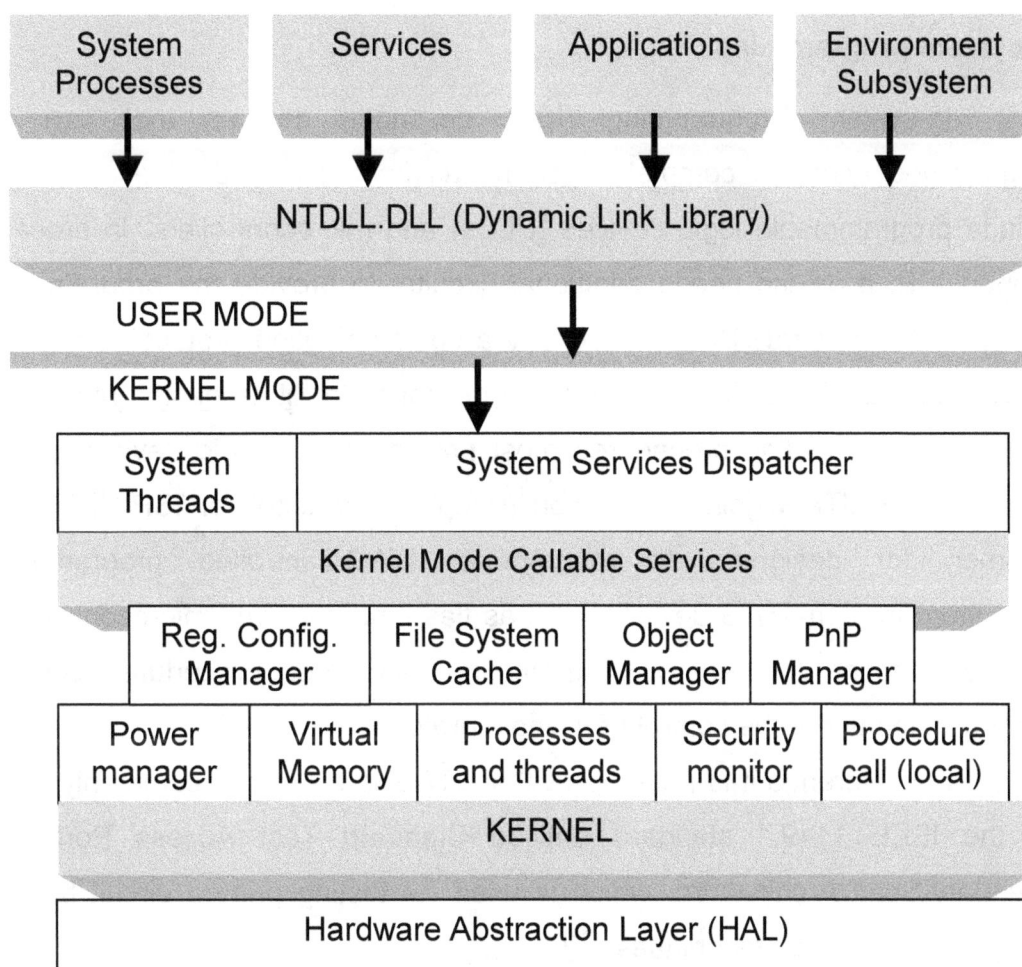

System Processes	Services	Applications	Environment Subsystem

NTDLL.DLL (Dynamic Link Library)

USER MODE

KERNEL MODE

System Threads	System Services Dispatcher

Kernel Mode Callable Services

Reg. Config. Manager	File System Cache	Object Manager	PnP Manager

Power manager	Virtual Memory	Processes and threads	Security monitor	Procedure call (local)

KERNEL

Hardware Abstraction Layer (HAL)

Figure 1.12 Simplified Windows NT 2000 Kernel Architecture [17]

Typically, a kernel includes an interrupt handler that looks after all requests or completed I/O operations that compete for the kernel's services. It will also have a scheduler that determines which programs share the kernel's processing time and in what order. With reference to Figure 1.12, in kernel mode all the processor services are performed and before accessing the hardware the services need to pass through a hardware abstraction layer (HAL). The windows HAL provides a link to the hardware interfaces such as buses, I/O devices, interrupts, interval timers, direct memory access (DMA), memory cache control etc. In the windows O/S the HAL layer was first introduced with Windows 2000 O/S and for this reason drivers for devices pre-Windows 2000 are different to post-Windows 2000. The introduction of the HAL layer implies that the O/S does not have direct access to the hardware and also, by suitably replacing the HAL, the O/S could easily run on different hardware platforms.

In-system programming

In-system Programming (ISP) describes devices that can be programmed after the complete system has been installed. These devices include programmable logic devices (PLDs) and microcontrollers. In order to support ISP, a device needs additional circuitry to provide the programming voltages for on-board RAM. Additionally a communication protocol is needed in order to load the code into memory. In order to facilitate easier integration with automated testing procedures most programmable logic devices use a variant of the JTAG (joint test action group) [18] protocol for ISP. It is also common for designers to incorporate JTAG-controlled programming subsystem for non-JTAG devices such as flash memory and microcontrollers. In this manner the entire programming and test procedure can be accomplished under the control of a single protocol.

For reference it is noted here that JTAG is the name commonly used for the IEEE 1149.1 standard entitled Standard Test Access Port and Boundary-Scan Architecture, which is used for testing printed circuit boards using boundary, scan techniques. [19]

1.11. Microcontroller programming

A microcontroller will become useful only after it has been programmed with suitable code. The code that has been developed and downloaded into the chip will run for as long as the chip lasts, and excepting some upgrade options, it is not intended to change during its lifetime.

All digital integrated circuits work in binary signal representation. That is, they can only recognise values of logical zero (0) and logical (1). These values are conveniently represented by a voltage level of +5V for logical (1), and 0V for logical (0). In fact many modern chips will quite happily work with 3.3 V to represent logical (1) in order to reduce power consumption.

In order to instruct the processor to perform a task, a sequence of binary numbers are programmed into memory. These numbers act as an instruction to the processor and it is convenient for us to represent these 8-bits at a time (8-bits = 1-byte). While we are on the subject, 4-bits (half byte) are called nibbles, two bytes are termed words (16-bit) and double words are 32-bits (4 x bytes). It has to be said that with the introduction of 64-bit CPUs this terminology has become somewhat blurred and some authors will refer to 32-bit words in their text. Strictly speaking this is not correct, but it is used to simplify the expression, i.e. 'quad-words' has not as yet been adopted as a standard expression.

All CPUs work on the FETCH-EXECUTE principle. This means that an instruction is fetched from memory, and once it is available, the CPU can execute it. When the execution is over, next instruction is fetched and so on, this is repeated until all of the instructions contained in the programme segment have been executed.

While the CPU will work best with binary numbers, the human programmer is much better at comprehending worded instructions. For this reason tools are available that enable the programmer to write the code in words, and then to have these converted to binary numbers by a special programme. Thus we have code written in a particular programming language, and according to the correct syntax of this language, which is then converted into machine code for execution on particular hardware. Figure 1.13 shows an example programme written in assembly language for the Intel 80x86 family of processors. Figure 1.13 a) shows the assembly language programme and the corresponding machine code is given in Figure 1.13 b).

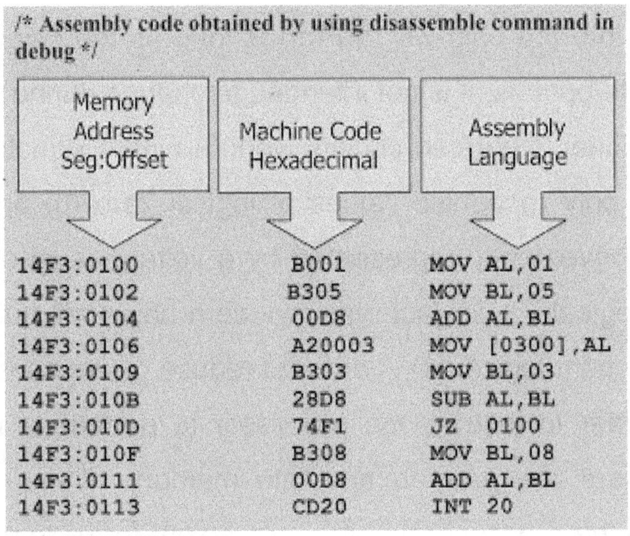

/* Assembly code obtained by using disassemble command in debug */

Memory Address Seg:Offset	Machine Code Hexadecimal	Assembly Language
14F3:0100	B001	MOV AL,01
14F3:0102	B305	MOV BL,05
14F3:0104	00D8	ADD AL,BL
14F3:0106	A20003	MOV [0300],AL
14F3:0109	B303	MOV BL,03
14F3:010B	28D8	SUB AL,BL
14F3:010D	74F1	JZ 0100
14F3:010F	B308	MOV BL,08
14F3:0111	00D8	ADD AL,BL
14F3:0113	CD20	INT 20

a) Assembly language (Intel 80x86)

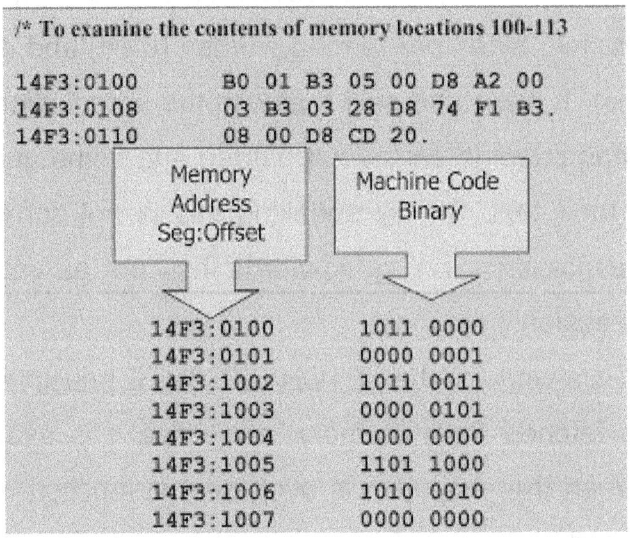

/* To examine the contents of memory locations 100-113

```
14F3:0100      B0 01 B3 05 00 D8 A2 00
14F3:0108      03 B3 03 28 D8 74 F1 B3.
14F3:0110      08 00 D8 CD 20.
```

Memory Address Seg:Offset	Machine Code Binary
14F3:0100	1011 0000
14F3:0101	0000 0001
14F3:1002	1011 0011
14F3:1003	0000 0101
14F3:1004	0000 0000
14F3:1005	1101 1000
14F3:1006	1010 0010
14F3:1007	0000 0000

b) Machine code (Intel 80x86)

Figure 1.13 Assembly code and the corresponding machine code

With reference to Figure 1.13 the assembly programme segment is shown below indicating a brief explanation of each line of code.

```
MOV AL,01; Load value 01 to accumulator register
MOV BL,05; Load value 05 to BL register
ADD AL,BL; Add the contents of AL and BL registers
MOV [0300],AL; Move the contents of AL to
          ; address 0300H
MOV BL,03; Load value 03 to register BL
SUB AL,BL; Subtract contents of BL from AL
```

```
JZ 0100; Jump if zero to start address
MOV BL,08; Load value 08 to BL register
ADD AL,BL; Add contents of register AL to BL
INT 20; Interrupt program
```

The assembler assembles the same code into the so-called machine code, which is in fact a hexadecimal sequence of numbers that represent the binary numbers, which are processed by the CPU. The hexadecimal numbers and their binary equivalents are shown in Figure 1.13 b). It should be clear from Figure 1.13 b) that writing in assembly is much easier than attempting to write in machine code.

With most microcontrollers the levels of programming are classified according to how high they are above the binary code that the CPU understands. In general we refer to programming in Machine Code, Assembly Language, and a High Level Language (for example C).

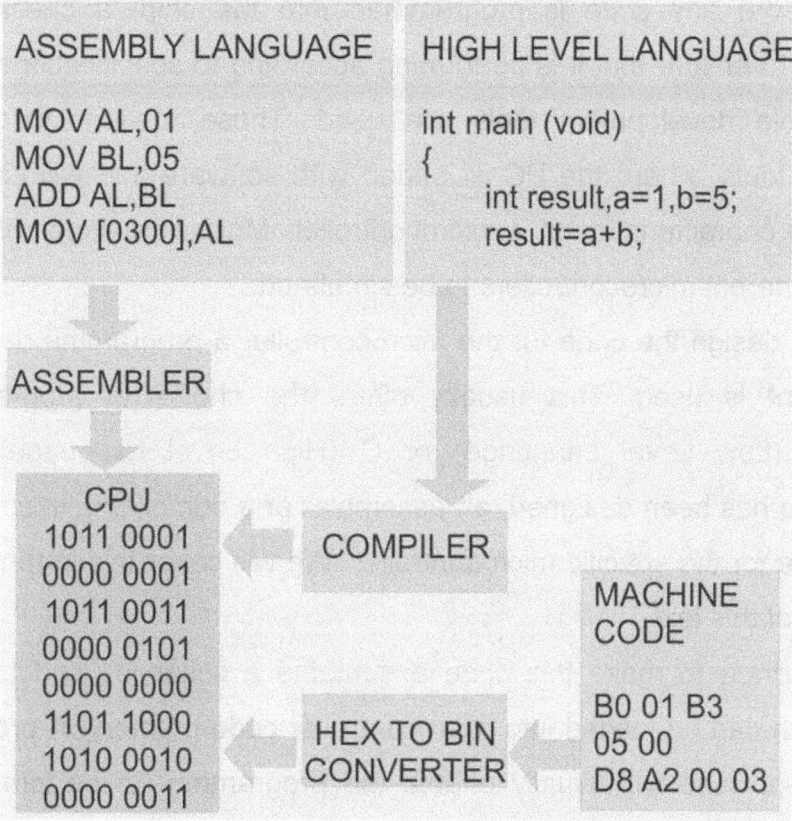

Figure 1.14 HL and LL programming

Figure 1.14 shows the comparison between programming in high level and low-level languages. This Figure also shows that the lowest level of programming is in Machine Code, since it is the nearest to binary number representation of instructions. Here actual numbers are coded in hexadecimal (i.e. base 16) notation and written into memory as bytes. It is worth noting that 4 bits in binary can represent 16 numbers in decimal (i.e. $2^4=16$). Thus, hexadecimal numbers 0-F are represented by 4 bits (half byte) called a nibble. To accommodate 16 numbers the notation uses numbers 0-9, and letters A-F to represent numbers 10-15. As an example, hexadecimal value B3 would convert to binary 1011 0011.

From Figure 1.14 it is seen that it is necessary to convert the written programme code into the binary instructions for the CPU. For this purpose, the assembly language uses the assembler, a high-level language uses the compiler and the machine code programme uses the HEX to BIN converter.

Embedded development tools

Before any code is programmed into the chip, a check must be performed to ensure that it is performing according to specifications. To make this possible development tools are used. These tools include software simulation tools, where the PC is loaded with software that will simulate the processing characteristics of a microcontroller. Most simulators will enable a range of different microcontrollers to be simulated.

To design the code for the microcontroller a programme development environment is used. This usually offers the choice of programming in Assembly (Low Level Language) or C (High Level Language). Once a programme has been designed, an assembler or a compiler is used to provide object code for the specific microcontroller. We will cover this in more detail in Chapter 3 of this text.

Further, to make this code executable a linker is used to generate code, which can be loaded into microcontroller code memory. A programming development suite will usually enable the programmer to perform all these tasks in a single process often referred to as a Build or Make.

Another useful tool for programmers is the Debugging tool, which enables us to examine programme execution during run-time and to check if it is functioning according to the specification.

It is worth noting that originally, microcontrollers were only programmed in assembly language, and later in C. Subsequently, microcontroller designers went on to include a built-in high-level programming language interpreter for greater ease of use. Very early on, the Intel 8052 and Zilog Z8 were available with the BASIC programming language. As a matter of fact, BASIC is used more recently in the popular BASIC Stamp MCUs. Java programming is also being used in microcontroller applications with many devices supporting Java Run-Time. For example the Imsys' Reconfigurable J2ME Java-Enabled Microcontroller. [20] Some other microcontrollers such as Analog Device's Blackfin processors can be programmed using LabVIEW, which is a high level programming language. [21]

C++ is starting to be more frequently selected for use with medium and large embedded projects. There are no clear criteria or benchmarks established for selecting a processor when C++ is the desired programming language. However, C++ supports object oriented programming which can in some cases result in programs that consume large amounts of memory. As a result of this embedded solutions tend to rely on hardware platforms that can support large code size. [22] In this text the programming tool that we will be using is the KEIL Integrated Development Environment (IDE) [13] and this will be discussed in Chapter 3. You may download evaluation software and use the on-line documentation to learn about the KEIL tools. The KEIL suit includes evaluation software for the following processors, ARM, C51, C166 and C251. Each evaluation tool set includes the assembler, compiler, linker, debugger, and IDE. These tools allow you to evaluate the quality of the generated code, the speed and flexibility of the debugger, and the ease-of-use provided by the µVision IDE. Before we look at KEIL software in more detail, let us first consider briefly the Intel family of microcontrollers.

Exercises

1.1   Describe the general characteristics of embedded systems.

1.2   If you wanted to use a microcontroller, do you need an operating system? Explain why or why not?

1.3   Explain the essential functions of a computer operating system.

1.4 Discuss the different levels of programming that an O/S typically supports.

1.5 What are the main features of a RTOS? Contrast the general purpose O/S with a RTOS and highlight the main differences as well as common aims.

1.6 Explain the role of the kernel in RTOS.

1.7 Explain the Windows NT internal Kernel architecture.

1.8 Within the NT kernel architecture, explain the memory management component.

1.9 Explain the essential features of CISC and RISC processors.

1.10 An integer multiply instruction on CISC CPU takes 110 clock cycles. A RISC processor does not support multiply but does support loop and ADD instructions. The loop instruction takes 5 clock cycles, and the ADD instruction takes 10 clock cycles. Assume that both machines are 16 bit, that they run at *100MHz* clock speed, and that the RISC processor has 20 CPUs running in parallel. Calculate the time that it would take each machine to perform the following multiplications, and compare all the results that are possible:

a) 50x4,   b) 25x1000,   c) 165,000x20.

1.11 How do optimising compilers work?

1.12 Why is power consumption an issue in embedded applications? What are the typical rated power consumption figures for common processors?

1.13 Advanced Risc Machines (ARM), is a UK company that started working with RISC architectures in the 1980s, under the name of ACORN and produced a PC named the Acorn Archimedes. Do a literature survey on the company to get an idea of its market share on the embedded scene. Also, who owns KEIL?

1.14 Describe the 3-state and the 5-state process models.

1.15 What are the three levels of scheduling that apply to the state diagrams above?

1.16   Explain the principle of priority based pre-emptive scheduling as used in RTOS kernels.

1.17   How are tasks allocated priorities in a RTS application?

1.18   Non-pre-emptive polices use scheduling algorithms to decide what tasks to schedule next. This makes sense because these tasks cannot be pre-empted. But, how do pre-emptive policies schedule tasks?

1.19   What is a context switch and how is it related to the RTOS kernel?

1.20   Explain the various levels of programming in computer systems.

1.21   Distinguish between monolithic and kernel based programming in RTSs.

1.22   Discuss the different levels of programming used with present day microcontrollers.

1.23   What is the advantage in low-level language programming over high-level language?

1.24   What are the benefits of programming in OOP language such as java?

Chapter 2 Computer hardware

2.1. Introduction

A typical microprocessor as an integrated circuit chip will comprise the functions that are needed to perform arithmetic and logic operations. In order to perform these it will need some memory to store values as it calculates them. This memory will normally be interfaced to the microprocessor in an addressable form. This means that the microprocessor will have an address for each memory location. The microprocessor will also need memory to store the programme code and some memory to store the reference values and other process information (i.e. the stack). Besides memory the microprocessor will need some I/O device that will enable sensor information to be acquired and actuator controls to be issued. The memory, I/O ports and a serial communication link (RS232) are therefore essential for the functioning of a computer-controlled system.

To enable dedicated systems to be developed IC (Integrated Circuit) manufacturers are providing a selection of microprocessor systems that include memory, I/O ports, serial link etc. on a single chip. These are commonly termed 'Microcontrollers' and abbreviated MCUs.

The discussion to follow will consider in more detail the various components of a microcontroller, namely the essential structure and functions of the central processing unit (CPU), memory types and addressing modes, I/O ports and interfacing techniques including signal conversion. Brief consideration of programming techniques will also be given.

A microcontroller is essentially a single chip computer contained in one IC package. This IC will comprise a CPU (central processing unit), ROM, RAM and several I/O lines. These chips are made up of many logic devices that have been integrated into a single IC. As a result these devices can be embedded into control systems without the need fro adding more components such as I/O ports etc. Thus, microcontrollers can be viewed as single chip microprocessor modules equipped (on-board), with the essential interfaces required for real-time control applications.

Microcontrollers (MCUs)

Figure 2.1 compares the basic features of the microprocessor and a microcontroller. The CPU of a microprocessor chip (i.e. Intel Pentium™) is solely dedicated to processing. Any additional functionality such as memory, input-output access or interrupts has to be added externally. The end result affords fast computing power but with the overhead of external buses and components that need to be interfaced to the CPU.

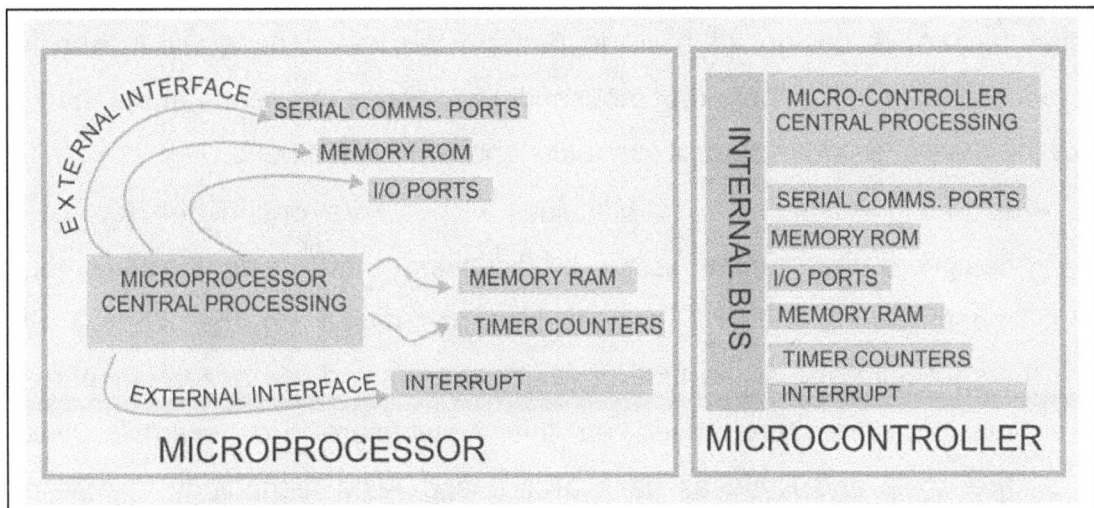

Figure 2.1 Distinguishing between a microprocessor and a microcontroller

In contrast to general-purpose CPUs, microcontrollers are designed to integrate all the RAM and non-volatile memory on the same chip as the CPU. Therefore these chips do not have an external address bus or a data bus. As a result of this, microcontroller chips require fewer pins and the chip can be made smaller and its power consumption is consequently reduced. In a general sense, microcontrollers can be described as computers on a single chip. Besides the CPU, which is found in all computers, a microcontroller will also have input-output ports, some memory and an interrupt mechanism as well as in some cases serial communications support. Consequently microcontrollers are able to provide a single chip solution to an embedded application. Microcontroller chips have a dedicated architecture, which makes them considerably cheaper than microprocessors and more versatile for embedded applications. Here the term architecture refers to the internal components inside the microcontroller chip, such as internal data bus, ports, memory etc., as shown in Figure 2.2. However, it must be said that the processing power of a microcontroller, including capacity and speed is inferior to a microprocessor.

Embedded chip manufacturers

Most microprocessor manufacturers also offer an embedded range of microcontroller chips. These are often termed Application Specific Integrated Circuits (ASICS). For example, if a mobile phone manufacturer needs to embed a new solution in their product range, they may ask a chip manufacturer to design an ASIC to perform the task. These will in turn be produced in large numbers (i.e. thousands) to service the needs of the market for the device. Some microprocessor designers are listed next.

- ARM Ltd Advanced Risc Machines Ltd [23], are one of the few CPU designers that profits solely by licensing their designs rather than manufacturing them. These designs are based on the 32-bit RISC architecture and at the time of writing there are a few dozen companies making processors based on this architecture. For example, Intel, Freescale and Renesas have all licensed ARM technology to develop embedded solutions in a variety of real-time systems including, mass storage, automotive, industrial and networking applications etc. Another important feature of ARM processors is their low electric power consumption, which makes them particularly suitable for use in portable devices. In fact low power consumption is the driving force behind modern embedded devices. As a result almost all modern mobile phones and personal digital assistants contain ARM CPUs, making them the most widely used 32-bit microprocessor family in the world, more so than the better-known 32-bit Pentium 4 processors found in many PCs. Today ARMs account for over 75% of all 32-bit embedded CPUs. [23]

- Advanced Micro Devices- AMD design mainly for the x86-compatible personal computer CPUs. (AMD Athlon was the first 64-bit CPU) [24] On the embedded side AMD offer the AMD Sempron™ Processor Model 2100+ enabling fanless designs for embedded systems (i.e. low power dissipation so no fan required) and offering AMD64 technology features in a 9W TDP (Thermal design power) processor. AMD is also offering another new choice for embedded systems with the introduction of the AMD Geode™ LX 800 @ 0.9W processor, which is designed to support extended temperature applications. Both are part of AMD's ongoing commitment to providing the embedded market with cutting edge features, a balanced approach to overall system design and a combination of high performance and low power. [24]

- Freescale Semiconductor- (formerly of Motorola) – design a wide range of microprocessors including embedded 8, 16, 32-bit microcontrollers PowerPC based processors. [25]

- IBM Microelectronics- Microelectronics division of IBM, which is responsible for many PowerPC based designs, including many of the CPUs used in video game consoles. [26]

- Intel Corp- Intel, a maker of several notable CPU lines, including IA-32, IA-64, and XScale. Also a producer of various peripheral chips for use with their CPUs. Pentiums, High Performance Chipsets. Also motherboards, PC chipsets, server RAID controller, microcontrollers, PCI bridges, Ethernet products, Flash memory, and a wide range of connectivity chips. [2]

- MIPS Technologies- MIPS Technologies, developers of the MIPS architecture, a pioneer in RISC designs. Vast range of devices and solutions. Developed more than 20 years ago at Stanford University, the MIPS architecture is a simple, streamlined, highly scalable RISC architecture. [1]

- Sun Microsystems- Sun developed the SPARC architecture, a RISC design. In embedded offering, The Java processor family consists of three lines: Pico JAVA, micro JAVA and Ultra JAVA. [27]

- Texas Instruments- The semiconductor division designs and manufactures many types of low power microcontrollers among their many other semiconductor products. [28]

- Transmeta Corporation- Creators of low-power x86 compatibles like Crusoe and Efficeon.. Additionally at the time of writing Linus Thorvald, the creator of the Linux O/S, has been engaged by Transmeta Corporation in order to develop the portable Linux. [29]

Other examples of common RISC chips include the Atmel range based on the industry-standard ARM 32-bit RISC processor architecture. i.e. AT91SAM7X and AT91SAM9 Smart ARM®-based microcontrollers offer [30]:

- Proven architecture based on ten years' experience in ARM-based standard products with significant enhancements.
- Deterministic behaviour, predictable response to a real-time event within a specified number of clock cycles.
- Peripheral DMA eliminates bottlenecks in memory-to-peripheral transfers.
- Advanced interrupt control enhances real-time performance.
- Single-instruction bit set/reset simplifies application code.
- Embedded Flash memory for flexible code and reference data storage.
- Connectivity: USB, Ethernet, SPI, USART, etc.
- Security: AES/TDES accelerators, memory locks bits, etc.
- Code compatibility across all products.
- Low-cost development tools.
- Extensive compiler, operating system, compiler and application support from industry-leading third parties.

The above is not an exhaustive range of examples but it does serve to show that the embedded market is very buoyant. Whilst it is always good to know what is available in terms of chips, the principles of embedded systems design need to be mastered before any actual chip is used to develop an applications. Any application is only as good as the person who designs it and the persons that implement it on the available technology. It is therefore imperative that a full understanding of the capabilities and features of the hardware are understood before any design can begin.

2.2.   Components of computer control systems

Microprocessor

Microprocessors come in families such as Intel, Motorola, Rockwell, National semiconductor etc. As an example of what is on offer in microcontrollers, Intel offer a family of 8-bit controllers including the 8048, 8049 and 8051. The 8051 has 4 k-bytes of ROM, 128 bytes of RAM and 32 I/O lines. In addition two 16-bit timers are provided for accurate real-time recording of events. It also has a full duplex (simultaneous transmission and reception) serial I/O port. The Intel MCS-96 family offers 16-bit microcontrollers such as the 8096, which has a 16-bit CPU, 8-Kbytes of ROM, 232 bytes of RAM, a 10-bit A/D converter, full duplex serial port and 40 I/O lines. In order to understand these specifications it is necessary to provide a brief overview of the terminology used and the functionality of the components of microprocessor based systems. There are three main components in a microprocessor,

- Central Processing Unit (CPU)
- Memory
- I/O devices or ports

These will be discussed briefly along with other elements relevant to embedded control applications. It must be appreciated that only general points will be discussed and more detailed description of the various components can be found in other literature.

Central Processing Unit (CPU)

The CPU performs numerical processing (addition, subtraction), logical operations and timing functions. It controls the overall operation of the system through a set of instructions programmed in memory. This programme is stored in non-volatile memory and is often termed micro-code. Also this level of programming is sometimes termed firmware (as opposed to software and hardware). In general the CPU operates by reading data and control signals from memory or I/O device, executing one instruction at a time and sending data and control signals to the outside world through the output port.

To perform this task all CPUs contain an Arithmetic and Logic Unit (ALU), registers and control circuitry. The ALU will contain an adder to perform binary arithmetic (some will also contain multiplication and division), and logic and data shifting operations. The ALU also contains flag bits that signal the result of arithmetic and logical operations such as sign, zero, and carry and parity information. Registers provide temporary storage within the CPU for memory addresses, status words etc. Each register is a set of eight flip-flops (FF) with each FF representing one bit (8 bits = byte, 2 bytes=16 bits = word, 2 words= 32 bits = double word). These FFs provide the fastest level of memory available. The control circuitry coordinates all microprocessor activity. Using clock inputs, the required sequence of events is maintained for the processing task. The control circuitry decodes the instruction bits and issues control signals to units inside the CPU and those outside it, to perform the processing action.

Memory

In embedded computer application the two most common types of memory are random access memory (RAM) and read only memory (ROM).

RAM: This is read and write memory and it can be Static (SRAM) or Dynamic (DRAM). This memory is volatile (i.e. it will lose its contents when the supply is switched off). Static RAM (SRAM) stores a bit of information in a circuit similar to a FF as with registers mentioned earlier, it is asynchronous and does not require a clock and its contents remain intact while the supply power is available. Dynamic RAM (DRAM) stores a bit of information as a charge. It uses the gate-substrate capacitance of a MOS transistor as an elementary memory cell. The obvious advantage is that this circuit is smaller than a FF and consequently DRAMs have a high memory density and they are cheaper but slower than SRAMs. Their disadvantage is that the charge will leak and the memory will lose its charge after a few milliseconds. To prevent loss of data DRAMs are refreshed every millisecond by reading from it and writing back to it. This will be performed on blocks of memory rather than single memory locations. Another disadvantage is that DRAM memory runs at the speed of tens of nanoseconds while SRAM is significantly faster and runs at speeds of a few nanoseconds. For best economy and performance a combination on SRAM and RAM is used where for example SRAM is used as a level 2 CACHE and RAM as main memory.

ROM: as the name implies this type of memory can only be read from. Once the memory is filled (programmed) with information this remains unchanged even if power is switched off. Five main types of ROM exist,

- Masked ROM,
- Programmable ROM (PROM),
- Erasable PROM (EPROM),
- Electrically Erasable PROM (EEPROM or E^2PROM) and Flash ROM

- **Masked ROM**: This is mask programmed by the manufacturer. The information to be stored in this type of memory is supplied as a bit pattern and the manufacturer makes the necessary connection mask for the production of the ROM. In view of the cost of producing a mask this type of ROM is usually subject to minimum quantity (i.e. minimum 1000 ROMs) and they are therefore intended for large production volumes.

- **PROM**: This is read only memory, which can be programmed directly by the user, using a special PROM programmer. The user can programme the required bit pattern but once this is done no changes can be made and the PROM becomes very much like ROM. Because it is not mask-programmed it is cheaper than ROM and for most systems requiring 10-100s units it is the preferred alternative.

- **Erasable PROM (EPROM).** These are read only memories programmable by the user which can be reprogrammed a number of times using a programmer and an eraser. Several technologies are used to implement EPROMs. Once programmed, an EPROM will retain its charge for a number of years. They are easily erased by exposure to ultra-violet light. For this reason EPROM chips have a quartz window that lets in UV light.

- **Electrically Erasable Programmable Read Only Memory (E^{2}PROM).** This type of memory can be read from and written to. The disadvantage is that writing to it requires a relatively long time (i.e. one millisecond) while the read operation can be done in a microsecond. It is therefore not suitable as a general-purpose read/write memory. In addition, it uses complex technologies resulting in low density and the necessity for multiple voltages. Typically, EEPROM will be used where it is necessary to store a small number of parameters infrequently. Its advantage is that it is non-volatile.

- **Flash programmable** ROMs are also electrically erasable and are becoming increasingly common in embedded applications. The main difference between E^{2}PROM and Flash devices is that flash technology cannot erase individual bytes. It can only be erased one sector at a time with typical sector sizes in the range of 256 bytes to 16KB. This is not a major disadvantage since in embedded applications it is often necessary to erase blocks of memory.

Input-Output devices

These are also called peripherals, and they provide the means by which the CPU communicates with the outside world. In a typical microcomputer system output devices are controlled via the output ports. These can be serial (RS232) or parallel ports (i.e. printer port). Parallel ports are 8-bits wide or multiples thereof. These ports are attached to output devices via a port controller chip. In serial communications this chip is termed the USART (Universal Synchronous Transmitter Receiver), which means that it can receive and transmit asynchronous and synchronous data. No such standard is available for parallel communication. Intel for example use the term Programmable Input Output (PIO) for the interface chip, Motorola use PIA, Rockwell use PDC etc. Whatever the term used, the essential function of these chips is to provide a basic input and output interface for 8-bits of parallel data. In addition the chip is programmable which means that it can be programmed to operate in a selection of modes.

Data, Address and Control buses

The CPU is connected to memory and I/O by a set of parallel wires or lines called a bus. As seen in Figure 2.2 there are three of these that interface the CPU to the system components, the data bus, the address bus and the control bus. A bus is essentially a set of communication lines that are grouped together and named according to their function.

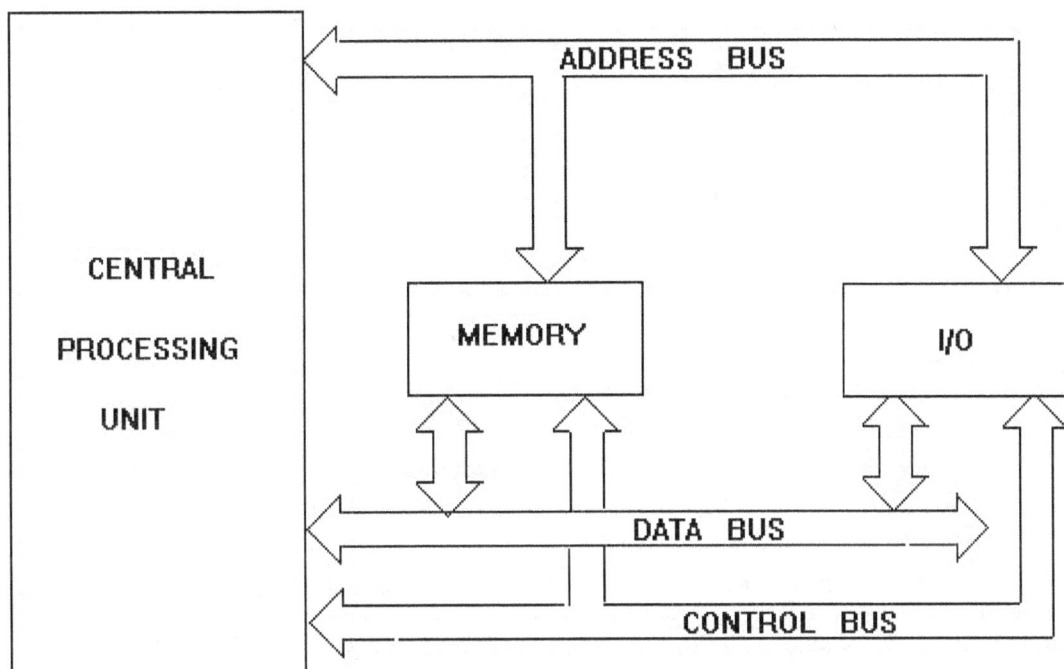

Figure 2.2 Block diagram of a typical microprocessor

Data travel between the CPU, memory, and I/O over the data bus. In microcontrollers the width of this bus is normally 8-bits but it can be 16 bit or 32 bits wide. By convention it is the data bus that defines the system architecture. Thus for example when the microprocessor is termed 16-bit or 32-bit, this refers to the width of its data bus. Typically the registers that are used in the microcontroller will be the same width as the data bus.

In order to communicate over the bus the system needs to know when the byte of information is sent and to which device. In order to send information to a device some information is required about its location. The address bus provides information about all the devices in the address space. The address bus therefore provides a unique address that corresponds to one of the memory or I/O elements of the system.

The control bus carries the control signals to the memory or I/O devices specifying when this is done and in which direction i.e. from the CPU to the device or the reverse. (i.e. read/write and other control information).

Bus cycles

As the microprocessor programme executes, data is transferred to and from memory and I/O devices. Each instance of data transfer from one part of the system to another is called a bus cycle. The timing of these cycles is done by the CPU clock signal. As the programme executes, the information that is communicated over the bus can be an instruction fetch, memory read, memory write, read from an input or write to an output port. The length of time taken to perform these is timed in the number of clock cycles. The duration of the unit clock cycle is determined by the CPU clock speed which in microcontrollers can range form *8MHz, 12MHz, 20MHz, 25MHz, 33Mhz, 40MHz* etc. This frequency is often converted to the length of the clock cycle. For example, a clock frequency of *8 MHz* will have one clock cycle duration of $\dfrac{1}{8 \times 10^6} = 125nS$.

All microcontroller activity is timed by the CPU clock and in many design considerations timing waveforms are used to describe how devices operate. Typically signals will be activated and this will cause a specific action to be performed. This can be seen from the Figure below.

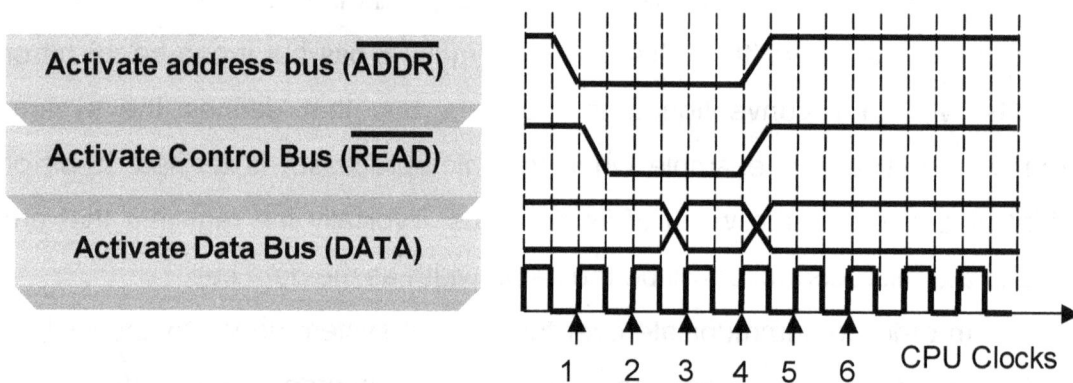

For example, at the beginning of a bus cycle the CPU issues a code to the address bus to identify the memory location or I/O device to be accessed. Next, the CPU issues an activity command on the control bus. Third the CPU either receives or transmits data over the data bus. Each of these activities will consume a certain number of clocks and this can be described using a hypothetical timing waveform shown below. Notice that the signals with a horizontal bar above them are active Low. That is they are active when they are logic '0'. The data signal is shown as taking either value because most data is made up of both '1's and '0's.

As the programme is executing, the CPU keeps track of the instruction sequence using the instruction pointer register, which contains the address of the next instruction to be executed. This instruction depends on the programme that is currently running and the CPU proceeds with executing all the instructions sequentially until the programme terminates. It is possible to accurately time the execution of instruction by considering the number of clock cycles that are needed to perform the required operation.

For example a memory read of 8-bit data may require 10 clock cycles which for an *8MHz* CPU clock will require *1.25μS*. This information is necessary in real-time control since for these the control loops have to be executed in a timely fashion. If for example the control algorithm executes in 5mS and the system response requires the control signal to be made available within 12 μS of a disturbance, then there is no prospect for real-time control even though 5mS is relatively fast.

Interrupts

An interrupt is the term used to signify an interruption of the sequential execution of the microprocessor programme. An interrupt can be software or hardware generated and will stop the execution of the programme when it is generated. What happens after the programme is stopped depends on the nature of the interrupt and the associated interrupt service routine (ISR). For example, if a programme sends a character to a printer to be printed out, then until the printer has finished the CPU has nothing to do but wait. With an interrupt the CPU sends the character to the printer and goes on to do other things that are needed. When the printer has finished printing the character, it will send an interrupt to the CPU to tell it that it is ready for another character. The CPU will respond to this interrupt by sending the character and going back to its original activity.

Often several interrupting devices will need servicing by the CPU and consequently interrupts are often prioritised. When two or more interrupts occur simultaneously, the one with the higher priority will be executed first. Once again it is important to stress that in real-time control applications it is necessary to ensure that the CPU does not lay idle for long periods of time. The CPU will need finite time to perform calculations and other functions and all these will affect the response of the control system.

Direct Memory Access (DMA)

From the standpoint of execution speed the efficiency of a microprocessor can be improved by using direct memory access (DMA). In ordinary I/O operations, the CPU supervises the entire data transfer this is to say that it executes I/O instructions to transfer data from the input device to the CPU and then from the CPU to the specified memory location. Similarly, data going from memory to the output device goes via the CPU. Some peripheral devices transfer information to and from memory faster than the CPU can accomplish the transfer under programme control. By using DMA, the CPU allows the peripheral device to hold and control the bus, transferring the data directly to and from memory without involving the CPU. When the DMA transfer is completed, the peripheral device removes the hold request signal and thereby releases the bus to the CPU. In order to enable DMA transfer a DMA controller (DMAC) is provided. A DMAC implements the transfer algorithm in hardware, which is much faster than would be possible in software. It therefore automates data transfer between memory and I/O device.

2.3. System hardware architecture

An important way to differentiate between internal processor architectures is by counting the number of buses used to communicate between the systems registers and its ALU. According to this principle a system is said to have a single-, dual- or triple-bus architecture. Most of the presently available monolithic microprocessors have adopted what is called Standard Architecture. The discussions to follow will describe briefly the alternative architectures although it is emphasised that most microcontrollers will have the standard architecture.

In a single bus system data is brought to the ALU along the internal data bus shown at the top of Figure 2.3. This bus is connected to both sides of the ALU. The result of the operation performed on the data is returned to the data bus via the result bus and are subsequently gated to the registers. In order to allow for this bi-directional flow of data along the bus the single bus is multiplexed in time. This means that the Read/Write operations are sequenced by the control signals to share the same bus. It is also worth noting that the result returned via the result bus has to be buffered from the ALU so that it does not corrupt the contents of the accumulator. For this purpose a buffer register is provided (not shown in Figure 2.3) to store the result before placing it on the bus.

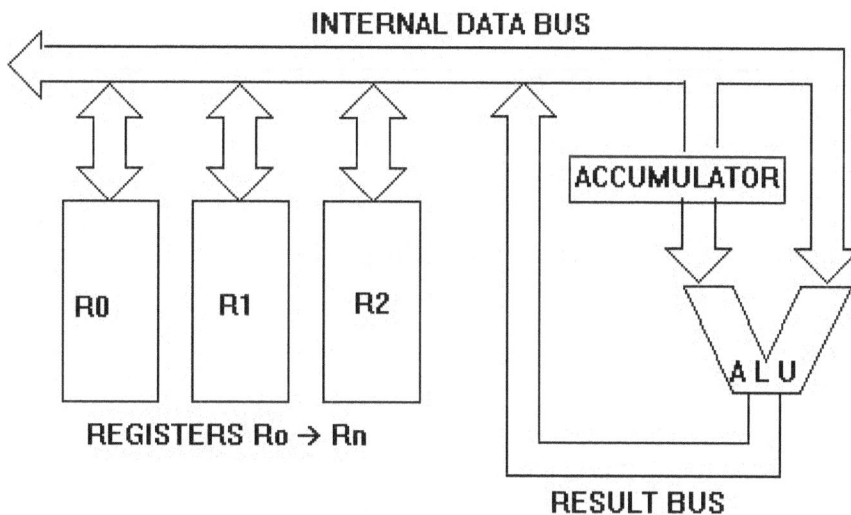

Figure 2.3. Single bus architecture

The main advantage of the single bus architecture is that it requires least bus area on the microprocessor IC. Its disadvantage is the fact that it is slow. In order to improve execution speed of a microprocessor the use of multiple buses is desirable.

Double and triple bus architectures

A double-bus system would use, for example, a single input bus, connecting to both inputs of the ALU, and a separate result-bus (D-bus) connecting the ALU back to the registers. As an example, many National Semiconductor products employ this architecture in order to improve speed. The architecture of a triple-bus system, shown in Figure 2.4 provides maximum performance. Two input buses are provided, the A-bus and the B-bus connected to either side of the ALU, which allows for both inputs to the ALU to be selected simultaneously. In addition they do not need to be buffered. The result can be gated on the D-bus independently from the source buses, which means that the buses do not need to be multiplexed in time. One disadvantage of this architecture is that it takes up a significant amount of chip space for the three buses. The physical size of the chip is limited and space is an important factor. The "standard" architecture therefore uses a single-bus system.

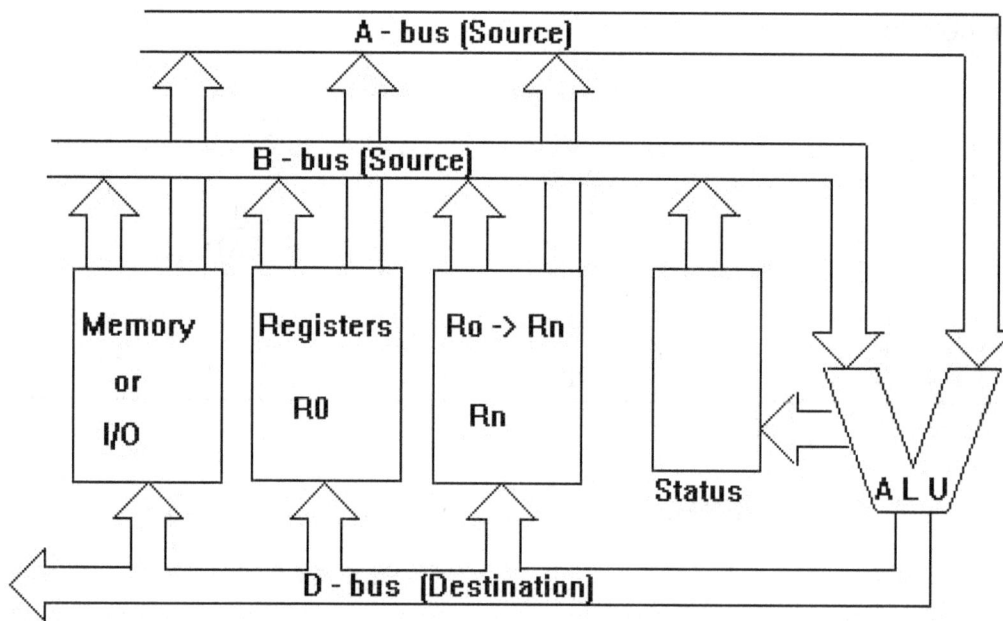

Figure 2.4. Triple bus architecture

Standard microprocessor architecture

The large majority of microprocessor chips on the market today implement the same architecture called the standard architecture shown in Figure 2.5. This is a single bus, accumulator based architecture, which makes efficient use of the chip area. A special accumulator register is added to one of the inputs to the ALU. The control box in the right of Figure 2.5 represents the control unit, which synchronises the operation of the entire system. It generates synchronisation signals between the ALU, the I/O and memory and it also decodes, fetches and executes instructions. The control unit also manages the control bus, which is used to communicate control information to the CPU and peripheral devices. The sequencing of the control unit is performed by an internal specialised programme called the micro programme, which is stored in ROM and is normally not accessible to the user.

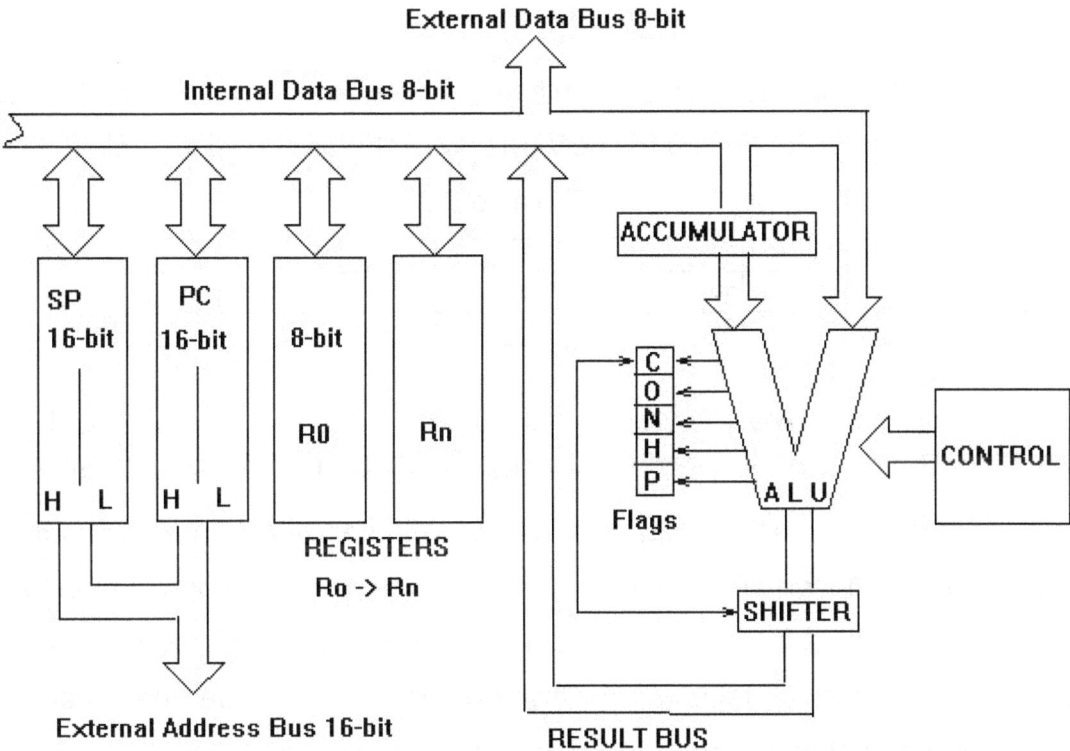

Figure 2.5. Standard computer architecture

Figure 2.5 also shows a number of flags associated with the ALU and the shifter operation. These will be described next by considering a simple example. Shifting operations are normally performed on register contents. These can range in size but for convenience we will consider operations on a byte of data. 8-bits form a byte and in binary arithmetic each bit is a power of 2 as shown in Table 2.1 below. When bits are manipulated for arithmetic and logic operations the result can cause overflow, zero, negative or other situations, which are monitored by a series of flags. Each one of these flags is either High or Low (i.e. On or OFF) to indicate whether the operation has caused the state of the flag to occur.

Table 2.1

Decimal	128	64	32	16	8	4	2	1
Power of 2	2^7	2^6	2^5	2^4	2^3	2^2	2^1	2^0
Binary	0	1	1	0	1	0	1	1

Where (MSB) - most significant bit, (LSB) - Least significant bit.

The binary byte 01101011 shown in Table 2.1 has a decimal equivalent,

$$0+64+32+0+8+0+2+1=107.$$

If for example the above byte were shifted to the left by one bit (i.e. each bit is shifted one position to the left) the new byte would be as shown in Table 2.2.

Table 2.2

128	64	32	16	8	4	2	1
2^7	2^6	2^5	2^4	2^3	2^2	2^1	2^0
1	1	0	1	0	1	1	0

The new binary byte 11010110 has a decimal equivalent of $128+64+0+0+16+0+4+2+0=214$, i.e., the number has doubled. Shifting operations are the quickest means of multiplication and division by a factor of 2. i.e. divide by 16 will be the same as shifting five bits to the right. In a regular shift the bit coming in on the right is a '0'. The bit falling off the left side is captured in a special "status register" where it is stored in order that it can be tested. In this context the bit that falls off the left is the carry bit and its status is held in the carry flag. The carry flag also monitors the overflow in arithmetic operations. For example if two of the above bytes were added together and the result was larger than 255, then a '1' as the ninth bit would be stored in the carry flag. This is shown in Table 2.3.

Table 2.3

	128	64	32	16	8	4	2	1	Decimal
	2^7	2^6	2^5	2^4	2^3	2^2	2^1	2^0	
	1	1	1	1	1	1	0	0	107
					+				
	1	0	0	0	0	0	0	0	214
					=				
1	0	1	1	1	1	1	0	0	321

Carry bit

Thus the overflow of the result generates a carry i.e. the ninth bit, which is stored in the carry flag. Other flags that are available for use are as follows,

Overflow (O): Overflow denotes the fact that an arithmetic carry within the word has modified the value of the most significant bit (MSB), resulting in a sign error in the case of a 2's compliment notation. Bit 7 (the MSB) in 2's compliment notation indicates the sign of the number (i.e. positive if logic '0' negative if logic '1'). Whenever 2's compliment addition is performed the result can inadvertently change the ninth bit and consequently cause an error by changing a positive into a negative number. In order to monitor this occurrence an Overflow flag is provided so that corrective action can be taken. Mathematically, the overflow is the exclusive OR (XOR) of the carry bit out of bit 7 and the carry generated from bit 6 to bit 7. The overflow will normally be used only when performing 2's complement arithmetic.

Negative (or sign flag) (N or S): The N bit is directly connected to bit 7 (MSB) of the result and indicates whether the result is positive or negative.

Zero (Z): The Z bit is set whenever the result of an operation is zero. It is used by arithmetic instructions to determine whether the result is zero and also by logic operations such as compare. Whenever the result of a comparison is successful, the Z bit is set to 1. This is because the compare operation implements a logical XOR between the word being tested and the pattern to which it is being compared.

Parity (P): This bit is not always present in microprocessors but when it is, it is used to test whether data has been transmitted correctly. The principle of parity is to count the number of 1's present in 8 bits. If this number is even the parity is even and conversely when it is odd. The parity test is normally used in communications and therefore it is usually implemented in a UART. Nonetheless, an even parity scheme will complete the number of 1's of a 7-bit word by adding either a 0 or a 1 so that the total number of 1's is even. Conversely, an odd parity scheme will set the eighth bit so that the total number of 1's is odd. The parity flag is used to detect whether the parity count is correct or not. Assuming for example even parity, the parity bit will be set whenever the number of bits within a word is not even, indicating parity error. The parity bit is an extra bit (bit 8) appended to the data and does not affect the value of the data.

Note: A byte has eight bits starting from bit 0 and going to bit 7. The MSB is therefore bit 7 and not bit 8.

Other status bits can be provided within the flags register. In particular Interrupt enable bit may be provided. Whenever it is set, outside interrupts will be accepted and conversely when it is cleared, external interrupts will be inhibited, i.e. they are masked.

Address registers

To the left of Figure 2.5 are two registers connected to data bus on the top and the address bus on the bottom. These are address registers intended for storage of addresses. They are 16-bit which means they are made up of two bytes a high byte (H) and a low byte (L). The only way to load an address register is via the data bus. Two bytes, the high and the low byte, need to be transferred for a 16-bit address. The low byte represents bits 0→7 and the high byte bits 8→15. At least two address registers are present in most microprocessors. In Figure 2.5 these are shown as the Stack Pointer (SP) and the Programme Counter (PC) registers.

Programme Counter (PC): The programme counter register must be present in every microprocessor. In some microprocessors such as the Intel 80x86 family this register is called the instruction pointer (IP) register. It contains the address of the next instruction to be executed. Being as the execution of the programme is sequential the microprocessor must know the address of the next instruction to be executed. In order that this instruction can be executed the memory address of its location needs to be supplied to the microprocessor. This address is stored in the programme counter and is deposited on the address bus when the next instruction is to be fetched for execution. This instruction will normally reside in memory and once it has been located its contents will be sent from the memory to the CPU for execution. The contents of this location are the instruction for the microprocessor to execute.

Stack pointer (SP): The stack pointer points to the top of the stack, which is an area in memory that is reserved for storing important information during the execution of a programme. For example, when an interrupt occurs, the stack will be loaded with the location of the current instruction being executed. In order to keep track of the top of the stack a 16-bit stack pointer register is used. The stack is a 'Last In First Out' structure shown in Figure 2.6. It is a chronological structure, which accumulates events in the order in which they are deposited. The oldest event placed on the stack is at the bottom and it is the last to come off it. As shown in Figure 2.6 events or symbols are placed onto the stack with a PUSH command and taken off it with a POP command. Stacks can be implemented in software or hardware depending on the specifications of the embedded system that is being implemented. Software stacks are cheaper and slower than hardware stacks. It is possible to provide a hardware stack by dedicating a set of internal registers to implement the stack. This is limited in size and the software stack is often the preferred alternative. In software the stack is implemented in microprocessor RAM. The base of the stack is selected by the programmer and is managed automatically within the SP register. The SP usually points to the first available word on the stack. The goal is to provide the fastest PUSH and PULL operations possible. The stack is particularly useful in interrupts when the contents for the important information are PUSHed onto the stack to be saved before control is switched to the interrupt service routine. When the programme is resumed the contents of the stack are POPed back. It is up to the programmer to decide what elements need to be PUSHed and POPed when an interrupt occurs.

Another useful feature is stack programming. Since the PUSH and POP instructions are very fast, stack programming loads words onto the bus that are pushed and popped, to be executed as a programme. This kind of programming is extremely fast since the fetch is very efficient, however it is only suitable for sequential programming where the sequence of instructions is known in advance.

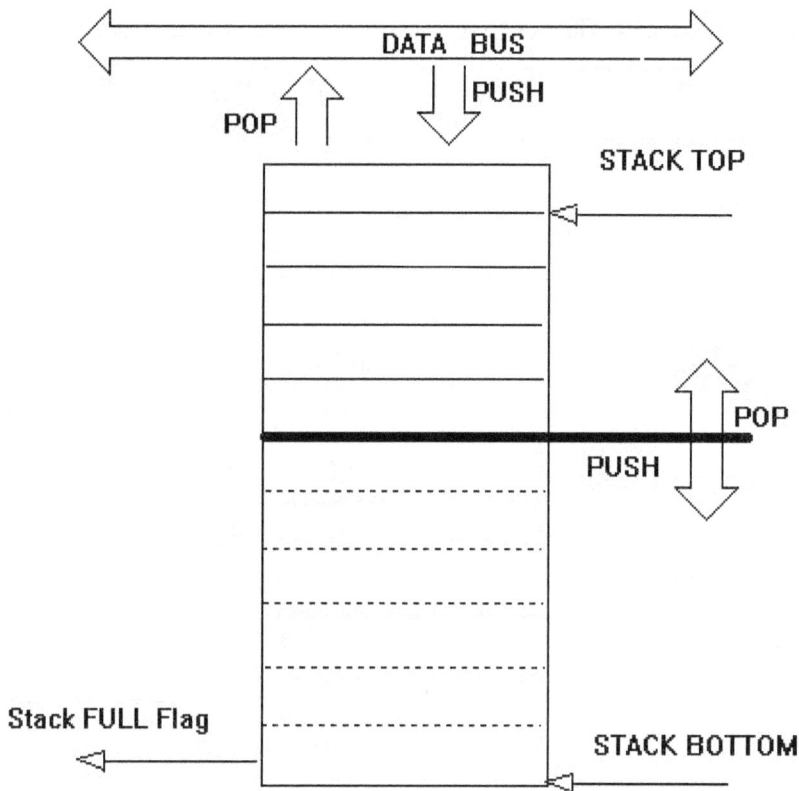

Figure 2.6 The Stack is accessed with PUSH and POP instructions

Execution of an instruction

The microprocessor needs to be told what to do and this is done by providing it with instructions in the programme. The execution of the instruction whether it is in ROM or RAM is done in a sequence of three steps,

- Fetch
- Decode
- Execute

This should make sense since the instruction resides in memory and needs to be fetched first. When it is fetched it has to be put somewhere so that it can be decoded. After it is fetched the instruction is stored as a bit pattern in a special register called the instruction register (IR) inside the control unit. Before this instruction can be executed it needs to be decoded by a decoder, which is also inside the control unit. The control unit then generates the appropriate signals and the instruction is executed.

An instruction can be longer than 8-bits and can consist of two or more words. The first word of the instruction contains the operation code (op-code).

In fact the 80x86 family of microprocessors use the first six bits of the instruction to describe the op-code. By decoding this op-code the microprocessor will know whether it needs to fetch more bytes from memory in order to execute the instruction. The control unit controls the complete fetch-decode-execute process.

2.4. Overview of Intel 8051 family of microcontrollers

Intel entered the microcontroller market in 1980's when it produced the 8051. The 8051 was one of the first microcontroller families, and remains one of the most commonly used. Although Intel have discontinued production of the MCS52, 251 families, the 8051 continues to be manufactured by other chip manufacturers such as Atmel, Dallas Semiconductor, Philips and others. Devices in the family include the 8031, 8051, 8052, 80151, 80251, and the extended 8051 series XA. [2]

2.5. 8051 Microcontroller architecture

In its standard form the 8051 includes several standard on-chip peripherals, including timers, counters, and UART's (Universal Asynchronous Receiver Transmitter), varying amount of on-chip programme memory and 128 bytes of data memory. As a result, 8051 devices are available from multiple sources, are relatively inexpensive, have good development tools, and have a rich repository of application specific documentation accumulated over a number of years and a variety of applications. Other variations include even more on-chip peripherals, such as analogue-digital converters, pulse-width modulators, I^2C bus interfaces, etc. A list of current devices with their basic features is available from the Intel web site. [2] Figure 2.7 shows all the components required in a stand-alone computer which include the CPU, ROM and RAM, I/O ports, interrupt control and counter timers. An external oscillator, which is not shown on the diagram, drives the CPU clock. Although many variants of the 8051 support faster clock rates, for the duration of this course we will assume a clock frequency of 12MHz, which is conveniently divided by 12 to produce 1MHz instruction cycle. The 8051 family of microcontrollers can have anywhere from 64 to 256 bytes of RAM. [2] Programme code refers to the actual software, which controls the operation of the microcontroller. It is specific to an application and once designed it is not intended to change during the lifecycle of the application. For this reason, programme code is stored in read only memory (ROM). On the other hand, variables and data that change during the execution of the programme must be placed in random access memory (RAM).

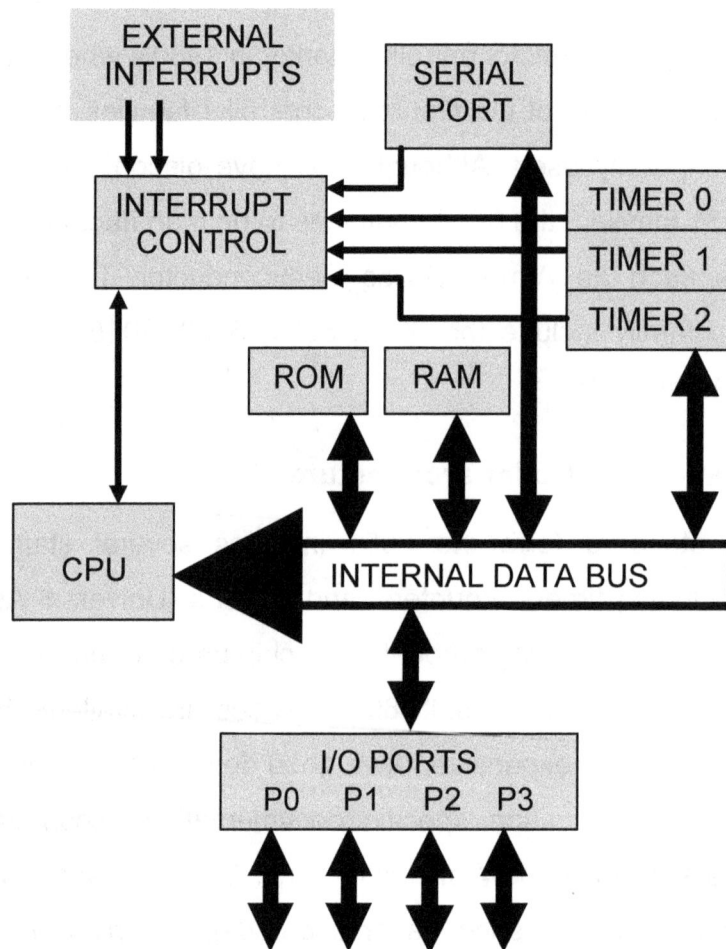

Figure 2.7. System hardware architecture for the 8051 family.

Since it is the programmer who ultimately decides what part of the programme is code, and what is data, it is important to bear in mind that anything written to ROM cannot be changed at Run-Time. Figure 2.7 also shows the basic connectivity between the on-board peripherals. Namely the serial port, timers and interrupt control. It can be seen that an interrupt can be received from the timer and also from the serial port. This allows the designer to programme a response to interrupts from these peripherals. More details are given in later sections of this course.

Programming the 8051 in C or assembly necessitates that the programmer is familiar with the internal architecture of the microcontroller. This architecture refers to the functional components that facilitate programme execution. The best source of information on the architecture is available from the users manual for the chip. However, a brief outline of some components will be covered next.

Special function registers (SFRs)

A powerful feature of the 8051 family is that they use a dedicated set of Special Function Registers (SFRs). These registers are located in RAM, and are used to access arithmetic registers and also to control the on-chip peripherals such as ports, timers and interrupts. The SFRs are labelled by symbols that are recognised by all 8051 assemblers and C compilers, however they can also be accessed directly by their exact memory location. The general layout of SFRs, including their names and addresses (in hexadecimal), is shown in Figure 2.8. The SFRs are mainly located to the left of the diagram. Let us briefly describe the function of each special function register.

Starting at the top of the diagram the first SFR is the programme status word (PSW) register, which contains the flags. It is worth pointing out that in computer programming, flag refers to one bit that is used to store a binary value, which has an assigned meaning. If the value of this bit changes, then the CPU is aware from the meaning of the flag, what has occurred? Typically, flags will be assigned a meaning based on what is happening in the accumulator register. Consider the example shown earlier in Table 2,3 where the accumulator register is used in the addition of two numbers and the result is larger then 255 (i.e. one byte range). It can be seen from table 2.3 that this produces a carry bit. The way that the CPU remembers that a carry has been produced is to use the program status word register to show that the carry flag has been SET. The same flag will be CLEARED when the accumulator is next used in the arithmetic operation. Other flags are used similarly to indicate the status after an operation and these will be briefly described next.

SPECIAL FUNCTION REGISTERS

```
                                                        ┌───────┐
                                                        │  ALU  │
                                                        └───────┘
 ┌─────┬─────┬─────┬─────┬─────┬─────┬─────┬─────┐
 │ CY  │ AC  │ F0  │ RS1 │ RS0 │ OV  │ --- │  P  │
 └─────┴─────┴─────┴─────┴─────┴─────┴─────┴─────┘
 │           ACC (E0)          │        FLAGS - PSW
 │             B (F0)          │
 │           IPC (B8)          │   INTRUPT
 │           IEC (A8)          │   CONTROL
 │           SBUF (99)         │   SERIAL
 │           SCON (98)         │   PORT
 │           TH1 (8D)          │
 │           TL1 (8B)          │
 │           TH0 (8C)          │   TIMER
 │           TL0 (8A)          │   CONTROL
 │           TMOD (89)         │
 │           TCON (88)         │
 │           DPH (83)          │       PROGRAM
 │           DPL (82)          │       CONTROL
 │           SP (81H)          │         PCH
 │         DATA RAM            │         PCL
 │         (20-7Fh)            │   20-2F BIT
 │      RBANK 3 (19-1Fh)       │   ADDRESSABLE
 │      RBANK 2 (10-18h)       │   30-7F GENERAL
 │      RBANK 1 (08-0Fh)       │   PURPOSE
 │      RBANK 0 (00-07h)       │
```

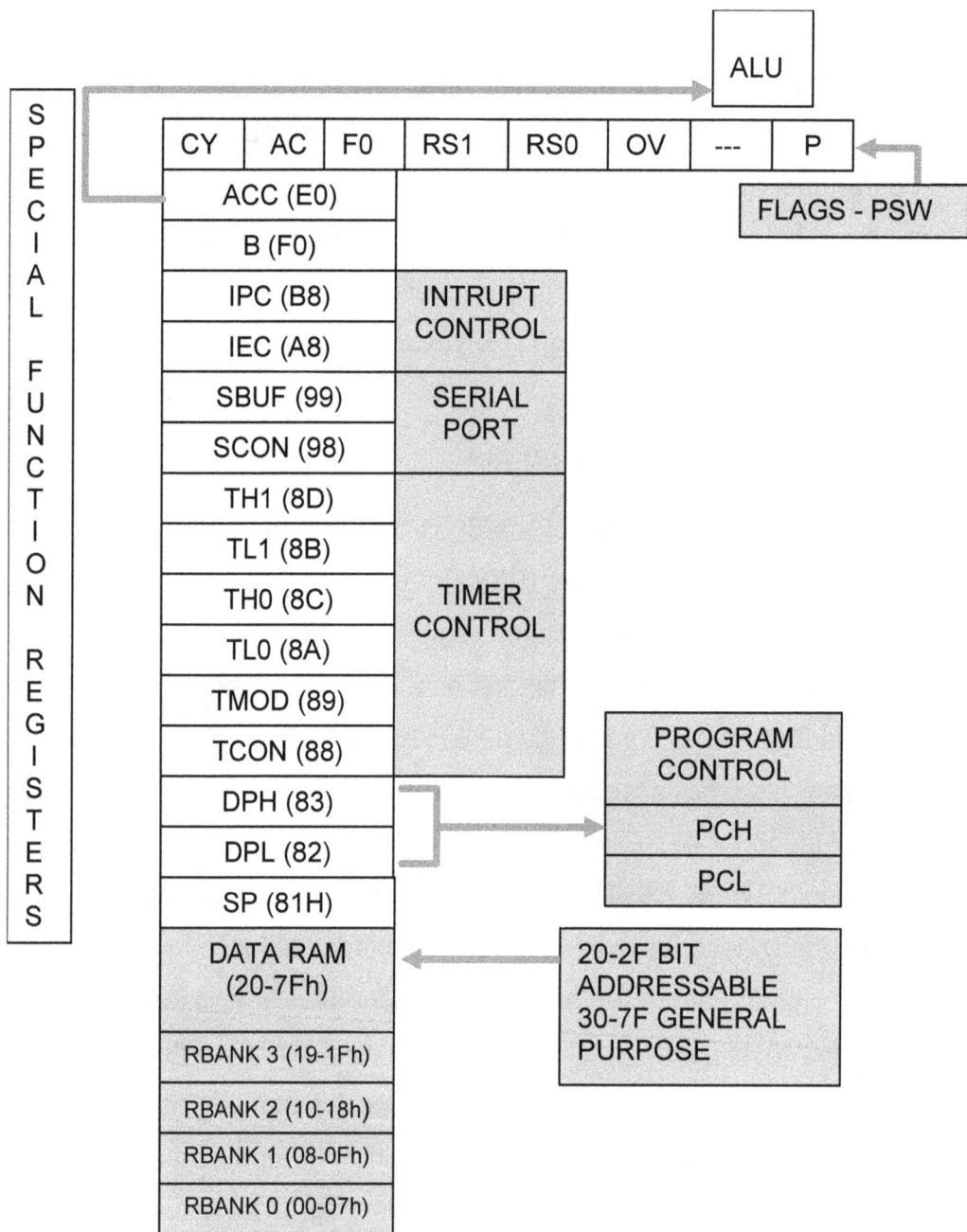

Figure 2.8 Special function registers

The diagram of Figure 2.8 shows how the individual flags are mapped onto the PSW. A brief description of the individual flags is as follows:

- **Carry (CY):** is SET if the latest arithmetic operation resulted in a carry bit, from low byte to high byte. It is also used as the Boolean accumulator for bit operations.

- **Auxiliary Carry (AC):** is SET if the latest arithmetic operation resulted in a carry bit, from low nibble to high nibble.
- **User Flag 0 (F0):** General-purpose flag, which is pushed onto the STACK as part of the PSW save.
- **Register Bank Select (RS0 and RS1):** These determine which of the four register banks is in use.
- **Overflow (OV):** is SET if the latest arithmetic operation resulted in overflow.
- **Parity (P):** reflects the parity of the Accumulator register.

Arithmetic registers: Next down are the arithmetic registers including the accumulator (ACC), which is the data, register used in calculations. The B register is dedicated for multiply and divide arithmetic, and in this event serves both as source and destination register.

Interrupt control SFRs: These are, the Interrupt Priority Register (IPC), which contains the control bits to set the interrupt to a desired level of priority. There are only two levels of priority represented by a 1 or a 0, 1 representing the higher priority level. The interrupt enable register (IEC) stores the enable bits for each of the five interrupts sources. Thus, each source can be individually enabled or disabled. This register also includes a global enable-disable bit of the interrupt system.

Serial port SFRs: The serial port control registers are the SBUF, which is used to store the data, and SCON, which is used to control serial communications. Programming the communications mode is achieved by setting the relevant bits in the SCON register.

Timer registers. There are two 16-bit timer/counters on the chip and these are labelled T0 and T1. They each have a high and low byte to store the timer count. These are respectively, Time/Counter 0 (High), Timer/Counter 0 (Low) and Time/Counter 1 (High), Timer/Counter 1 (Low). Additionally the TMOD register contains the bits that select which operations each timer/counter will perform. The timer control register (TCON) contains the bits to start/stop counters and to control timer overflow and interrupts.

External memory access: The 16-bit data pointer register (DPTR) is used for external memory access. Memory expansion for the 8051 is possible by interfacing external memory using the I/O space and locating this peripheral using the DPTR register and the Programme Store Enable (PSEN) control signal.

STACK register: The STACK pointer SFR stores the address at which the last byte was pushed onto the STACK, that is to say, the top of the STACK. As mentioned earlier the STACK is an area of memory, which the CPU uses to store important programme information. This information is primarily concerned with storing where the programme should go after an interrupt and what information must be stored before it occurred.

Below the SFRs on the memory map are the 128 bytes of user RAM. We will discuss details later on but for now it worth mentioning that this area is split up into Data RAM, which starts at 20h and ends at 7Fh. This data RAM is in turn split up into 16 bytes (128 bits) of bit-addressable memory in the range 20h –2Fh.The bit addressable area can be used as individual flags which can be a very useful programming tool. The range 30h-7Fh is user data memory.

Parts of the 8051 internal memory can be accessed as four register banks – each register bank is a group of 8-bytes. These are designated R0 through R7 and are used for rapid moving from one activity to another. Again, labels Rn are used to identify these to the assembler but their physical locations can vary depending on the set-up in the Programme Status Word (PSW) register. Next we consider the 8051 hardware architecture from the programmer's standpoint. This is to say that the programmer needs to understand how the memory arrangement corresponds to the programming instruction set. For example, the 8051 uses the data pointer register (DPTR) as a 16-bit register that is specifically designed to access external ROM. When this is needed all the address space (i.e. 2^{16}=64K) is used for external access. In hexadecimal this range is form 0000h to FFFFh. On the other hand when internal RAM is accessed the address range 0000h to 0080h is available to access SFRs and other memory locations available. It should be fairly evident that the programmer must understand the variety of addressing modes and what they correspond to in order to make the best use of the available resources. For this reason the 8051 memory model is briefly covered next.

8051 Memory model - hardware view

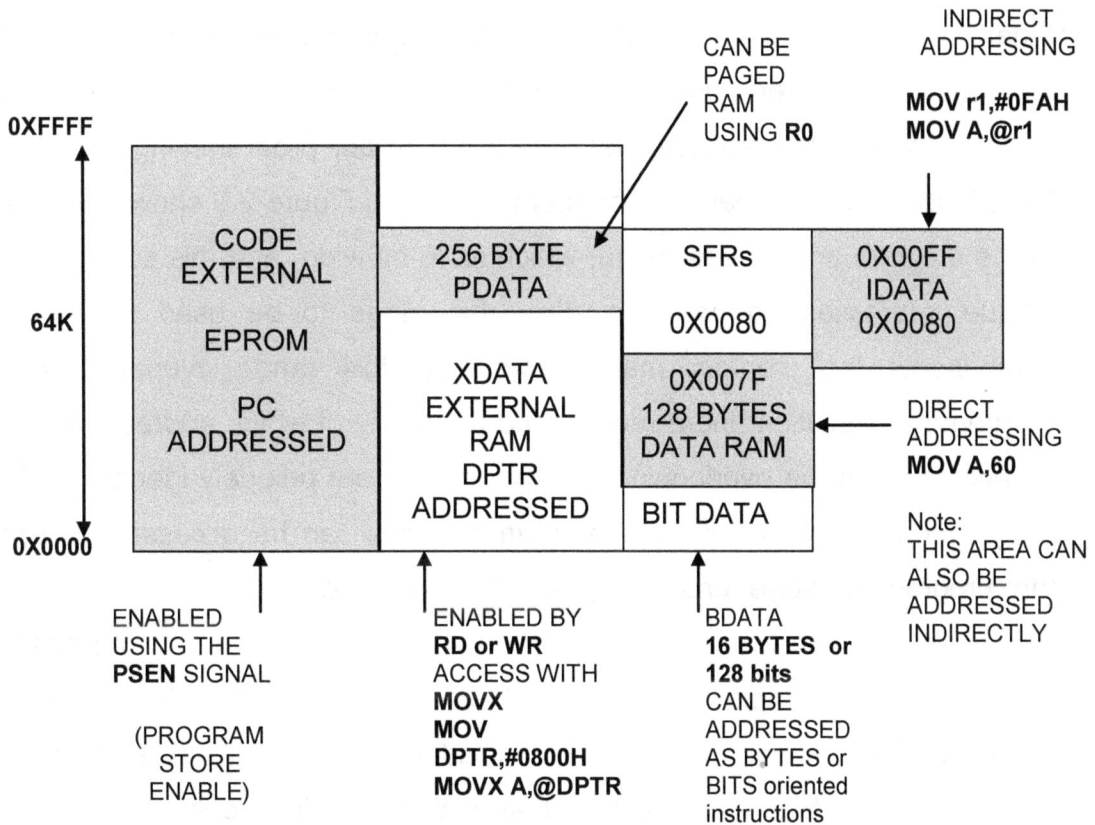

Figure 2.9. The 8051 memory model

Efficient programs execute fast and take up the least amount of memory while performing a specific task. As mentioned earlier computer memory is divided into two main categories:

- Random Access Memory (RAM) which is used for temporary data storage and which can be written to or read from.

- Read Only Memory (ROM): This can only be read from and is therefore used as permanent storage and is therefore used to store programme code. Additionally ROM can also be used to store data that does not change, such as constants and look-up table data.

In embedded design it is very important that the programme developer is fully aware of the memory capability of the hardware. Memory is expensive, and it does consume power, so storing redundant information, which takes up memory, is not advisable. Additionally, the developer should maintain variables at their lowest possible size, so that programme memory (RAM) is conserved.

Assembly language programming is generally more memory-efficient because the programmer allocates the memory for data and code. On the other hand high-level languages declare a memory model, which the compiler supports for the given hardware. In this case memory allocation is performed in accordance with compiler rules. We will consider programming models for the 8051 in the next chapter. The memory map in Figure 2.9 shows to the left of the diagram an address range, which is 16-bit wide, and this supports 64K unique addresses. In order to allow this range to be used by different components the memory map shows how this range overlaps. During programme execution, there must be no ambiguity of which address needs to be accessed so the overlapping memory ranges are uniquely identified to the programme. Thus, for example programme code can be accessed by using the programme store enable signal (PSEN). When this is the case, the overlapping range of addresses shown in Figure 2.9 is not accessible. However, if for example access to the SFR range is required, then the PSEN signal can be removed, and the required address range for the SFRs can be placed onto the bus. The memory that is available is accessed in different ways. For example the CODE memory shown in the diagram above is addressed using the Programme Counter (PC) register. This register is 16 bits and therefore the amount of EPROM code that can be accessed is 2^{16}=64K. The address range is therefore from 0x0000 to 0xFFFF (the x represents Hexadecimal notation). Clearly, the fact that this is ROM means that the programme variables cannot be stored in this memory range. The reason for this is that variables are expected to change during the execution of the programme, and their values have to be written to memory, which ROM will not permit. Thus, only the read operation will work with CODE memory.

The 8051 architecture supports a signal called Programme Store Enable (PSEN), which is used to ENABLE the CODE ROM chip. This is so that it can be differentiated from RAM access. Later on in this chapter we will consider a typical interface of the 8051 to RAM and ROM chips. There you will see that signals from the 8051 CPU to start a Read (RD/) and Write (WR/) cycles are suitably connected to the corresponding memory chips.

Data is stored in RAM, and the same address range is used. That is, the range 0x0000 to 0xFFFF of RAM is available for XDATA. The X here indicates that the data is external to the 8051 chip. (Not to be confused with 0x000 that uses the x to signify that the value is hexadecimal). The fact is that 8051 architecture supports interfacing of external RAM of up to 64K. Since both the READ and WRITE signals are available with RAM these are used to ENABLE the RAM chip. An example of this interface is briefly discussed later in this chapter. The 8051 allows XDATA to be represented as PAGED memory. Thus the memory space is divided up into equal size pages (256 bytes to be precise). It follows that 256 of these pages can be defined in the 64K memory range. This memory range is referred to as PDATA (P for Paged). To access this memory arrangement two 8-bit ports are used. One port is used to address the 256-byte page, the other to access 256 of these pages. This is shown in Figure 2.10.The choice as to whether to use paged or non-paged memory is left to the programme developer.

Note: Port 0 is multiplexed as Data/Address High

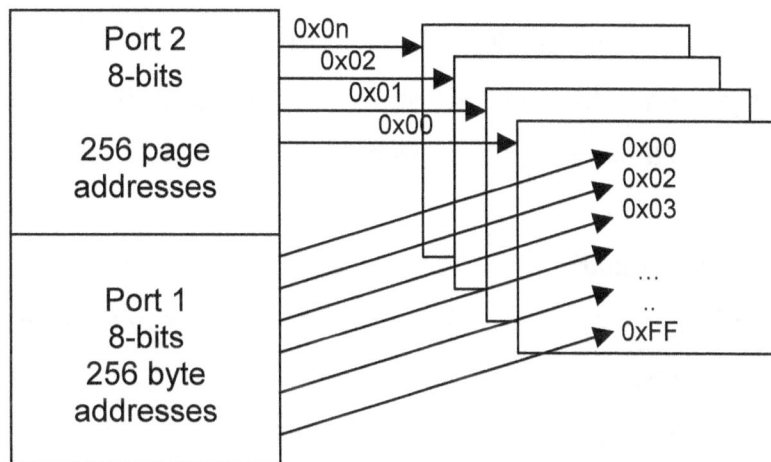

Figure 2.10 16-bit address space from two 8-bit ports

8051 RAM address space – programmers' view

Figure 2.11 shows the memory map of the standard 8051. To the left of the Figure is the memory range in hexadecimal and to the right the explanation of the use for this range. It is clear that the memory range 0x000 to 0x00FF contains 256 bytes. The lower 128 bytes in the range 0x0000 to 0x007F are RAM as mentioned earlier. The 128 bytes above this, in the range 0x0080 to 0x00FF are used to store the SFRs. These are shaded grey in Figure 2.11.

0x00FF - 0X0080	SFRs	IDATA
0X007F - 0x0030	General Purpose DATA RAM	
0X002F - 0X0020	BIT DATA BITS OR BYTES	
0X001F - 0X0018	register BANK 3 R0 to R7	
0X0017 - 0X0010	register BANK 2 R0 to R7	
0X000F - 0X0008	register BANK 1 R0 to R7	
0X0007 - 0X0000	register BANK 0 R0 to R7	

Figure 2.11 8051 programmer's view memory model

Thus, it is seen that the standard 8051 comes with 128 bytes of user RAM. This memory is accessed using the internal address bus. The lower addresses 0x0000 to 0x001F are used to provide the developer with 4x8-byte register banks; these are labelled BANK 0- BANK 3. Each of these banks holds 8 bytes of space to hold the registers labelled as R0-R7. It should be evident that labels R0-R7 could refer to any of the BANKS 0-3. Potentially this can cause programming errors, and to prevent this from occurring, ONLY ONE register BANK can be active at any one time. The actual BANK that is active is selected in the Programme Status Word (PSW) register bank select bits (RS0 and RS1). Alternatively the absolute address of each byte of a register BANK can be used for accessing the data so that there is no possibility of mistaking the register. For example, address 1A refers to R2 in BANK 3. In the address range 0x0020 to 0x002F is the 16 bytes of Bit-Addressable RAM. This memory is useful for storing bit values, such as for example flags, to indicate if run-time values have exceeded a particular pre-set limit. Whether accessed as bit or byte, this RAM has to be addressed by location. The relevant addresses are given in the Table 2.3.

Table 2.3

Bit Address locations															
20	21	22	23	24	25	26	27	28	29	2A	2B	2C	2D	2E	2F
Byte address locations															
00-07	08-0F	10-17	18-1F	20-27	28-2F	30-37	38-3F	40-47	48-4F	50-57	58-5F	60-67	68-6F	70-77	78-7F

This area of RAM can be accessed as bytes directly by using the Byte Address in table 2.3. If Bit addressing is required then the location of the bit has to be given as per table above.

In assembly programming, the bit operator SETB is used to access the individual bits, while in C we need to use the `sbit` operator, discussed in Chapter 5. It is worth noting the possibility of confusion here, in that the address 0x00 for example could refer to the first byte of register R0 while we are in fact attempting to access a bit value. However, since bit operations are distinctly identified in programming, there is no possibility of confusion. For example, SETB 0, will only perform the action on BDATA space.

RAM memory range 0x030 to 0x07F is the general-purpose data RAM. This is used for data storage. It is a good idea to put the STACK in this memory space so that the STACK operations do not affect any of the register banks or BDATA space.

We recall here that virtually all microcomputers use a STACK. As mentioned earlier, the STACK is an area of memory that is used to store temporary values needed by the CPU. For example, when an interrupt occurs, the current programme execution is interrupted, and the programme is directed to another memory location in order to service the interrupt. Following this servicing of the interrupt, programme control needs to be returned to the point that it was at when the interrupt occurred. This information is temporarily stored on the STACK, and is made available automatically by the RETI instruction. Thus, whenever an interrupt occurs, the address of the next instruction to be executed is stored on the STACK to be retrieved when a return from the interrupt service routine is made with the RETI instruction. In a multi-tasking system with many interrupts, many values are placed on the

STACK and this can cause the STACK to grow and invade memory space of registers and BDATA, which can cause errors. Additionally it is very important to note that when the system is reset the STACK is placed at address 0x07, which interferes with register BANK space. The developer must therefore change the location of the STACK as appropriate.

Special function registers (SFRs)

The RAM range from 0x0080 to 0x00FF holds the special function registers (SFRs). (See Figure 2.8). The basic function of these registers is to enable the programme developer to control the on-board peripherals, which is done by writing information to the relevant SFR.

Programming the SFRs will be covered in later chapters but for now it is worth noting that the same memory address range, namely addresses 0x0080 to 0x00FF are also used for indirectly accessed data (IDATA) as shown in Figure 2.9. To distinguish between accessing an SFR or IDATA the 8051 provides a different addressing mode. Thus, when accessing IDATA RAM we use the indirect addressing mode i.e. (MOV A, @Ri), where the location of the data is contained in a register (Ri). This register can be either in banks R0 or R1. Recall that R0 and R1 are 8-bit registers and can hold 2^8=256 addresses, ranging from 0x00 to 0xFF. However, only the address range 0x80 to 0xFF is available, and this range gives 128 bytes. In 8051 applications it is generally recommended to use IDATA RAM for the STACK because the STACK is well suited to indirect addressing and this prevents STACK interfering with user memory or vice-versa.

Programming the SFRs

Within the 8051 family of MCUs, SFRs are designed to enable programmers to access the hardware. By writing the correct bytes of information to each SFR the programmer can control the operation of a particular device. Precise details of these registers and the settings that need to be used for specific operation are available form the user's manual. [31] The programming bits that correspond to any function are given in the user manual for the microcontroller, and we do not need to reproduce these here. It is sufficient at this point to simply state that the bits need to be programmed in accordance with the function specified in the user's manual. Once we have specified the necessary values of these bits, it is a relatively simple matter to write these values to the address of the appropriate SFR. Please note that this course is not aimed at describing every possible combination of programming SFRs. Some discussion on the general principles of programming SFRs including the use of `sbit` operator is covered in Chapter 5. We will look at some examples of how to programme SFRs in the laboratory exercises of Chapter 5 of this course.

2.6.   Decoding the EPROM (CODE) and RAM (XDATA) memory

To illustrate the address overlap in CODE and XDATA memory ranges it is worth showing a typical hardware interface combining both ROM and RAM. Figure 2.12 shows a ROM-less CPU, the 8031 version of the microcontroller, which relies on external ROM to store the programme code. An interface is therefore required for an external ROM chip. (EPROM in the diagram above) The diagram does not show details, but indicates that the ROM chip is enabled using the programme store enable signal (PSEN/), which is only active for external ROM access. This is seen on the diagram by the (PSEN\) pin connecting to the chip enable pin (CE/) of the EPROM chip. On the other hand, RAM is accessed by using the read (RD/) and write (WR/) signals. Note that the backslash on these symbols indicates that they are active low. In other words the signal is active when the value is logical '0' and conversely it is not active when the value is logical '1'.

The RAM and ROM can be located in the same address space since they are enabled by separate signals that are mutually exclusive. That is the WR/ and PSEN/ signals will never be LOW at the same time, since writing to ROM is not possible. This means that the same memory range can be used for both RAM and ROM, but they are selected separately by the status pf the

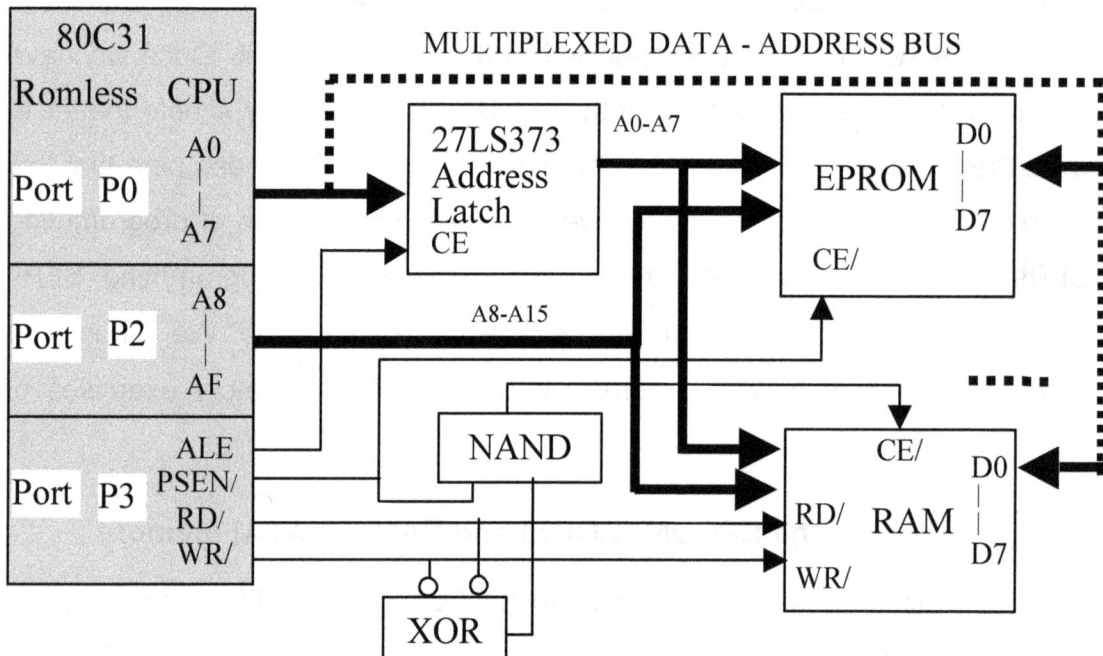

Figure 2.12 Interfacing ROM and RAM chips to the 8031

The diagram of Figure 2.12 also shows the use of an address latch chip (27LS373). This enables a whole port (P0 in this case) to be multiplexed in time. That is to say, it is used at different times for a different purpose. This chip is enabled using the edge triggered Address Latch Enable (ALE) signal available from the Intel 8051 family of chips. This arrangement supports the multiplexing of 8-bit data and address lines. When used for addressing the 8-bits are used to latch the low byte of the 16-bit Programme Counter (PCL) address value. That is to say, ALE latches addresses A0-A7 from port P0 on the -ve edge. Note that high byte of the Programme Counter (PCH) is available directly from P2.

NOTE: Port P0 is data/address multiplexed, Port P2 is not multiplexed. When P0 is not used to latch PCL, it is used to deliver 8-bit data. This multiplexing arrangement is workable because CODE and DATA access is separate in all cases. Once again, please note that I am using the backslash here (PSEN/) to indicate that the signal is active low. This is to say, it is active when it is a logical '0' rather than logical '1'. If there were no backslash this would make the signal active high and no backslash would be used as is the case with the ALE signal.

In summary therefore, there are two signals that are used to control external memory. PSEN/ is edge triggered and only goes active low during external read cycle. When it is not active, access is intended to internal memory of the 8051. ALE on the other hand is active high and it is used to enable the latch, which is used to distinguish between port use for address and for data. The two signals, PSEN/ and ALE combine to control the usage of port P0. External memory is 64K and therefore 16-bit address values are needed for access and so PSEN/ needs to combine with ALE to provide 16 bits for addressing. This information is aimed mainly to show how the memory map can be decoded using the port multiplexing features of the 8051 and the ALE chip. More details on general interfacing techniques are provided in Chapter 8 of this text.

Earlier on we mentioned that for efficient use of memory space assembly programming is the preferred option. This is particularly true in applications where code efficiency is required, such as for example in critically constrained real-time systems. Now that we have covered basic architecture let us consider the programming environment. In the next chapter we will look very briefly at assembly programming so that the reader can have a feel for comparison between C and assembly programming.

Exercises

2.1. Discuss the main differences between a microprocessor and a microcontroller.

2.2. Give examples of embedded systems applications that may use a microprocessor controller and others that can use a microcontroller. Discuss the basis on which the choices are made.

2.3. Explain the types of memory that are used in embedded systems and discuss possible applications for each of these.

2.4. What is a bus-cycle in computer chips?

2.5. Explain the single, double, triple and standard bus architectures. Also, discuss the relative disadvantages and advantages between them.

2.6. Describe typical flags found in a computer system and explain their purpose.

2.7. Explain what the Programme Counter and Stack Pointer registers are and what they are used for.

2.8. Describe the systems hardware architecture of the Intel 8051 microcontroller family. In your answer include a brief description of all the on-board peripherals.

2.9. Figure 1 below shows a partially completed memory map of a typical 8051 microcontroller. Explain what each block is typically used for and also the addressing mode that is used to access it.

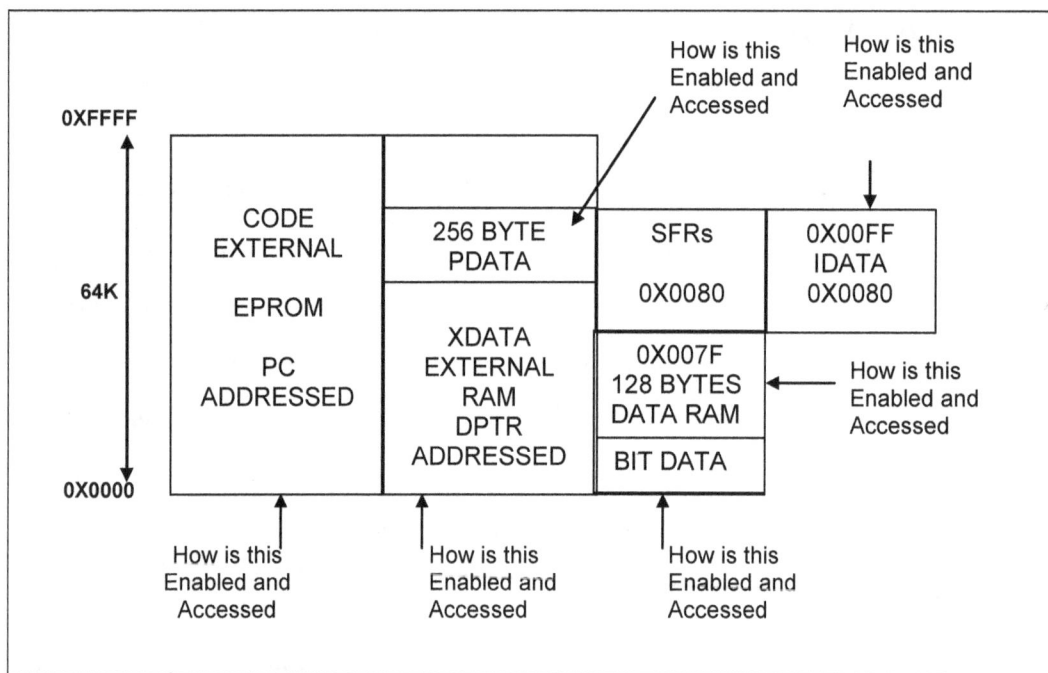

Figure 1 Memory Map for 8051

2.10. Draw a diagram of the internal architecture of the 8051 microcontroller and explain briefly each component. In your answer also explain the location and function of each of the Special Function Registers

2.11. Explain how port multiplexing can be used to enable 16-bit access for addressing ROM/RAM with 8051 derivative microcontrollers.

2.12. Design a detailed interface to the 8031 ROM-Less microcontroller to 8K-bytes of RAM and a further 8K-bytes of ROM. In your design, show details of signals and gates used.

CHAPTER 3 SOFTWARE DEVELOPMENT TOOLS

3.1.   Introduction

All microprocessors and microcontrollers are digital electronic devices that are packaged as integrated circuits (ICs). The task of programming these ICs reduces to writing worded instructions and storing this as source code. This source code is then converted into a code that the digital IC can execute. Thus, all programming efforts are aimed at producing executable code which is in binary format (i.e. 00101000), and which will instruct the hardware to perform in a specific manner.

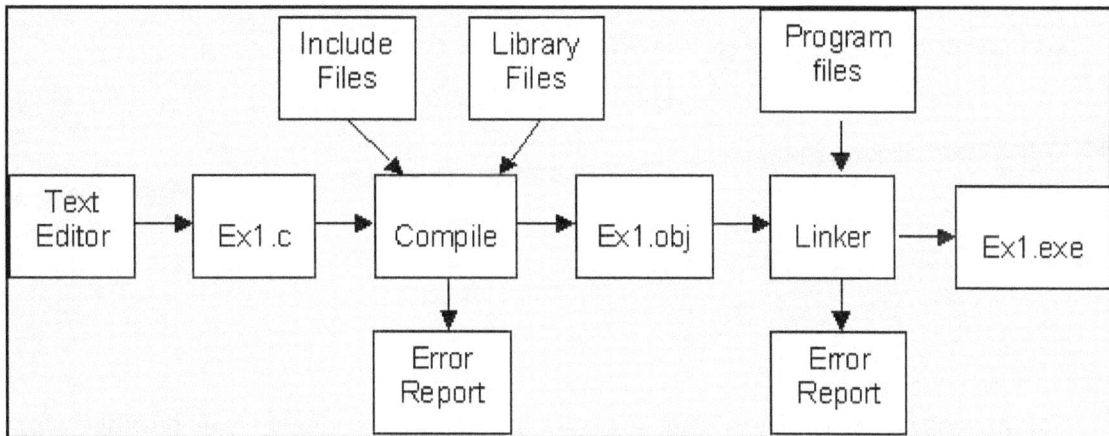

Figure 3.1 Process of converting source code into executable code

The actual coding is in a language that is easier to understand by the programmer. This can be a high level language (HLL) such as C or a low level language such as assembly. Programming languages include the tools to translate the language code instructions into the binary machine code for the hardware to execute. These tools include, compilers, assemblers, linkers as well as editing and debugging tools. This process of converting a source file into executable programme code is shown in the diagram of Figure 3.1. Typically a source code written in a programming language is entered in the text editor. For example, with reference to Figure 3.1, the source code Ex1.c is written in the C programming language. This file is saved, and used wherever it may be needed in the various stages of programme design. This is to say that a particular source file may be used in more than one development project. Next, the compiler converts the source file into the object file. This is done with the help of include and library files, which we will cover in Chapter 5 of this text.

At this point it is worth noting that C uses libraries or header files which contain pre-coded functions that a programmer may need to use. A very common example of this are the `printf` and `scanf` functions that are contained in the `stdio.h` header file. Note that in C you can only use the functions and variables that have been declared previously. Therefore, include statements must appear before any other statements in order for the compiler to be certain of having seen the functions before they have been used. An example of this would be as follows,

```
#include "stdio.h" // Header file
main()
{
printf ("hello world/n"); /* Function contained
in stdio.h */
}
```

In actual fact, when the include statement is used, the compiler will process the complete header file (`stdio.h`) as though it were a part of the C source file. Thus, when the compiler encounters the function `printf`, it will recognise it, for it is contained in the `stdio.h` file.

If you need more information about the contents of the header files please note that the C reference manual, which is normally supplied with the compiler will list all the header files and the functions that the compiler supports so that programmers can make use of them.

During the compile stage, any errors in the language syntax are highlighted. Syntax errors are generated when the compile encounters instructions in the source file that it does not recognise. These can be spelling errors or incorrect use of a variable or a function.

However, it should be said that errors in the algorithm, or rather inaccuracies in the results produced by the programme, are not detectable at this stage. Programming errors of this type are checked using the debugger facility.

With reference to Figure 3.1, once the object file Ex1.obj, has been produced it needs to be converted to an executable file. To do this it is necessary to complete the link phase of programming. At the link stage all the object modules, which participate in the programme that is being compiled, are linked together. This stage needs to be completed whether there is a single file, or multiple files that participate in the complete programme. Thus, the linker will access all other files needed, which should have been compiled into object form. In case of errors during the link phase an error report will be generated. Once again, any errors reported will only deal with availability of files used in the link process; the actual accuracy in performance of the code will not be checked. As previously mentioned this requires the debugger.

The output of the link phase is the executable file in this case Ex1.exe. It must be pointed out however that an executable file can only run on the platform that it has been compiled for. For example, a file written in C and compiled to run on the 8051 microcontroller will not run on correctly in DOS.

3.2.   Integrated Development Environment (IDE)

Integrated development environments such as µVision IDE [13] that we shall be using in this course, provide tools to help programmers to produce executable code. These tools usually include an editor, a compiler, and a make and/or build facility as well as a debugger. A debugger allows the user to run the programme in a special debug (get rid of programming bugs) mode. Along with other features, debug mode of execution gives the programmer full access at run-time to variables, their instantaneous values, and also allows execution to be stepped through line by line. Within debug, breakpoints can be set at selected lines of code, which are considered important or critical. In this event, execution of the code is allowed to proceed uninterrupted until the breakpoint is encountered. At this point, the programme stops and the user can examine the state of variables and other programme features. The screenshot shown in Figure 3.2 show the typical components of an IDE.

Figure 3.2 IDE components

Debuggers usually support a watch feature, which is aimed at following the state of a selected variable during programme execution. Thus, for example, a watch can be placed on a variable and the definition of the watch is to stop the programme when the variable reaches a certain value. The programme will run, and if the condition of the watch is satisfied the programme will stop. Once again it has to be stressed that this feature is only possible in debug mode. Furthermore, in order to make the debug facility available the compiler must be configured to include debug information, during the compile phase. As an example the µVision IDE does this through the dialogue box as shown in Figure 3.3.

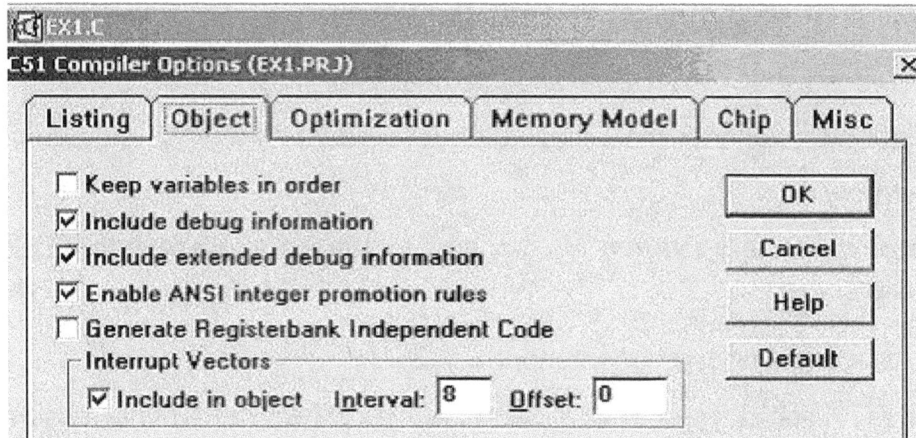

Figure 3.3 Dialogue box to set-up options in the KEIL IDE

This dialogue box is accessed from the menu, under options, and selecting C51 compiler from the drop down menu. (Note: This is also available for the A51 assembler in a similar selection format). More details on the use of the debugger for running programs and analysing status of variables will be covered in Chapter 5 of this text.

3.3. Introduction to KEIL software suite

µVision for Windows is an integrated software development (IDE) platform that supports the KEIL [13] software development tools for the 8051 family of microcontrollers. On their website, KEIL provide an evaluation version of their IDE platform, which is fully functional except for the fact that it is limited to the size of programme code that can me compiled. In this text I shall be working with an older version of the KEIL IDE software, but the tools and the general principles of use should be similar to the newer versions. Figure 3.4 shows a screen shot of a selection of KEIL software windows. The development environment includes features as follows,

- **Windowed user interface:** allowing multiple windows to be displayed on the screen.
- **Full function editor:** enabling source files to be created and code to be written in different programming languages. (i.e. assembly, C, PLM)
- **Project manager:** allowing projects to be created that comprise single or multiple source files.

81

- **Make facility**: enabling programmes to be assembled/compiled, and linked so that object files and hexadecimal files can be created. When required, hexadecimal files can be downloaded to microcontroller memory.
- **Integrated help system:** This covers the topics relevant to the IDE.

There are two major components to the IDE:
- The μVision development platform which allows the writing, assembling, compiling and generally developing programmes, and
- The dScope Debugger platform, which enables the programmes to be tested for run-time errors and performance.

   Programming can be done in assembly, C or PLM. During this course we will concentrate on C programming with some reference to assembly, which will primarily serve to compare performance between the two programming languages. PLM will not be considered.

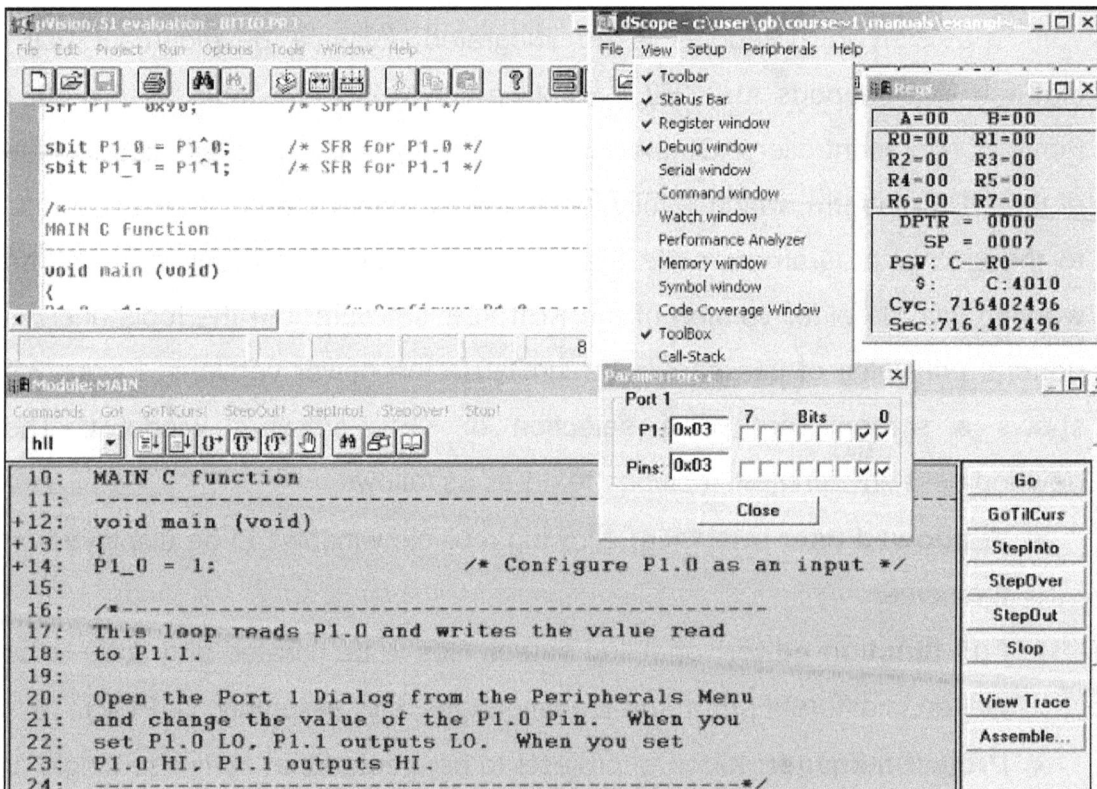

Figure 3.4 Screen shot of the IDE tools

Basic features of µVision

µVision IDE offers a range of built-in features to enable the programmer to create and edit source files, create a project file (with automatic make information), and build a target (usually an absolute object file). Figure 3.5 shows the editor where the source code can be entered. After writing the programme code in the syntax of the programming language selected, the programmer makes the choice of assembly or C programming when they save the file. The different programming languages will be saved under different extensions. For example assembly programs are stored as *.A51 and C programs as *.c. It is worth mentioning that KEIL IDE will not accept alternative extensions for these files.

µVision enables software development projects to proceed in a number of ways. During development or testing, you may wish to compile a single source file to locate warnings and errors. Later you may want to create an absolute object or Intel HEX file for generating your target programme. µVision supports both of these development models. It has to be said at this point that downloading the code to the MCU requires that this code be transferred using the Hexadecimal format. For this reason the compiler generate a *.Hex file.

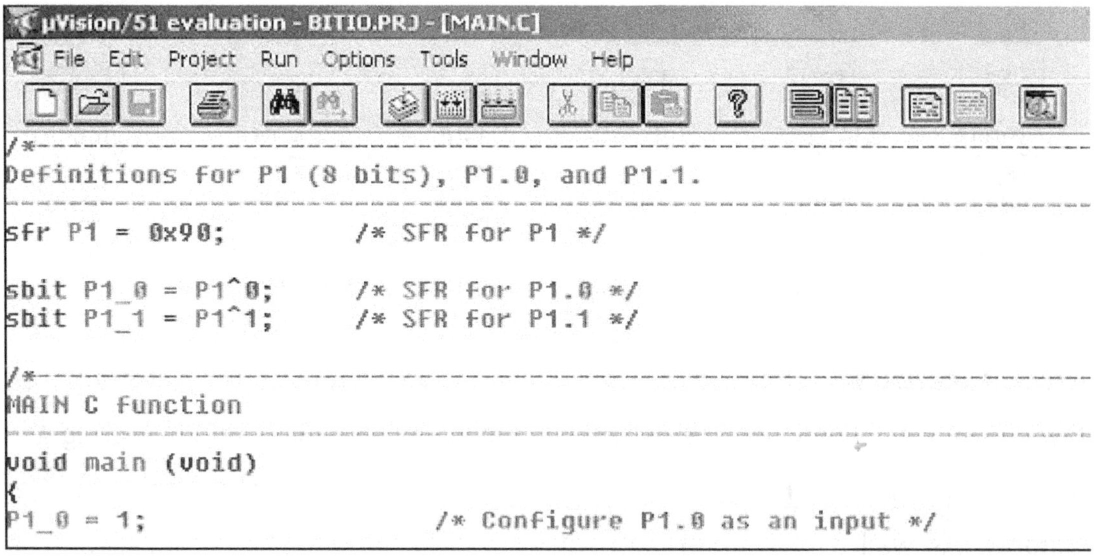
µVision/51 evaluation - BITIO.PRJ - [MAIN.C]
File Edit Project Run Options Tools Window Help
/*--
Definitions for P1 (8 bits), P1.0, and P1.1.
sfr P1 = 0x90; /* SFR for P1 */
sbit P1_0 = P1^0; /* SFR for P1.0 */
sbit P1_1 = P1^1; /* SFR for P1.1 */
/*--
MAIN C function
void main (void)
{
P1_0 = 1; /* Configure P1.0 as an input */

Figure 3.5 Editor for writing the source code

To help the developer during the software development process, the following features are provided with the IDE:

A pull-down menu system: These are standard Windows based interface with menus that offer pull down selection after mouse click. The main Menu Bar (MMB) is shown below.

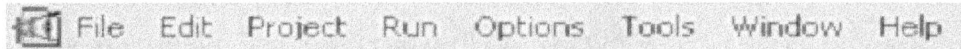

File   Edit   Project   Run   Options   Tools   Window   Help

Before you begin, you must select a tool set to use for your development. The tool set you choose determines which compiler, assembler, linker, and other tools are included in the environment. Additionally, below the menu bar, icons are provided as shortcuts to some commonly used options. These are shown in Table 3.1. These are self-explanatory and offer shortcuts to speed up development. The function of each icon is displayed when a mouse pointer is dragged across it slowly. All action begins from the Main Menu Bar (MMB), which contains the standard Windows set of options. Some of the more important selections from the menu as far as development is concerned are given next.

Table 3.1

New File	Open	Save	Print	Find	Repeat Find
Compile	Update	Build All	Cut	Copy	Paste
Help	Tile Horizontally	Tile Vertically	Colour Syntax	Show Occurrences	Debug

Project manager: The Project manager is found under the project button on the menu bar. These options provide complete project file support during the development phase. Figure 3.6 shows a screen shot of the project manager window. As well as the automated make facility for building target files. The project manager performs the following tasks,

- Maintains a project file that stores all information about your project.

- Keeps a list of all source files required to build your target file.
- Saves the options for the tools.
- Checks dependencies of your source files (by scanning your include files) and determines which source files are current and which need to be rebuilt.
- Compiles and assembles the source files into object files that comprise your target file.
- Combines object files into a library or absolute object module.
- Converts created object modules into Intel HEX files.

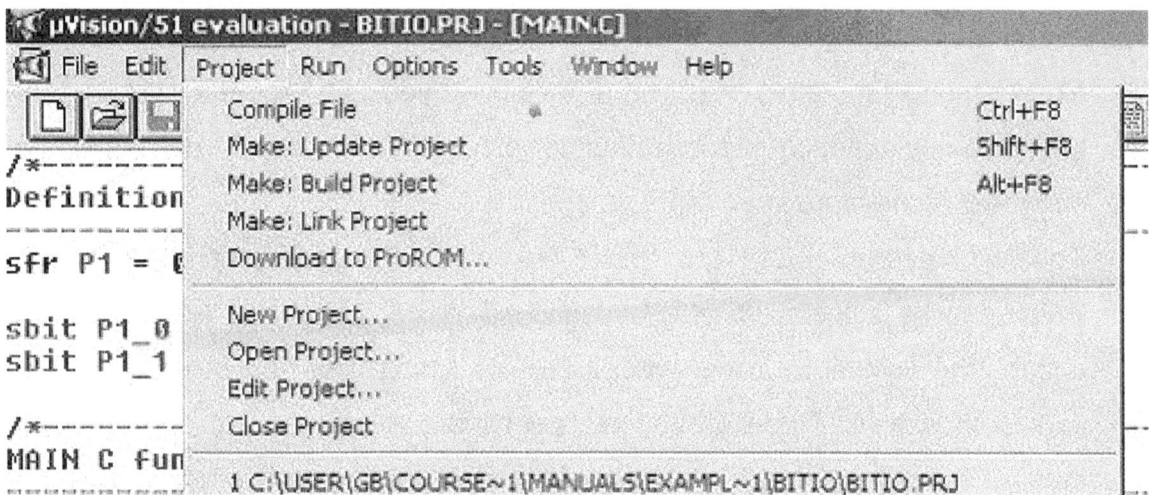

Figure 3.6. Project manager window

Essentially, the project manager provides a method of maintaining a project so that the target programme is always up-to-date. All aspects of a project are saved in a project file including the following,

- List of the source files that make up the target programme,
- Compiler, assembler, and linker command-line options,
- Debugger and simulator options; and the make facility options.

Before you start using the IDE it is worth spending some time to discuss the features that you may find useful during programming and development of projects. Some of the more important features are covered next.

Option Dialog Boxes: These are found under the options button on the main menu (MMB) and allow the user to perform all environment and development tool settings as shown in Figure 3.7.

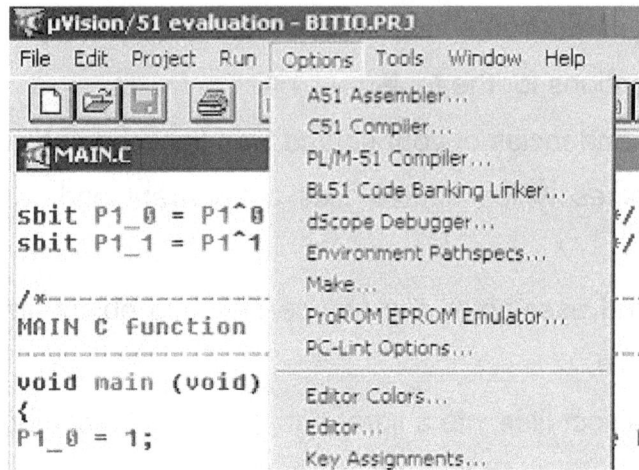

Figure 3.7 Options dialogue box

Note: During laboratory exercise 1 to follow, you can use the HELP menu button to explain each of these dialogue boxes in more detail. Here is a brief summary of the more important components.

The A51 Assembler Options: These are provided through a series of options, which can be selected from a dialogue box. The dialog box lets you select options the assembler uses when it creates listing files and object files from your source files. Three groups of options are available in this dialog box, these are: Listing, Object, and Miscellaneous. Option choices are selected or deselected by checking the relevant check box as shown in Figure 3.8.

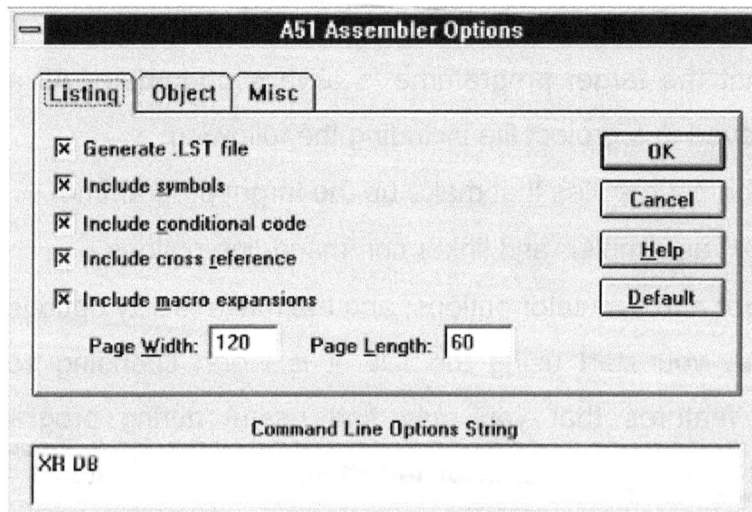

Figure 3.8 Setting A51 assembler options

The option choices and their brief explanation are given in the Table 3.2.

Table 3.2

Listing	Object
Generate .LST file: Produces a listing of the programme, which enables the programmer to examine code more clearly.	Include debug information: Includes debug information in the object file. This is equivalent to the DEBUG assembly directive. It allows you to define symbols on the command line. This is equivalent to the SET assembler directive.
Include symbols: This option includes symbols in the listing file. This is equivalent to the SYMBOLS assembly directive	Exclude line numbers: Leaves out line numbers from debug information in the object file. This is like the NOLINES assembly directive.
Include conditional code: This option includes conditionals in the listing file. This is equivalent to the COND assembly directive.	Define 8051 SFRs: This option allows the special function registers to be defined. This is equivalent to the MOD51 assembly directive.
Include cross-reference: This option includes cross-reference in the listing file. This is equivalent to the XREF assembly directive.	Register bank used: Specifies the register bank used. There are four banks, numbered 0-3. This is equivalent to the REGISTERBANK assembly directive.
Include Macro Exp: This option includes macro source in the listing file. This is equivalent to the GEN assembly directive.	Macro processor: Specifies the type of macro processor used to interpret the macros. The options are Standard for default macros, MPL for Intel ASM 51 macros, and disabled ignores all macro definitions.
Command Line options string: Shows the current command line option for the assembler. The test displayed in this box reflects the selected options.	

Other menu-bar options

Tools: There are two tools that help with the source code and these are self-explanatory. The first is the check C braces tool that makes certain that all the braces in C balance. The other is the insert template editor function, which replaces text with template text from the template file. (See Figure 3.9) This is a very useful tool in particular when you are developing applications with re-usable code that can be placed in a template file and inserted as required into source files.

Figure 3.9

Window: These allow the window layout to be modified according to the given cascade options. Further, the option to select the toolbars to be displayed is provided. The HEX/ASCII switch option allows you to display the code in either ASCII or HEX as shown in Figure 3.10. The last detail is the files that are currently opened. All of these are self-explanatory and their usage is very much down to user preferences.

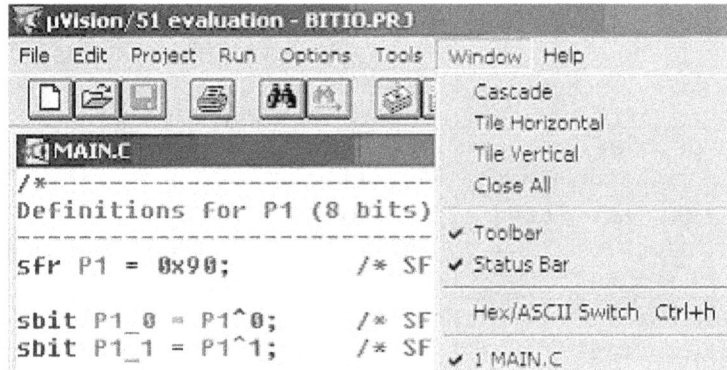

Figure 3.10 Window options screen shot

Help: All the features supported by the IDE are covered in help, which has a standard layout. Perhaps the best way to see what is on offer is to spend some time going through the help facility and familiarising with it.

Run: This option offers the post-compile actions that the user can invoke. These include the following,

- **dScope debugger:** We discussed this briefly in the early sections of this chapter, and we will cover it in more detail in Chapter 5. For now it is sufficient to say that the debug option can be called up from the run menu button as shown in Figure 3.11. Note that the debug can only be run after the project files have been suitable compiled and linked. The combined term for this is under the menu option to Build a project.

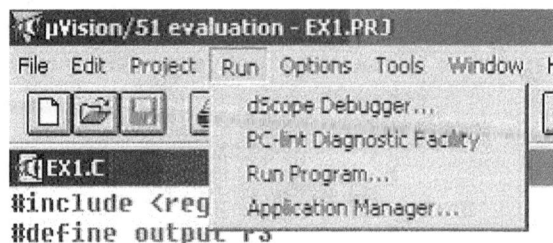

Figure 3.11 dScope debugger option

- **PC-Lint Diagnostic Facility:** This is a software package that finds errors in C programs using the Kernighan and Ritchie [32] and ANSI standards [33] for C. The purpose is to determine potential problems prior to integration or porting, or to reveal unusual constructs that may be a source of subtle errors. PC-Lint often finds problems that the compiler alone cannot. It is much fussier about details than the compiler. During this course we will not be using this feature.

- **Run Programme:** This option runs the programme.

- **Application manager:** The Application Manager lets you link external programs into the Run menu. The dialog box displays a list of user-defined programs (applications) as shown in Figure 3.12.

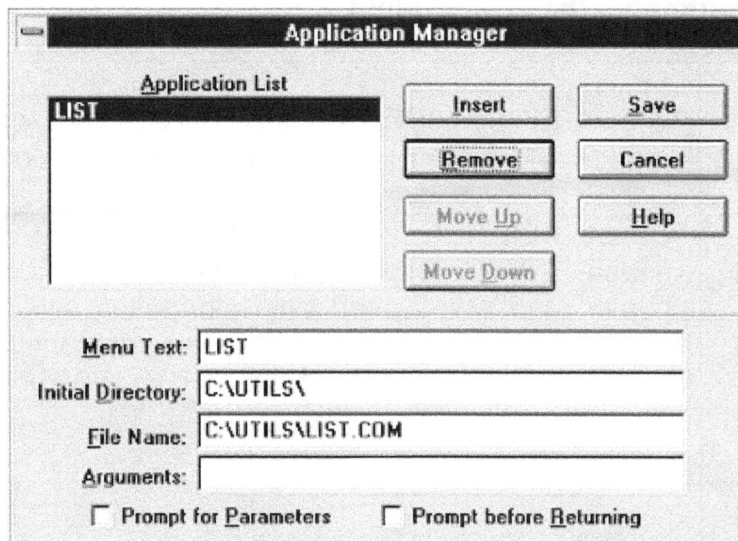

Figure 3.12 Application manager windows

You may insert, remove, or change settings for the applications. You may also move applications up or down in the list. Up to nine external applications may be added. Now that we have briefly discussed the general features of the IDE it is a good idea to experiment with these by performing the laboratory exercises.

Exercises

Lab A: Working with projects and files with KEIL IDE

This exercise presumes that you have a suitably installed and functional version of the KEIL IDE software installed on your PC. The version used here will be different and you may have a slightly different set of menus than on another version. The process of developing a software application however should be the same in any version.

Objectives: After completing this lab you will be able to,

- Create a project file and associated source files.
- Compile, Link and build a project.
- Run the programme in dScope debug environment.

Exercise 1: Setting up the environment

Log onto Windows and start the μVision IDE	To start μ**Vision IDE** click the **Start** button and follow the menu to →Programs → KEIL PK51-Eval→μVision-51
Set up the environment	To use KEIL IDE you need to set up the environment variables. These options were discussed briefly earlier in this chapter, and if you need any information you can use the Help facility in KEIL IDE. To set up environment variables use the options button on the main menu bar (MMB). Here you will see that we have a range of options to set up environment variables. In this course we will only need to set up the A51 assembler and the C51 Compiler. We will do this now.

Setting up A51 options	Select Options->A51 assembler from the MMB. You will see a dialogue box such as the one below. Select **Listing** and be sure to tick the relevant check boxes in your dialogue box.
	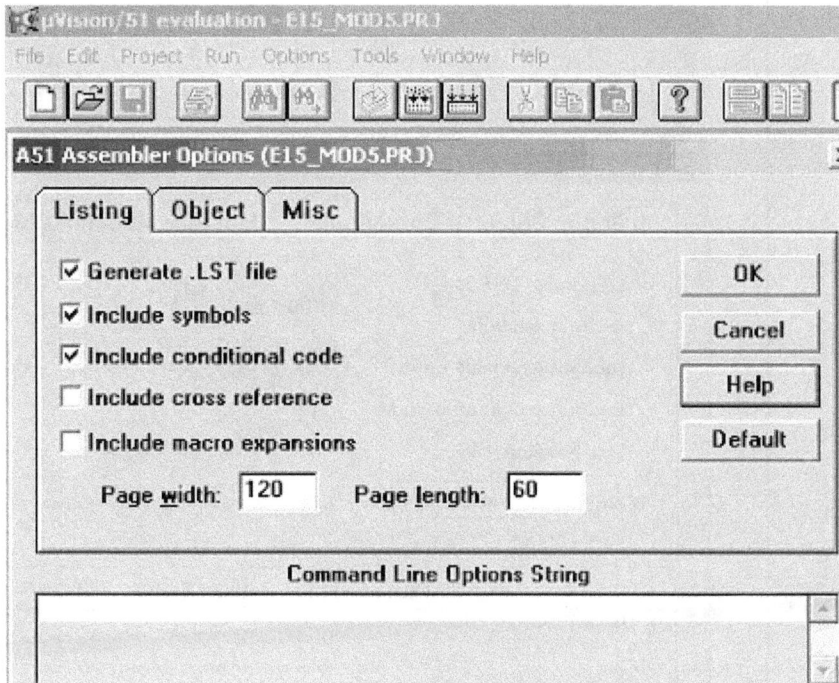
	Next, select Object and select check boxes as shown below.
	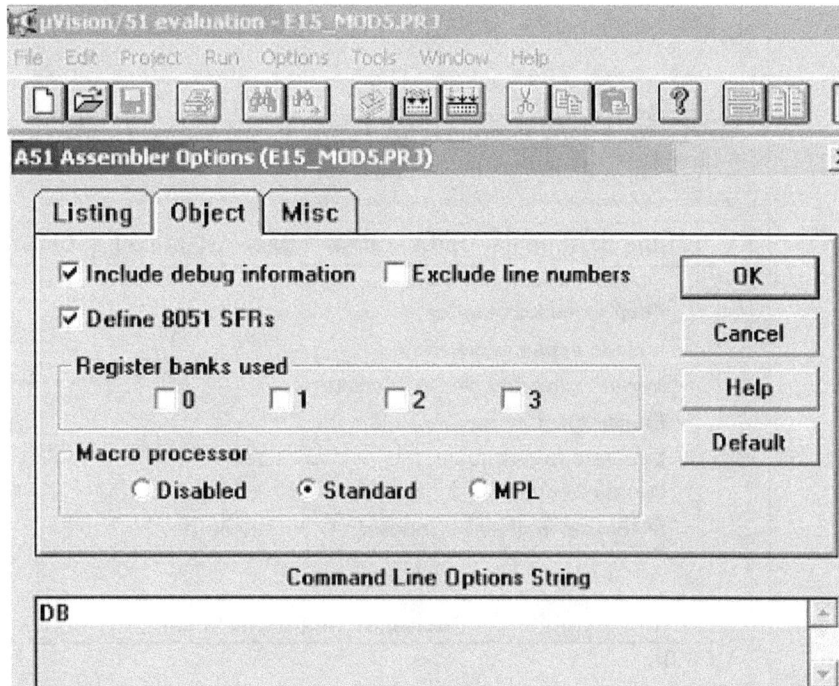
	There is no need to set up Miscellaneous options, as we will not be using these within this text.

Setting up C51 options	Select Options->C51 Compiler from the MMB. You will see a dialogue box such as the one below. Select **Listing** and be sure to tick the relevant check boxes in your dialogue box. **uVision/51 evaluation – E15_MOD5.PRJ** File Edit Project Run Options Tools Window Help **C51 Compiler Options (E15_MOD5.PRJ)** ✕ [**Listing**] [Object] [Optimization] [Memory Model] [Chip] [Misc] ☑ Generate .LST file Page width: `132` [OK] ☐ Include symbols Page length: `60` [Cancel] ☐ Include assembly code ☑ Include conditional code [Help] ☐ List #include files [Default] Warnings [Level 2 ▾] **Command Line Options String** `DB OE`
	Next, select Object and select check boxes as shown below. **uVision/51 evaluation – E15_MOD5.PRJ** File Edit Project Run Options Tools Window Help **C51 Compiler Options (E15_MOD5.PRJ)** ✕ [Listing] [**Object**] [Optimization] [Memory Model] [Chip] [Misc] ☐ Keep variables in order [OK] ☑ Include debug information ☑ Include extended debug information [Cancel] ☑ Enable ANSI integer promotion rules [Help] ☐ Generate Registerbank Independent Code Interrupt Vectors [Default] ☑ Include in object Interval: `8` Offset: `0` **Command Line Options String** `DB OE`

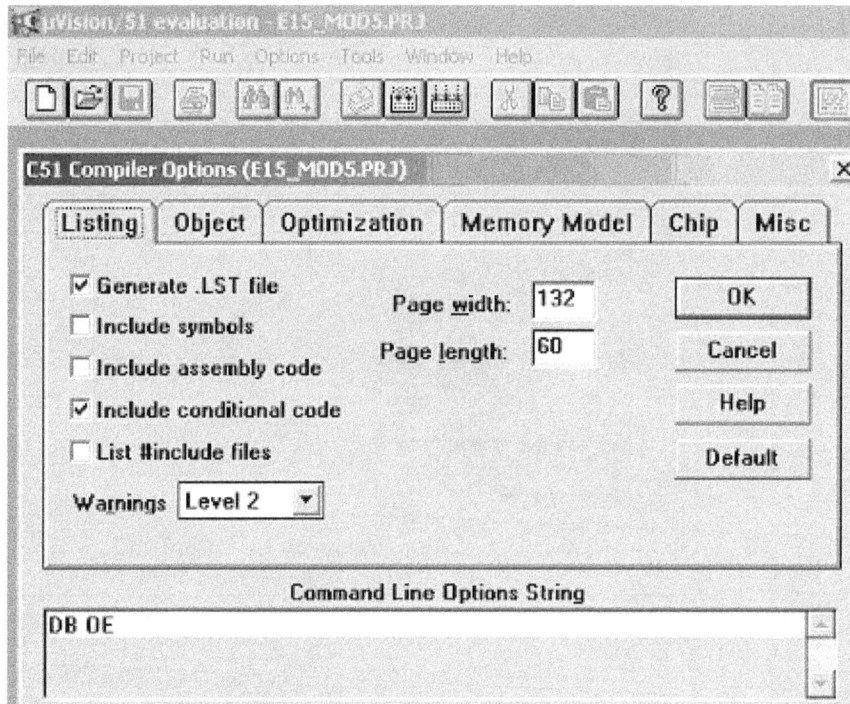

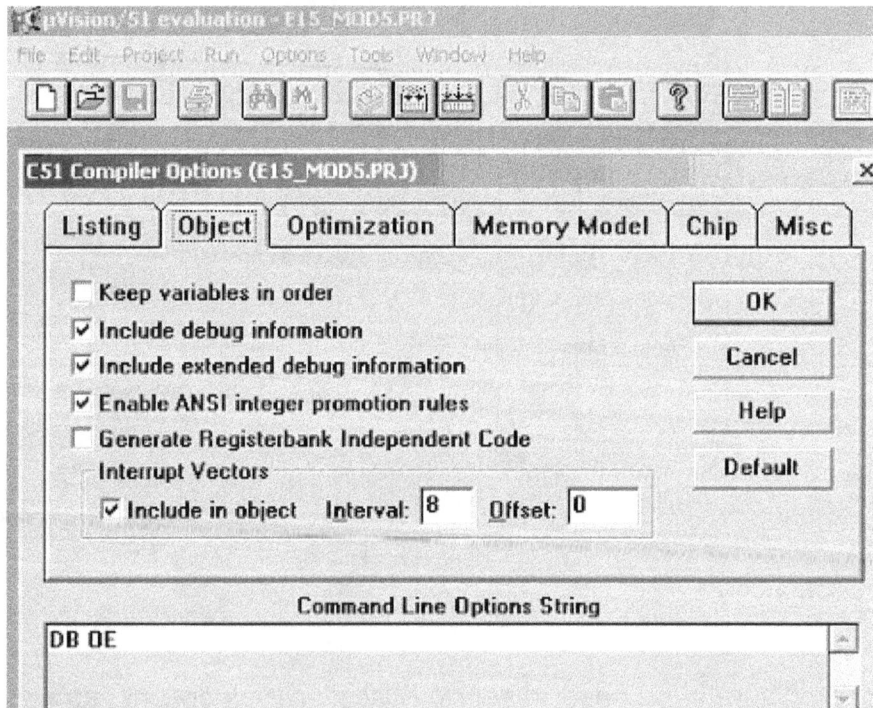

Next, select Optimisation and select check boxes as shown below.

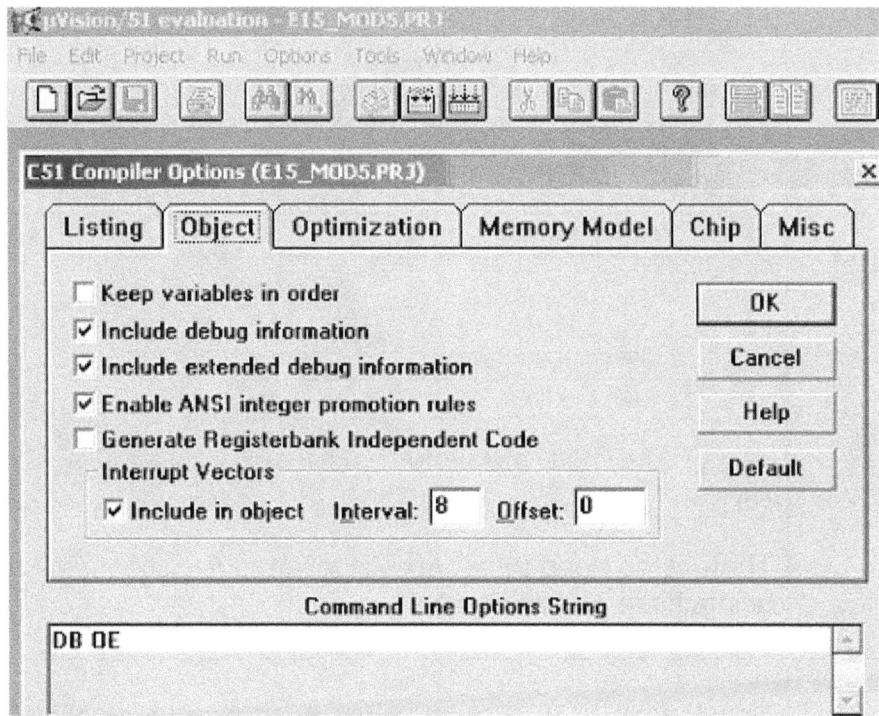

Next, select Memory Model and select check boxes as shown below.

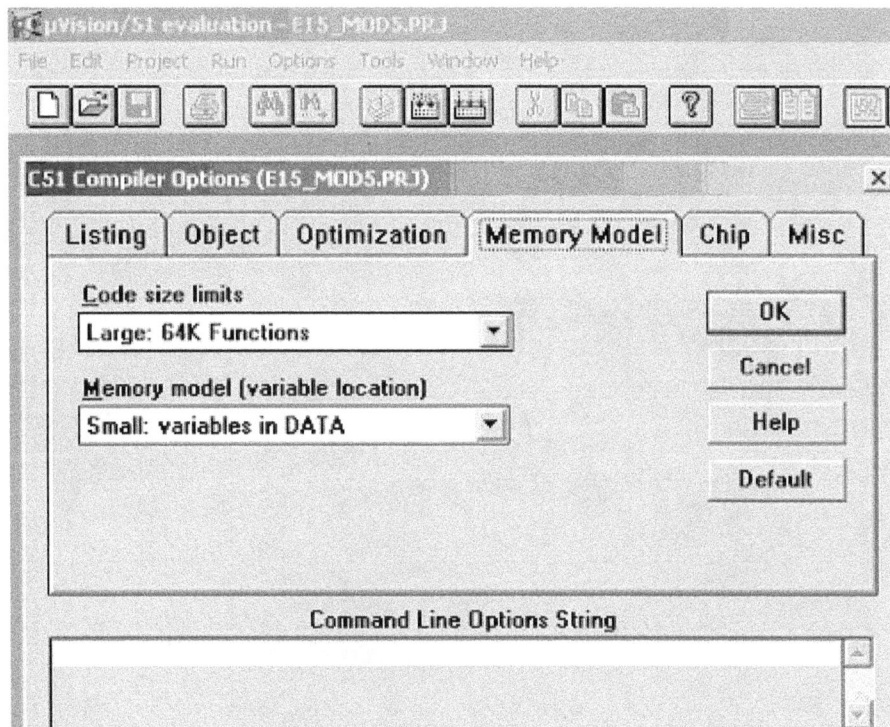

Next, select Chip and select check boxes as shown below.

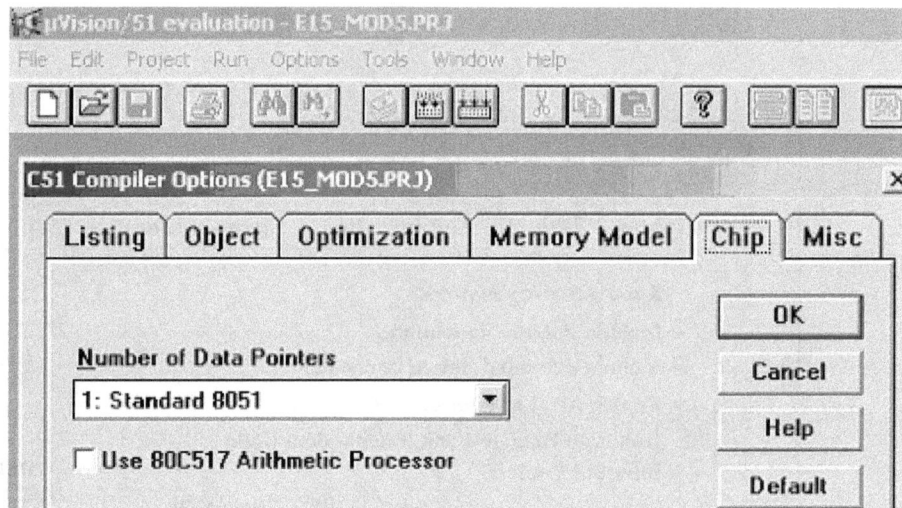

There is no need to set up Miscellaneous options, as we will not be using these on this course.

Now that you have set up all the environment specifications that are needed for this course we can begin using the KEIL IDE.

Exercise 2: Open a project file and prepare it for execution

Task	Detail
Start the μVision IDE	To start μVision IDE click the **Start** button and follow the menu to →Programs → KEIL PK51-Eval→μVision-51

Create a New Source file	From the μVision IDE menu-bar select **File**, and from drop-down menus select **New**.
	This opens a text file named untitled.
	Type the following code in the text window:
	
	``
	void main(void)
	{
	}
	``
	
	From the File menu, select **Save as** and **type ex1.c** in the dialogue box.
	    Click Ok

	You have now created and saved a source C file. This programme does not do anything but the code syntax is correct and it should compile without errors. Before we can compile this file we need to put it into a project in order that we can proceed with the development.
Create a New Project	From the μVision IDE menu-bar select **Project**, and from drop-down menus select **New Project**. This command displays the **Create New Project** dialog box. To create a new project file, select the drive and directory into which you want to place the new project file. In the File Name type: **ex1.prj**, to start a new project called **ex1**. **Click OK** Project dialogue box appears as shown in the graphic below. Click **Add** to fill the project with source files. The **Add File** dialogue box appears (as shown below in the same Figure).

Navigate through the folders until you reach the file **ex1.c** that you created earlier. Highlight this file and click **Add**, and then click **Close**, to close this dialogue box.

This will return you to the project dialogue box. Click **Save**, to save the added file to your project.

You have now created a new project called **ex1.prj**, which contains the file **ex1.c**.

You can **Edit** this project and make changes to the files that it contains.

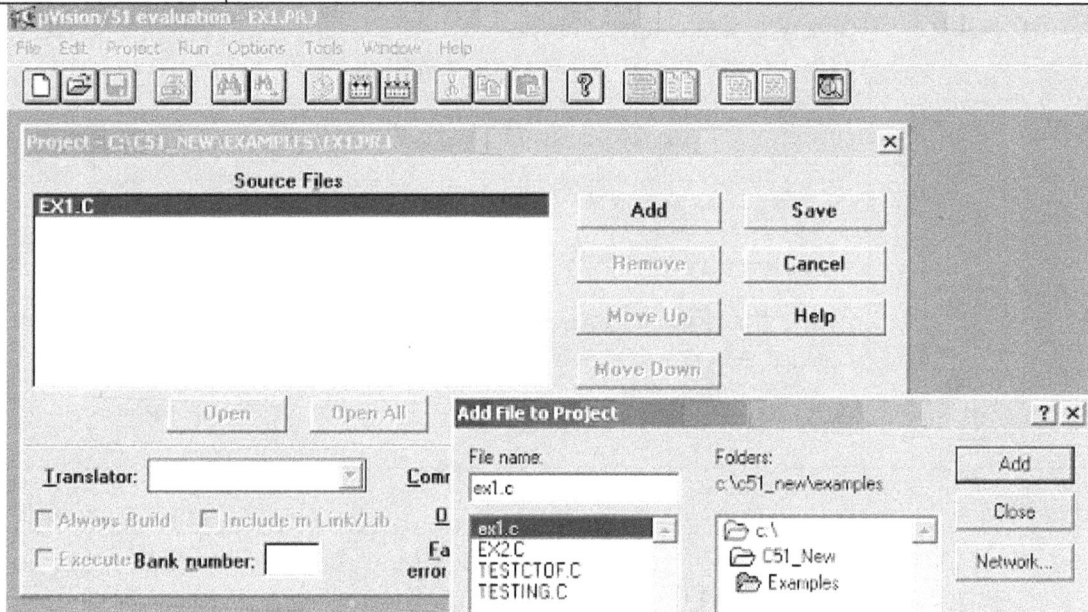

| Open and Edit an Existing Project | To open an existing project file, from the **μVision IDE** menu-bar select **Project**, and from drop-down menus select **Open Project**.

This command displays the Open Project dialog box, which is very similar to the dialogue box given earlier for creating a new project.

To open an existing project file:
1. Select the **drive** that the file is in from the **Drives** list box,
2. Select the **directory** that the file is in from the **Directories** list box,
3. Select the **project filename** from the **File Name** list box.
4. Select the **OK** pushbutton.

To edit the project **ex1.prj** that you created earlier, navigate |

	through the folders until you reach this project, Highlight this project and click **Open**. This will open the project, but if you wish to make programme modifications you will need to access the files within. To **Edit** a project that has been opened, from the µ**Vision IDE** menu-bar select **Project**, and from drop-down menus select **Edit Project.** This will present you with the project dialogue box. Click **Edit**, to access the file **ex1.c**, alternatively click **Edit All** if more than one file is contained in the project. Click **Cancel** button on the project dialogue box when the files that you need have been opened. This action will open the relevant files in the editor for you to work with and modify as necessary. You can **save** any changes to files from the file menu drop-down selections. This will also be updated in the project file.

Editing and Saving changes to Files	In the edit window of **ex1.c**, modify the source to include the following C code. At this time, do not concern yourself much with the meaning of the different instructions, since on this occasion we are demonstrating the IDE tools.
	
	``
	#include <reg51.h>
	#define output P3
	#define input P1
	void main(void)
	{
	  while (1){
	  output=input+1;
	}
	}
	``
	
	When you have finished, click **save** on the MMB to commit the changes.

Compiling Files	From the µ**Vision IDE** menu-bar select **Project**, and from drop-down menus select **Compile**. If, as is the case, the compile is successful the following dialogue box appears

| | ```
Project Status (EX1.PRJ)

    Source File:   EX1.C

    Object File:   EX1.OBJ
    _____

    Total Time:   00:00:01

    Status:  Compile Successful


                              [  OK  ]
```<br><br>Thus, the file contains no errors and we can proceed with the process of linking. Click **OK** to continue. |
| | You have now learned how to create projects as well as edit and compile files within.
Let us now consider what to do when the compiler reports errors during the compile phase.
We will modify a file so that it has a mistake in the syntax in order to demonstrate the process of complier error reporting. |
| **Compiling Files with ERRORS** | In the μ**Vision IDE** modify the variable **output** in the code to read **outputs**, as follows: |
| Modify the Source Code to contain an error.<br><br>Use the variable **outputs** instead of the declared variable **output** | ```c
void main(void)
{
  while (1){
  outputs=input+1;  /* this simply adds 3 to
the input port and outputs it */
  }
}
``` |
| | From the menu select **Project**, and from drop-down menus select **Compile**.
If, as is the case, the compile is unsuccessful the following dialogue box appears, |

```
EX1.ERR
Compiling: C:\C51_NEW\EXAMPLES\EX1.C
Error 202: 'outputs': undefined identifie
```

Project Status (EX1.PRJ)

Source File: EX1.C

Object File: EX1.OBJ

_____

Total Time: 00:00:05

Status: Error(s) Reported

[OK]

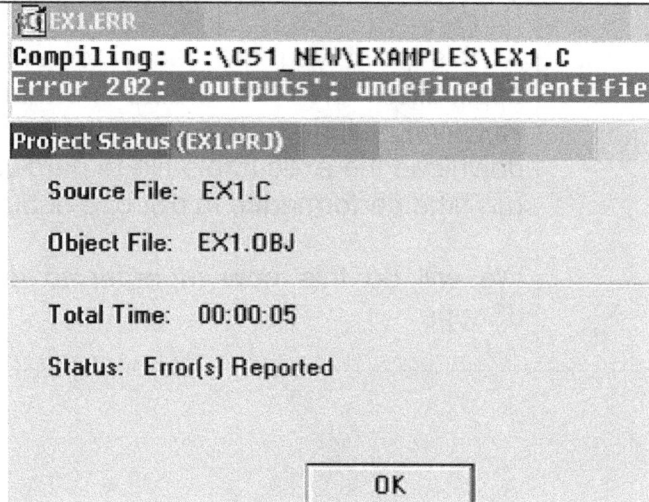

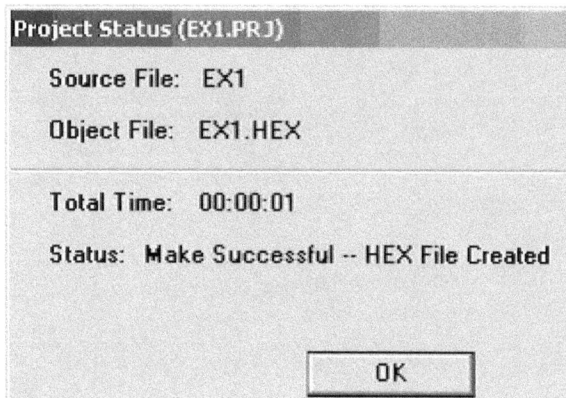

Thus, the file contains errors and we cannot proceed with the process of linking. Click **OK** to continue.

Double click on the line red highlighted to enter μ**Vision** editor where the line containing the error is highlighted in green.

You can now correct the error and compile the file once again so that there are no errors in the code.

Linking Files	After you have corrected the errors introduced in the previous activity, compile the file again to ensure that the errors are no longer present. The file is now ready for linking. From the μ**Vision IDE** menu-bar select **Project**, and from drop-down menus select **Make: Link Project**. If as is the case, the **link** is successful the following dialogue box appears **Project Status (EX1.PRJ)** Source File: EX1 Object File: EX1.HEX Total Time: 00:00:01 Status: Make Successful -- HEX File Created [OK] Thus, the file contains no errors and we can proceed with the process of linking. Click **OK** to continue.

At this point you are ready to run the file. In embedded application the file would normally run on hardware. However, during the development phase, before we download the executable file to hardware, we can simulate its run-time performance in dScope debugger.

We will do this now in order to demonstrate the use of dScope.

Exercise 3: Run the file in dScope debugger

Executing a file	Having compiled and linked **file1.c** in the previous example we will now run it in dScope debugger in order to demonstrate some of the debug features. Go to the main menu in **µVision**, select the **run** button and **DScope** option as indicated below.

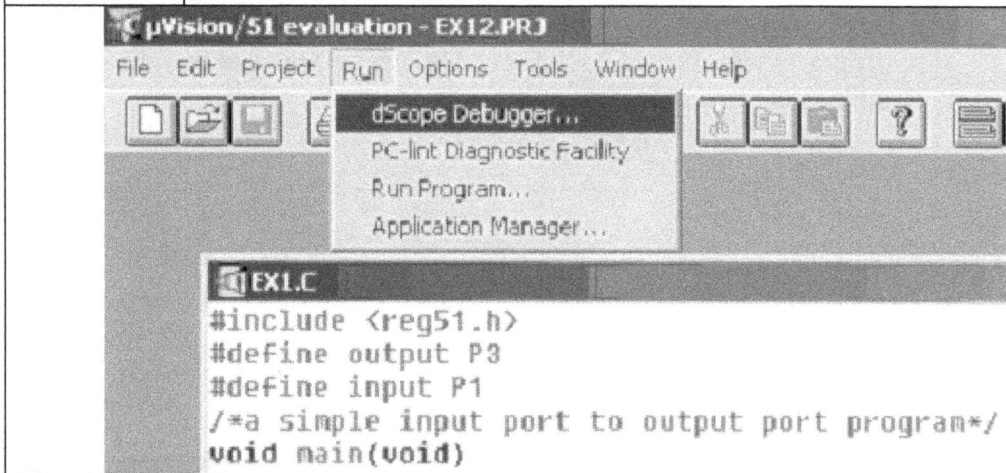

	A window showing the debugger will appear. It will look similar to the one shown below.

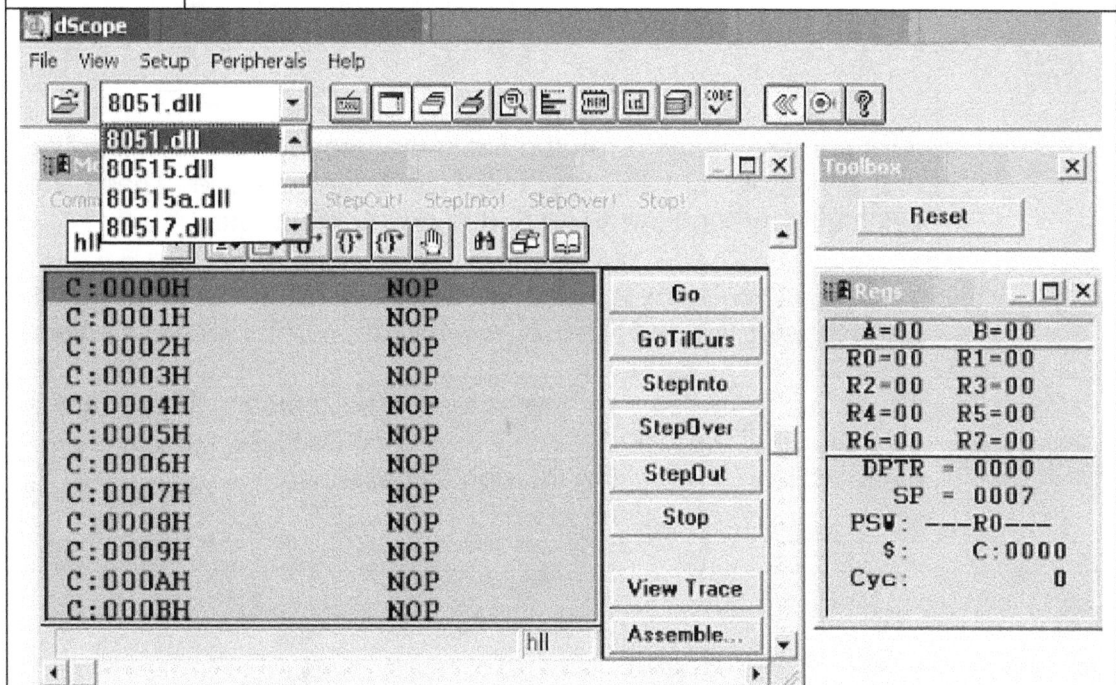

At the menu of **dScope** you need to select the 8051 CPU in the drop down window as seen in the previous Figure. Scroll down and select 8051.dll. This will load the driver that will allow the Debugger to simulate 8051 CPU performance.

Next you will need to load the object file that you wish to run in the debugger. In this case it is the one that you have created when you complied Ex1.c earlier. On the main menu, select File -> Load Object file. The list of files that are available will appear in a dropdown menu. Select **Ex1.** file as shown below. Note that this file has no visible extension.

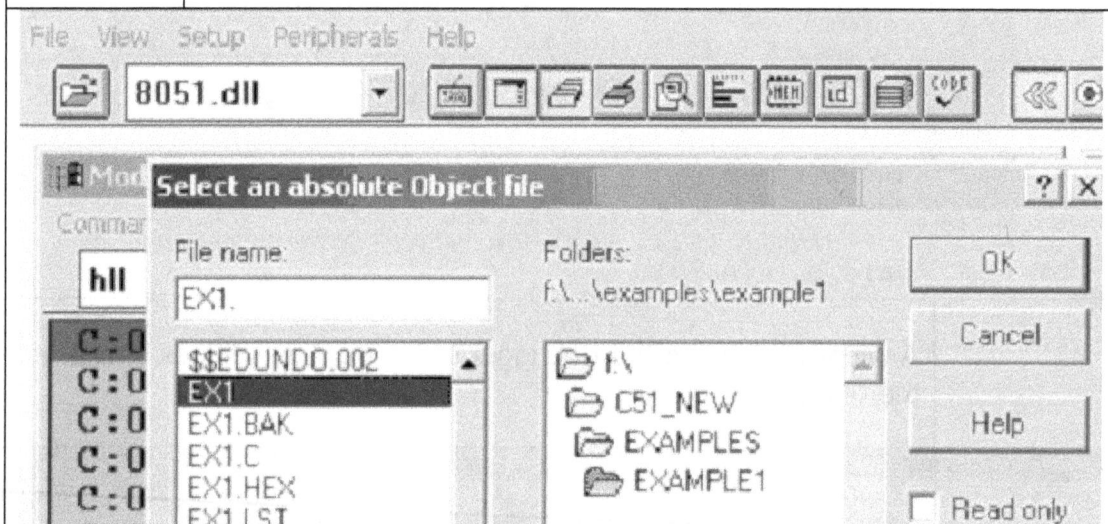

File   View   Setup   Peripherals   Help

8051.dll

Select an absolute Object file   ? X

Command

hll

File name:
EX1.

Folders:
f:\...\examples\example1

OK

Cancel

C:0 $$EDUNDO.002
C:0   EX1
C:0   EX1.BAK
C:0   EX1.C
C:0   EX1.HEX
C:0   EX1.LST

f:\
C51_NEW
EXAMPLES
EXAMPLE1

Help

☐ Read only

Now you are ready to run the file in the debugger. You will notice that a number of windows appear in your interface. These are selectable through the **View** button on the menu bar.

You will notice from the graphic below, that the Toolbar, Status Bar, Register Window, Debug Window and ToolBox are selected.

These are also seen on the screen. The toolbars shown are a selection that we will be using in this course. Be sure to select these while you are going through this exercise.

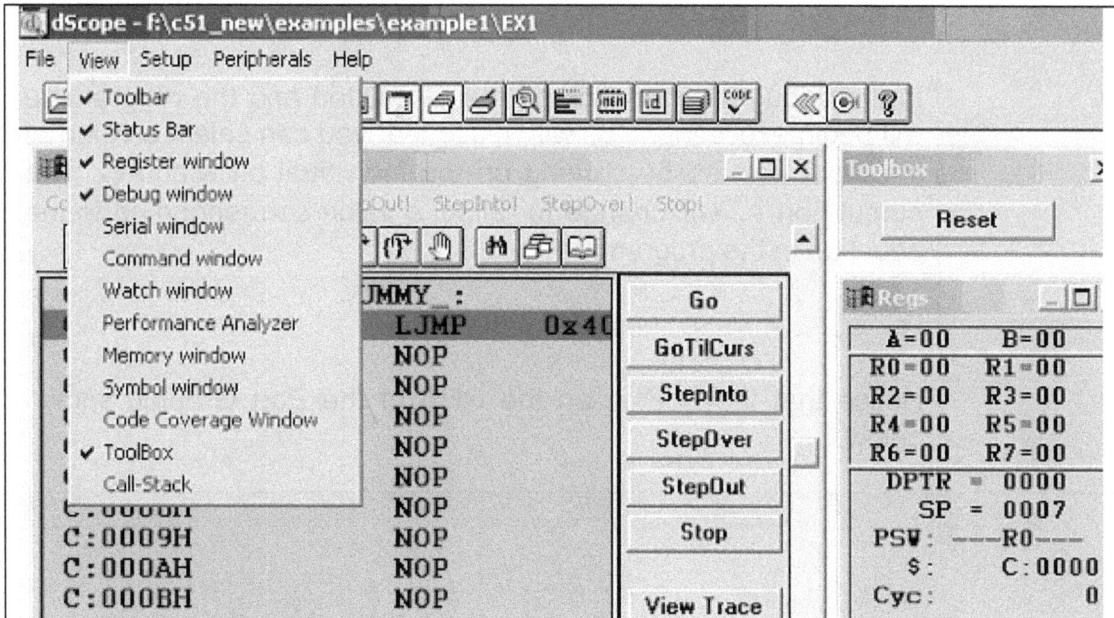

The programme that we are running in this particular exercise uses output ports P1 and P3. In order to see the contents of these ports as the programme is executing we need to select them for display. This is done from the peripherals menu shown in the graphic below.

Be sure to select ports 1 and 3 and to display their content on the screen.
The programme is now ready to run.

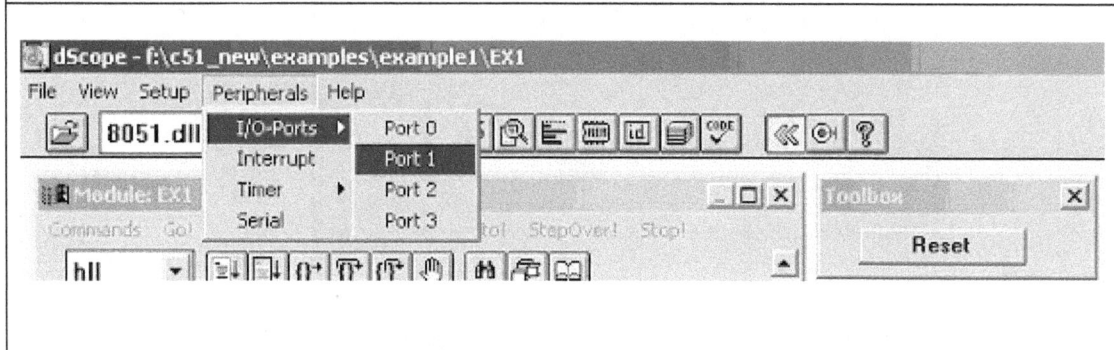

In the debug window click on the Go button and the programme will begin executing. You will notice that you can select a value of the input port P1 by clicking on the individual bit windows. The output port P3 will change to reflect a value corresponding to the equation in the programme.

i.e. `output=input+1;`

Notice that the LSB is on the RHS of the Port Graphic shown below.

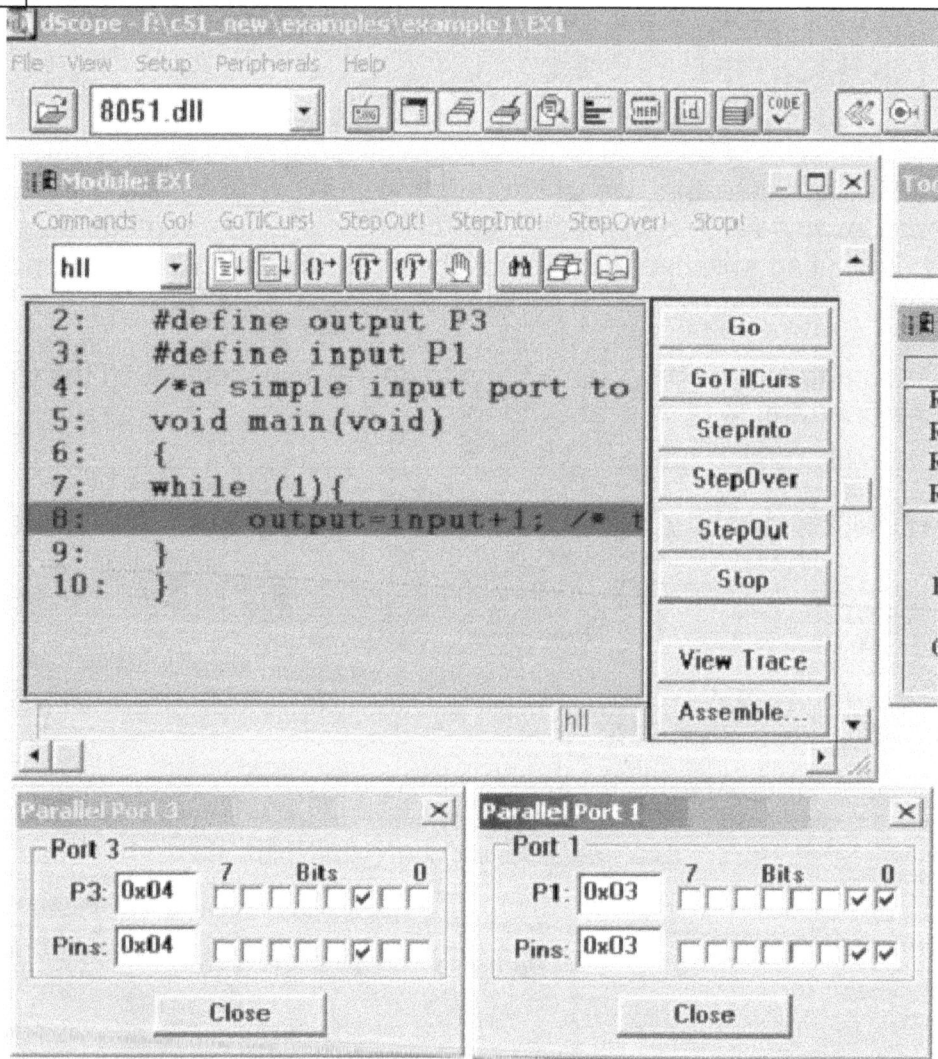

You can click **Stop** to terminate execution and if you need to perform execution again, you can click the reset button on the Toolbox component.

Other features of the debugger window are as follows:

- **GoTilCurs:** Allows you to specify the point to which your programme should execute. This point is called a breakpoint, and you select it by double clicking on the desired line of code in the debug window.
- **StepInto:** Allows you to execute a line of code and stop at the end of this instruction. This effectively enables you to step though each line of code.
- **StepOver:** Allows you to execute a complete instruction without stepping through each step. This is useful when the instruction involves a loop and you do not want to step through every iteration of the loop.
- **StepOut:** Allows you to step out of a step and execute the line of code. Useful in jumping out of loops that you may have started stepping.

Note: More details on each of these are available under the Help menu in dScope. You may wish to spend some time reading through this.

You have now become familiar with the main features of the KEIL IDE. It is necessary to go through more programs in order to practice using these tools.

Task:
1. Write the following programs and build them to make executable files.
2. Execute each file in dScope.
3. Explain what each programme is doing

Please note: I have provided the line numbers for reference. When writing the programme do not include these line numbers.

```
/*Programme 1: Simple loops for timing */

1. #include<reg51.h>      /*special      function      register
   definition*/
        /* reg.h contains SFR defs & sbit */
 /* definitions for standard 8051.*/
2. main()
3. {
4. int i;
5. for(;;) /* forever loop or while(1) { } */
6. {
7. P1=0xff; /* port1 all on. takes only hex or bits */
8. for(i=0;i<=50;i++); /* delay for about 0.5 secs */
9. P1=P1-1; /* port1 all 00 */
10.   for(i=0;i<=50;i++); /* delay loop */
11.   }
12. }
```

Explain what the programme is doing.	The above programme sets a value of 255 (all 1's in binary) to port P1 and decrements it after a short delay. Then it waits another short delay before returning the value of P1 to 255.
	Let us look more closely at the above programme I shall go through it line by line:
	Line 1: This is the include statement that calls for the inclusion in the programme of the header file reg51.h. This file contains the information on all functions provided by the 8051 CPU. In the above example it holds the definition for P1, which is an I/O port.
	Line 2: This is the start of main(), no other comment needed.
	Line 3: Opening braces for main(), no other comment needed.
	Line 4: Declare integer variable i, to use as a count variable in the for loop.
	Line 5: This is the declaration of a forever loop, same as while(1) {}. These loops will run forever until the programme is stopped.
	Line 6: Opening brace of the for loop. These contain all the statements to be executed within the loop. In other words, all the statements inside the braces are treated as a single statement of the for loop.
	Line 7: Assigning the value of the port P1. Basically the value FF, in hexadecimal is written to P1. This means that P1 holds all ones in binary (i.e. 1111 1111 = 0xFF). The x indicates to the compile that the number is hexadecimal.
	For the same effect we could have written: P1=255; which is decimal notation for all 1's on the port.

	Line 8: is a `for` loop structure, which reads, `"for i starting at 0 and up to 50 do the loop` `and increment i"`. The loop is empty, there are no braces and all we are doing is counting up to 50 and creating a delay in the software. **Line 9:** This is what gets done after the loop completes. The value of `P1` is decremented, and set to 254. (FE hex). **Line 10:** This creates another delay loop before we return to the forever loop. The forever loop will reset `P1` to 255 and so the whole programme simply changes bit 0 of `P1` from 0 to 1 and this is done with a delay. **Line 11:** Closing brace of the `for` loop. **Line 12:** Closing brace of `main()`.
Task	Compile and run this programme in dScope and confirm that you understand what the programme is doing.

```
/*  Programme 2 more complicated I/O programme reading a
table of Degrees Fahrenheit */

   1. #define uchar unsigned char
   /*variable type declaration +ve integer range 0-255 =
   char range */

   2. #include <reg51.h>
   3. #define output P3
   4. #define input P1

   5. uchar code cftbl[]={32,34,36,37,39,41};/*table of */
   /* values to read using an array */
   6. uchar degf, degc; /* declare variables of type uchar
      */

   7. uchar ctof(uchar degc) /* function named ctof */
            i. /* to read Fahrenheit in array as per degc
               */
   8. {
   9. return cftbl[degc]; /* the function returns */
   /* table reading corresponding to degc array index */
   10. }


   11. void main(void)
   12. {
   /*a simple input port to output port programme*/

   13. while (1){
            i. degf=input; /* take variable degc from */
                        i. /* input port */
         ii. output    =    ctof(degf);    /*     write
            corresponding */
                        i. /* array value to output */
   14. }
   15. }
```

Explain what the programme is doing.	The above example is similar in that it works with I/O ports. In fact it reads from P1 and writes to P3. The value that it reads is used as an index in an array of 6 elements. Please note that in C the first element of the array is the 0th element. That is array subscripts start at zero. i.e. ARRAY [0,1,2,3] has four elements.
	Let us look at the code in more detail. Once again I have included line numbers for convenience but you should not type these if you intend to compile the programme.
	Line 1: Definition of a variable named uchar as an unsigned character.

	Line 2: This is the include statement that calls for the inclusion in the programme of the header file `reg51.h`. This file contains the information on all functions provided by the 8051 CPU. In the above example it holds the definition for `P1` and `P3`which are I/O ports.
	Line 3: Definition of the variable `output` to represent port `P3`.
	Line 4: Definition of the variable `input` to represent port `P1`.
	Line 5: Declaration of an array and immediate assignment of values. The array is named `cftbl`, it is stored in code section of memory, and the elements are of the `type uchar` as defined earlier.
	Line 6: Declaration of variables `degf` and `degc` (degrees Fahrenheit and Celsius) both of which are of the `type uchar` as defined earlier.
	Line 7: This is, the body of function named `ctof()`. The function returns a `uchar type` variable, and passes `degc` as the parameter, which is also of `type uchar`. (Returning values from a function is covered in Chapter 5)
	Line 8: Opening brace of function `ctof()`.
	Line 9: The only statement of the function is the `return` statement. Here the value returned is a pointer to an element in the `cftbl` array. The pointer is evaluated from the variable `degc`.
	Line 10: Closing brace for the function `ctof()`.
	Line 11: Function `main()`
	Line 12: Opening brace of function `main()`.
	Line 13: While loop (forever),
	    (i) Assign the variable `degf` the value on the input port.
	    (ii) Assign to output port the value obtained by calling the function `ctof()` and passing the variable `degf` as a parameter.
	Line 14: Closing brace for the while loop
	Line 15: Closing brace for the function `main()`

Task	Compile and run this programme in dScope and confirm that you understand what the programme is doing.
	You have now learned how to use the KEIL IDE debug environment and in the process you have come across some C programming. Chapter 5 will cover C programming in more detail. The next Chapter will have a brief look at assembly programming so that you can appreciate the differences between C and assembly.

CHAPTER 4 ASSEMBLY LANGUAGE PROGRAMMING

4.1. Simple assembly programming

As mentioned earlier assembly is a low-level programming language, which enables programmers to keep close track of their code in relation to the microcontroller hardware. This is to say that assembly allows for development of very efficient code. Figure 4.1 lists what are perhaps the most often encountered instructions for the 8051 family of processors. [31]

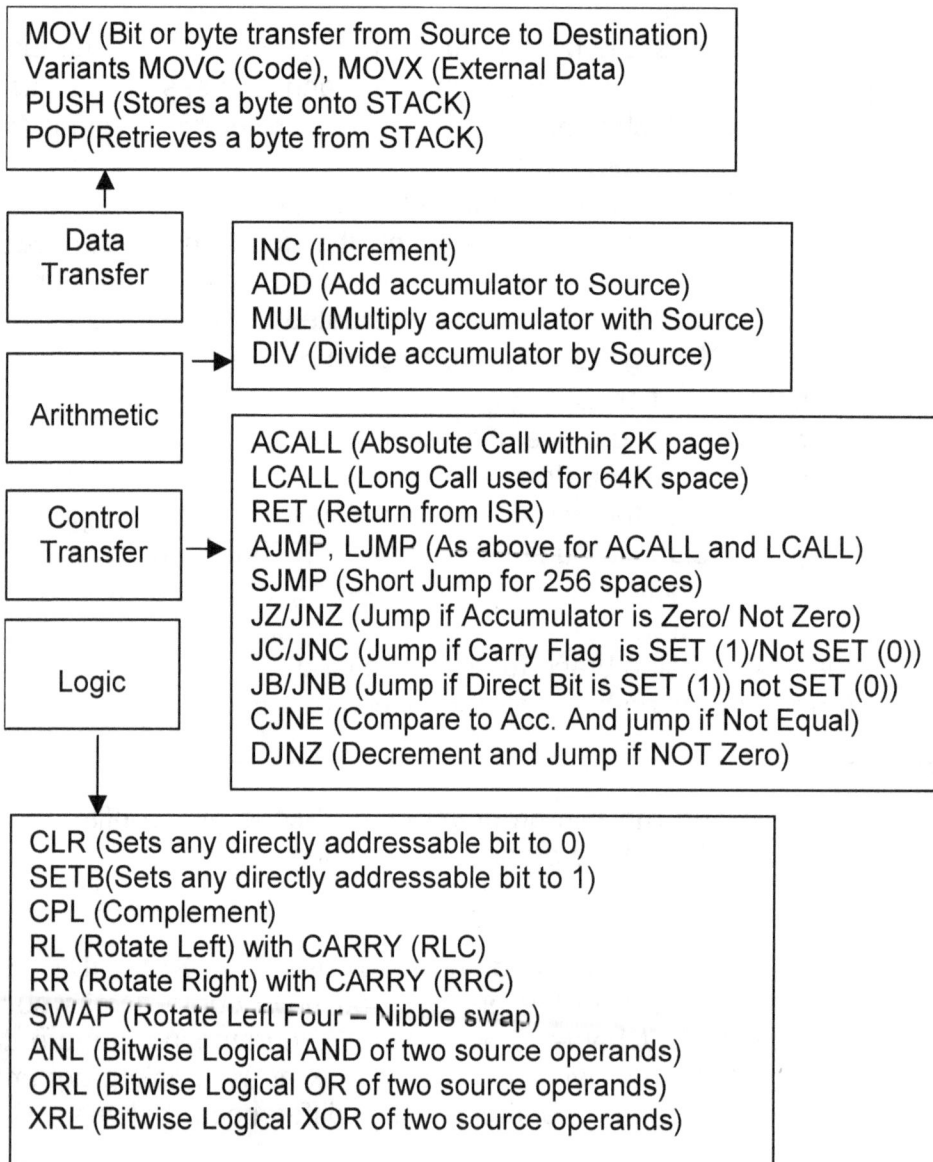

MOV (Bit or byte transfer from Source to Destination)
Variants MOVC (Code), MOVX (External Data)
PUSH (Stores a byte onto STACK)
POP(Retrieves a byte from STACK)

Data Transfer

INC (Increment)
ADD (Add accumulator to Source)
MUL (Multiply accumulator with Source)
DIV (Divide accumulator by Source)

Arithmetic

ACALL (Absolute Call within 2K page)
LCALL (Long Call used for 64K space)
RET (Return from ISR)
AJMP, LJMP (As above for ACALL and LCALL)
SJMP (Short Jump for 256 spaces)
JZ/JNZ (Jump if Accumulator is Zero/ Not Zero)
JC/JNC (Jump if Carry Flag is SET (1)/Not SET (0))
JB/JNB (Jump if Direct Bit is SET (1)) not SET (0))
CJNE (Compare to Acc. And jump if Not Equal)
DJNZ (Decrement and Jump if NOT Zero)

Control Transfer

Logic

CLR (Sets any directly addressable bit to 0)
SETB(Sets any directly addressable bit to 1)
CPL (Complement)
RL (Rotate Left) with CARRY (RLC)
RR (Rotate Right) with CARRY (RRC)
SWAP (Rotate Left Four – Nibble swap)
ANL (Bitwise Logical AND of two source operands)
ORL (Bitwise Logical OR of two source operands)
XRL (Bitwise Logical XOR of two source operands)

Figure 4.1. Instructions for assembly programming of the 8051

The language itself consists of a set of instructions, which can be listed in a sequence to form a computer programme that produces the desired result when executed. Thus, we use the term Instruction Set to describe a set of instructions that the assembler recognises. A table of the full instruction set for the 8051 family is included in the Appendix.

Comparison between Assembly language and a High Level Language

A high level language such as C is quicker to use, but the compiler rather than the programmer does the allocation of microcontroller resources. Often, this will produce executable code, which is less efficient than that produced in assembly language. That said optimising C compilers are available which will produce compiled code that is almost as efficient as assembly code. Furthermore, many C compilers also support in-line assembly, where sections of code written in a C programme are actually written as assembly code. As mentioned already in the introduction, all microprocessors execute binary code. It is convenient for us to represent this binary code as hexadecimal numbers. Programs stored in memory are often seen to be a list of hexadecimal numbers representing bytes. A byte will contain two hexadecimal numbers, so that for example B6 would represent a binary number 1011 0110. Each microcontroller has a number of instructions that it recognises and can execute and these are called the instruction set. The programmer describes these instructions in assembly language, which reads in simple English form except the data is moved from right to left i.e.

```
MOV A,#0FFh ; Move to accumulator the value 0FFh
```

It should be evident from the above example that the reader must know the meaning of instructions in assembly in order to understand the programme. Nevertheless, the instructions listed are fairly intuitive, and as a general rule assembly uses the format,

```
Operation destination, source   ;Comment ignored by
                                ;assembler
```

Thus the above assembly code would read as follows: Move the hexadecimal value FF (255 decimal) into the accumulator register. The CPU can only recognise this instruction when it is assembled into a binary code represented by a hexadecimal number, such as for example, '74FF'. The assembler performs this conversion of instruction code to binary form. The full programme code, representing a series of instructions, is therefore a list of hexadecimal numbers. For example, the following list of numbers could be stored in ROM.

```
74 FF 14 70 FD 08 B8 FF F6 09 C0
E0 E9 90 60 00 F0 D0 E0 B9 FF E8
```

4.2. Machine code and disassembly process

The representation of a programme as a sequence of hexadecimal numbers as shown above is referred to as Machine Code. It is fair to say that this representation makes much less sense to us than a listing in assembly language of the same code. At this point it is worth mentioning that it is possible for knowledgeable programmers to look at machine code and decode it back into assembly language. Thus, the programmer will use the hexadecimal numbers and knowledge of the instruction set to disassemble a piece of code into its assembly form.

Thus, for example the hexadecimal code '74FF' would disassemble into: MOV A,#0FFh. That is: 74 is the machine code instruction, which corresponds, to 'Move to Accumulator' and FF corresponds to the number that needs to be used in this case #0FFh. This process of converting machine code into assembly language format is generally referred to as 'hacking' the code. This is to say that the programmer could read a list of memory locations, convert them from binary to hexadecimal and step through each byte to disassemble the code into assembly language.

Perhaps the best way to introduce assembly is to go through some examples. These are given in the Lab A for this chapter, which follows. Going through these lab exercises will give the reader a basic understanding of assembly that will help in the overall understanding of programming the microcontroller.

4.3.   Lab A: Basic assembly programming

Objectives: After completing this lab you will be able to:

- Use assembly language to programme the microcontroller to perform simple tasks.
- Appreciate the difference between C and assembly programming languages and their impact on the produced executable code.

General note on Assembly and C programming within the μVision IDE

The μVision IDE that was introduced in Chapter 3 can be used for assembly programming as well as to programme in C language. Except for the difference in the respective syntax of the programming languages, the main difference is in the source programme window, which should be set-up to save the file as a *.a51 file rather than *.c. The assembly code is then entered as normal text in the editor window, and then it is saved as a *.a51 file. The assemble and build actions of the project are done through the run menu for either of the two programming languages.

Likewise, dScope is invoked in the same way and much of the simulation remains the same. The only difference in dScope is that when the original programme is written in C, the debug window can display HLL (high level language), assembly or mixed code. Programming in assembly requires that you know the instruction set of the microcontroller which in all cases will be supplied with a user manual. For reference purposes, I have included in the appendix a copy of the 8051-instruction set, which is obtained from the MCS-51 use manual. [31]

Exercise 1: Creating timing delay in software loops

Executing code takes time and it is possible to execute otherwise redundant code for the sole purpose of causing a time delay. It is often useful to produce these delays when hardware timers and counters are not available. On a general note however, it must be said that executing redundant loop is very wasteful of CPU time and consequently software delay loops are not recommended for use in real-time systems.

Task	Detail
Log onto Windows	Log onto windows and start μVision IDE
How to Programme Software Loop?	Software loops are a convenient means of generating timing delays that can be used to time and sequence external events.

Create a New assembly source file	From the μVision IDE menu-bar select File, and from drop-down menus select New.
	This opens a text file named untitled.
	Type the following code in the text window:
	
	`mov a,#0fh`
	`loop: dec a`
	`jnz loop`
	
	Click File → save to save the file on the subdirectory c:\user.
	Select file type *.a51 (assembly file) and save it as loop.a51.

Create a New Project	Click project and a window appears offering project options. Give the new project the name loop and select ADD. This brings another window with a choice of files to add to your project. Select file type *.a51 and the file stored earlier will appear in the window. Select ADD and close the project dialogue. You are back in the project window with the selected file listed. Select save to exit this window and return to μVision. Thus, a project file named Loop.prj containing a single file named loop.a51 was saved.

Compile file and read file listing	The IDE enables the user to assemble, list, edit and perform other operations on this project. Whenever changes are made to the project or any of its files, the whole project needs to be re-built. Click on project → compile file. Note that an error appears showing a missing end statement. The corrective measure is obvious, but in a more complicated case it would be useful to look at the file listing. To see the listing file perform the following: Select file→ open and choose file type *.lst. Open loop.lst, which comes up in a new window. The file is only a short programme, but the usefulness of a listing can nonetheless be appreciated.
Build Project file	Go back to the source window (loop.a51), correct the error by adding an End statement as the last instruction and compile the file again. You should not have any more errors, and compile successful loop1.obj file created will be the response. Click OK to proceed. Before this code is executed it need to be linked. Select Project → Make and the response is make successful hex file created.

Look at the HEX file	The hex file that was created can be viewed using notepad. It is reproduced here in order to show the actual CODE that will be stored in programme memory:
	`:05000000740F1470FDF7`
	`:00000001FF`
	`[File size 36 bytes]`

Debug File using DScope	Now you will use DScope debugging environment to run the absolute programme code.
	
	Click Run → DScope and a DScope GUI appears. Select view and select the following options;
	
	    ○ Toolbar
	    ○ Status bar
	    ○ Register Window
	    ○ Debug Window
	    ○ Toolbox
	For now de-select all other options.
	
	Click File → load object file. You will be given a list of OMF files (*.) to load. Select loop and click OK.
	
	The object file created earlier, is now loaded for use with DScope and the debug window will be used to check what is going on in the programme.
	This window has the options to run the file (GO), stop execution (Stop) or step through the programme line-by-line, step over or step until cursor.
	
	You can position the cursor on any line by clicking the line in the debug window. GoUntilCursor will take programme execution to this line.

Use Debug to Test the Loop programme	Step through this programme and note the value of the A register after each decrement. Note any changes in the Register window as you are stepping through the programme.
Task: Draw flow-chart	Looking at the code draw a flow chart of the above programme.
Task: Read clock cycles	While still in DScope, press reset. Double click the first NOP to set a breakpoint. Execute the programme with GO. The lower part of the register window shows how many machine cycles have executed. Number of cycles executed = _____

	Press reset once again, and use step into to step through the programme. Note the number of cycles that are shown as you are stepping through the programme. How many clocks are used up for the MOV, DEC and JNZ instructions? Since each cycle of execution takes a number of instructions each of which takes time, it is clear that loops such as this one can be used to programme delays in your code. The trick is to calculate the amount of delay, which is produced. All of the 8051 family of microcontrollers use a time unit called a machine cycle which is 12* clock cycle ($1/f_c$). Thus, machine cycles constitute an integer multiple of clock cycles. A complete list of instructions is available in the 8051 users manual [31] and I have included a table summarising these in the appendix. In summary however, most instructions are 1 machine cycle (12 clocks), some like ANL are 2 machine cycles (24 clocks), multiply and divide are 4 machine cycles (48 clocks), DEC A = 12 clocks, and JNZ takes 24 clocks.
Task: **Clock** **Calculation**	Using this information calculate the total number of clocks used up in running your programme.
Task: **Time** **calculation**	If the microcontroller clock is *12MHz* calculate the amount of time delay that the execution of this programme will create. (Remember: t=1/f)
	If you wanted to generate longer delay you could place a Loop inside a loop. Thus, if the above loop were repeated 256 times this would increase the total delay 256 fold.

Task: Compare with delay loop in C	You can use the principle of delay loops above and your knowledge of 'C' programming to produce a similar loop but in C language. Let the loop run 15 times as before.
	
	This is an example programme which uses the `while` statement in C:
	
	<pre>#include <reg51.h>
void main(void)
{
int count;
count=0;
 while (count <= 15) {
count+=1; //increment count
 }; // delay lop 15 times
}</pre>

Look at the HEX file	The hex file that was created during the compile phase of the above C programme is reproduced here in order to show the actual CODE that will be stored in programme memory: <pre>:0E400000E4FFFE0FBF00010EEF64104E70F5DE
:01400E00228F
:0300000002400FAC
:0C400F00787FE4F6D8FD758107024000C0
:00000001FF
[File size 125 bytes]</pre>
Task: Timing calculations and comparison	Compare the timing calculations between the assembly and C programs for the loops, by running the new programme in the debugger. *C Loop (while): Each increment is 2 cycles and jump is 5 cycles.* *Asm loop: each decrement is 1 cycle and 2 cycles for jump.* *In the C loop, there is a long jump to start of programme, which takes 389 cycles. Total executions = 490 clocks.* *In assembly there is no long jump and the programme completes in 46 cycles.*

Task: Alternative loop in C	As an alternative, C allows other loop options and an example is the `for` loop; The above task can be achieved by the following C programme:
	
	``c
	#include <reg51.h>
	void main(void)
	{
	int i=15;
	  for(i=15;i>=0;i--); // delay
	}
	``

Look at the HEX file	The hex file that was created is reproduced here in order to show the actual CODE that will be stored in programme memory:
	`:0F4000007F0F7E00EF1F70011EBEFFF8BFFFF5A0`
	`:01400F00228E`
	`:03000000024010AB`
	`:0C401000787FE4F6D8FD758107024000BF`
	`:00000001FF`
	`[File size 127 bytes]`

Comparing the HEX files	Hexadecimal files contain the actual machine code for the CPU to execute. The size of code determines the amount of memory that is needed to run the programme. It is seen that by comparing the three hexadecimal files, the one created in assembly is 36 bytes, and those compiled in C are 125 and 127 bytes, roughly three times bigger. So, it can be seen that although C programming is easier and more elegant, it does produce a code overhead.

Exercise 2: Writing to I/O ports

The 8051 has four 8-bit ports, which can be used for communicating with the outside world. These ports can be accessed as SFRs by name `P0, P1, P2` and `P3` or directly by their address `80h, 90h, A0h, A8h` respectively.

In assembly, writing and reading to/from ports can be done using the `MOV` instruction (i.e. `MOV P0,#0FFh` that will write the number `FFh` to port `P0`). In C this can be done using assignment (i.e. `P0=0xff`)

Looping inside a loop:	The task is to modify the your programme in exercise 1 so that you have an inner loop (loop2) counting 0-255, repeating in an outer loop (loop1) 255 times. As an additional feature, we can write the counts of the outer loop to an output port. The flow chart is as follows:
	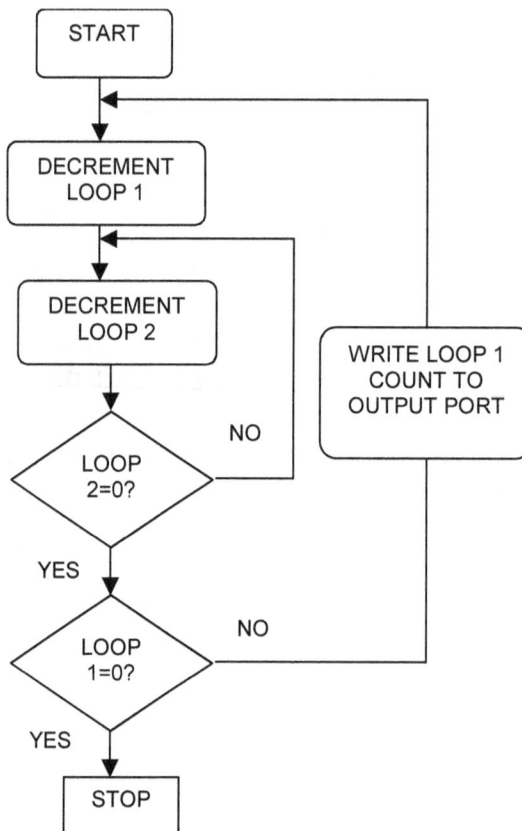

Assembly Listing for Loop inside a loop.	A possible example of this code is given below. You may retype this or design your own.
	
	``asm
	mov r0,#0h ;load outer loop counter with zero
	mov r1,#0h ;load inner loop counter with zero
	start1: nop ;do nothing
	start0: nop ;do nothing
	mov a,#0ffh ;load delay count 256d
	loop: dec a ;decrement count
	jnz loop ;loop until count is zero
	inc r0 ;increment inner loop counter
	cjne r0,#0ffh,start0 ;jump to inner loop if counter
	<ff
	inc r1 ;increment outer loop counter
	mov P0,r1 ;write outer loop counter to port o
	cjne r1,#0ffh,start1; jump to outer loop if counter
	<ff
	end
	``
	
	Compile the modified programme and run DScope.
	
	When in dScope select File →load CPU driver. From the list of CPUs select 8051.dll.
	
	Click File→ load object file and select the new file, which you have assembled above.
	
	Note that the menu on dScope now includes the Peripherals option, which is a feature of the 8051 microcontroller.
	
	Select peripherals → I/O ports port 0. A window with port bits in hexadecimal and binary is displayed.
	
	On the main menu, under view option, enable the watch and command window. This will bring up the two new windows.
	You will now set up watch on registers R0 and R1.
	
	In the command window type in ws R0 (return) and ws R1 (return). Notice that values for R0 and R1 appear in the watch window. On the main menu select setup→update watch window.
	Alternatively you can set-up watches using the menu options setup → watchpoints → define watch
	
	Run the programme in the debugger and notice the changing values in the watch window as well as the changing bits on P0 as the programme is executing.

CHAPTER 5 C PROGRAMMING

5.1. Introduction

Arguably the most versatile programming language that supports procedural concepts is the C programming language, which was originally developed by Dennis Ritchie [32]. Although it was primarily intended to run under UNIX, C is equally capable of running under Microsoft operating systems and other platforms, provided of course that a suitable compiler is in place to compile the C code for the required platform. Also, due to the simplicity and ease of writing a C compiler, it is the preferred high-level language available on microcontrollers and embedded development platforms. This is because it allows the programmer a wide range of programming operations from high level down to a very low level, approaching the level of assembly language.

Due to this diversity of application, C is a very useful language to learn. It also forms the basis of the C++ programming language that is widely used in object-oriented development (OOD). As a matter of fact the Windows O/S was developed in C++.

In this chapter we will specifically address C programming for the 8051 family of microcontrollers. The syntax and rules of C will remain unchanged and for detailed description of these the reader is best of referring to the text by Kernighan and Ritchie [32]. Additionally, there are a large number of texts that deal with C programming and some of the work presented in this chapter is derived from text is derived from a publication entitled procedural programming in C. [34] Before we move onto C programming it is necessary to consider the programming models that are supported by the KEIL IDE.

As we mentioned earlier the compiler controls memory allocation in C. Every C development environment will support a range of memory models that will suit different applications. Due to the fact that embedded applications are often subjected to real-time performance constraints, as well as cost related constraints, efficient use of memory is a common requirement. Next we consider the memory models that the KEIL IDE supports for the 8051 family of microcontrollers [13].

C51 support for the 8051 memory models

The user interface shown in Figure 5.1 provides a choice for the options that are available for the memory models in the C compiler. The choice of model determines how much memory the compiler will reserve when compiling a programme. It is therefore up to the programmer to decide which model to select. For example, within the context of this text, all the exercises will be using the small memory model.

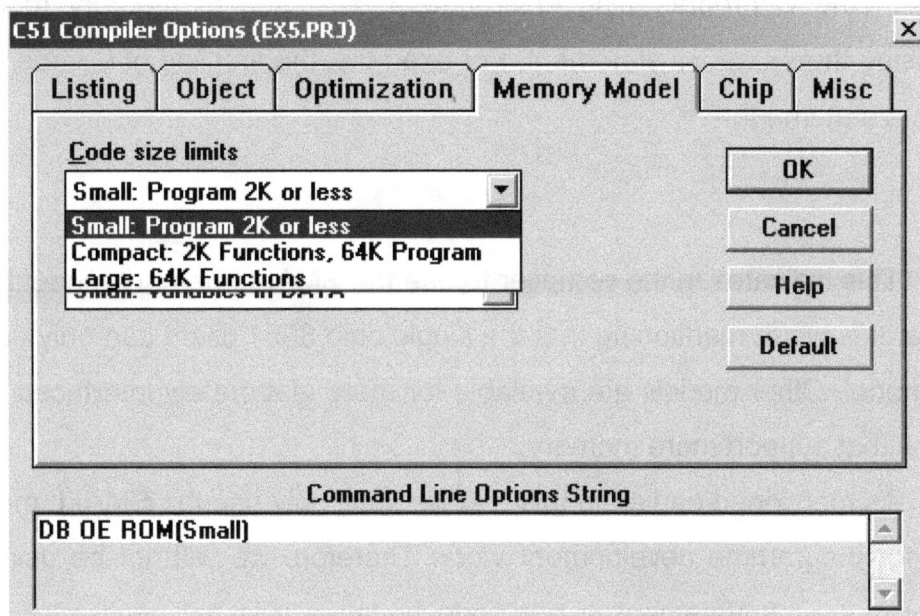

Figure 5.1 C51 Memory model options

With the µVision IDE, which includes the C51 by KEIL the 8051 programming models that are supported, are as follows:

SMALL memory model: Supports 128 bytes of RAM (on-chip). Additional RAM is supported if externally fitted.

COMPACT memory model: Supports 128 bytes or 256 bytes of RAM (on-chip). Additional 256 bytes of RAM are supported if externally fitted. (Off-chip)

LARGE memory model: Supports 128 bytes or 256 bytes of RAM (on-chip). Additional 64K bytes of RAM are supported if externally fitted. (Off-chip). This memory configuration can exploit five memory areas for data storage, as follows:

- DATA   128 bytes
- IDATA   128 bytes
- CODE   64 Kbytes
- PDATA   256 bytes paged
- XDATA   64Kbytes non-paged

(Please refer to Chapter 3 to see how this relates to the 8051-memory map)

In the C programming environment, selection of memory model is done using the `#pragma` statement. For example, the first line of C code would contain a statement,

```
#pragma small
```

This indicates to the compiler to use the SMALL memory model for the compile. It is worth mentioning that the single chip 8051 users can only use the small model. Other models are available for more elaborately interfaced target systems that support more memory.

As mentioned earlier, in this text we shall only use the SMALL memory model for programme development work. Therefore we will not be using the `#pragma small` statement in our code because it is not necessary in our case.

The choice of variables that are use when programming in C will have an impact on how much memory is required to compile and run the programme. For example, and integer variable will take up 16 bits of memory, however if it is known that the variable will not exceed the range 0-255, then it is best to declare it as a `uchar` variable. We will now consider some of the variable declarations in C. Much of the material in this chapter derives from reference [34] with the author's explicit permission.

5.2.   C programming - Declaring variables and constants

In all programming languages it is necessary to tell the compiler the type of constants and variables that the programme will use. The types refer to whether the variable or constant is an integer, floating-point number or a character or any other type that the compiler supports. The main reason for this is so that the compiler can allocate memory to the variable or constant. Types differ in range of values that they support and also in the amount of space they occupy, i.e. their bit-size. In C programming every variable, constant or function must be suitably declared, before it can be used. C51 supports the following type declarations:

Type	Size (number of bits)	Range
Bit	1	$0 \rightarrow 1$
Char	8	$0 \rightarrow \pm127$
Unsigned char	8	$0 \rightarrow 256$
Int	16	$0 \rightarrow \pm32K$
Unsigned int	16	$0 \rightarrow 64K$
Long	32	$0 \rightarrow \pm2G$
Unsigned long	32	$0 \rightarrow 4G$
Float	32	$\pm 1.2 \times 10^{-38} \rightarrow \pm3.4 \times 10^{38}$
Pointer	24/16/8	Variable address

By definition constants are not supposed to change, and consequently they can be stored in ROM. This does not mean that they cannot be stored in RAM. Sometimes a variable will be constant throughout the lifetime of application, but can change in another instance. For example, the present VAT rate has been fixed for some time, but will change at some point in the future. On the other hand, PI = 3.142…. is a constant which is never going to change. Therefore, it follows that VAT rate should be placed in RAM, while PI should go to ROM.

Programming guidelines

For embedded programming in C the C51 primer [35] is a very detailed reference that includes a wealth of information. Besides the programming detail it also recommends some general points regarding the general approach to programming in C. The following rules will allow the compiler to make the best use of the processor's resources.

- Always use 8 bit variables the 8051 is strictly an 8-bit machine with no 16-bit instructions. `char` will always be more efficient than `int`.

- Always use `unsigned` variables where possible. The 8051 has no signed compares, multiplies etc., hence all sign management must be done by discrete 8051 instructions.

- Try to avoid dividing anything but 8 bit numbers. There is only an 8 by 8 divide in the instruction set. 32 by 16 divides could be lengthy.

- Try to avoid using bit structures. Until v2.30, C51 did not support these structures as defined by ANSI. Having queried this omission with KEIL, the explanation was that the code produced would be very large and inefficient. Now that they have been added, this has proved to be right. An alternative solution is to declare bits individually, using the "bit" storage class, and pass them to a user-written function.

- Additionally, I have to add, since C is case sensitive I simply write my entire C code in lower case.

The ANSI standard [33] states that the product of two 8-bit numbers is also an 8-bit number. This means that any `unsigned` chars, which might have to be multiplied, must actually be declared as `unsigned int` if there is any possibility that they may produce even an intermediate result over 255.

For example consider the following C programme segment:

```
{
unsigned char z;
unsigned char x;
unsigned char y;
Z = ((unsigned int) y * (unsigned int) x) >> 8;
}
```

Here the two eight bit numbers x and y are multiplied and then divided by 256. The intermediate 16-bit (`unsigned int`) result is permissible because y and x have been loaded by the multiplier library routine as `int` types.

Calculations, which consist of integer operands but which always, produce an 8 bit (`char`) due to careful scaling result thus:

```
.. .. .. ..
unsigned int x, y;
        unsigned char z;
    z = x*y/256;
```

will always work, as C51 will equate z to the upper byte of the integer result.

Constants stored in ROM:

To declare a constant to be stored in ROM, we use the `code` declaration to indicate that it should be stored in read only memory. Constants can also be stored in RAM if they are suitably located so that they cannot be over-written.

```
code unsigned char base_voltage=0x02;
```

This example stores the variable named `base_voltage`. It is assigned a value `0x02` in hexadecimal (it could also have been declared in decimal), and it is of the `type unsigned char`. This means that the range that this variable can take is 0-255 decimal. The variable is declared as stored in `code`, which means that it is a constant stored in ROM.

Variables stored in RAM:

To declare a variable, we use the declaration to indicate that it should be stored in RAM.

```
unsigned char multiplying_factor=128;
```

This example stores the variable named `multiplying_factor`, whose value is 128 and it is of the `unsigned` character `type`. Once again the range of the variable is 0-255. By NOT specifying `code` in the variable declarations, we are telling the compiler that the variable is NOT stored in ROM and in fact this tells the compiler to store it in RAM. When we associate a value with the variable at the time that we declare it, the variable is initialised to that value, but being a variable it is allowed to change.

We recall from Chapter 4 that the 8051 supports addressing of up to 64Kbytes of external memory. To access this memory we use the `xdata` declaration to indicate that it should be stored in external RAM. **For example,**

```
xdata unsigned char motor_rpm;
```

Here the variable `motor_rpm`, which is of the `type unsigned char`, is directed to external memory by the use of the `xdata` statement.

Bit-wise operations:

The use of the bit-addressable space is relatively straightforward in assembly programming, where bit operations are allowed. This feature is particularly useful in embedded applications where it is often necessary to operate on a single bit within a byte. In particular, the 8051 family of microcontrollers use bit addressing to set specific bits within the special function registers, in order to control operation of a peripheral device (i.e. Times, interrupts etc.)

Bit operations in ANSI C are not permitted and therefore the required bit has to be identified from within a byte. This is done by a MASK operation, where a logical AND is applied to the whole byte, with all zeros except for a one where the bit (s) needed are. Therefore if it were necessary to establish the value of `bit 2` in any given byte, then the whole byte would be AND-ed with 0000100. The byte 0000100 in this case is the MASK. It is known that logical AND operation will leave unchanged, those bits corresponding to the logical 1 in the mask. Where the mask has logical 0 will make the resulting AND operation a 0.

Thus, the variable stored in the byte would be AND-ed with 0x40 (hexadecimal for 0000 0100). This is shown in Table 5.1.

Table 5.1 Bit masking operation using logical AND

Bit number	7	6	5	4	3	2	1	0
Byte	1	0	1	0	1	1	0	0
Mask	0	0	0	0	0	1	0	0
AND result	0	0	0	0	0	1	0	0

The MASK operation is rather cumbersome and in C51 IDE this can be simplified with bit operations using the `sbit` data `type` operator.

Using `sbit` operator

With typical 8051 applications, it is often necessary to access individual bits within an SFR. The Cx51 Compiler makes this possible with the `sbit` data `type`, which provides access to bit-addressable SFRs, Ports and the bit-addressable memory space. Usage, [35]

```
sbit source = address
```

For example:

```
sbit EA = 0xAF;
```

The expression to the right of the equal sign (`=`) specifies an absolute bit address for the symbolic name. Which in this case, is given as `0xAF` in hexadecimal notation.

This declaration defines `EA` to be the SFR bit at address `0xAF`. On the 8051, this is bit 7 of the IE (Interrupt Enable) SFR, which is the enable all interrupts bit. Any symbolic name, such as `P1`, `P2`, `EA`, `TCON`, `SCON`, etc, can be used in an `sbit` declaration.

There are three ways of specifying the address of the source byte for bit operations. Briefly, the first takes in the name of the SFR and the second takes its address. These two use the carat sign (^) to indicate which bit is required.

The third way is to calculate the absolute address of the bit. Here the base address of the SFR is given and the offset added. These three methods are described in more detail next. These are all derived from the C51 primer. [35]

Method 1: `SFR_name ^ int_constant`

This method uses an `SFR` (SFR_name) as the base address for the `sbit` declaration. The `SFR` must be specified before it is used, even though it is available through the `reg51.h` header file. The compiler will generate the error if the SFR is not suitably declared before being used.

The expression following the carat symbol (^) specifies the position of the bit within the SFR, in the range 0-7, to which this declaration refers. For example:

```
SFR PSW = 0xD0; // absolute address of the PSW register

sbit OV = PSW^2; // identifies bit 2 as the Overflow flag in PSW
sbit CY = PSW^7; // identifies bit 7 as the Carry flag in PSW
```

Method 2: `int_constant ^ int_constant`

Here an integer constant is used as the base address for the **sbit**. The base address value must be evenly divisible by 8; otherwise the wrong bit position within the byte will be referenced. Referencing bit position is as in method 1. For example:

```
sbit OV = 0xD0^2; // Overflow bit is bit 2 of the byte
located at address 0xD0 - which is the address of PSW

sbit EA = 0xA8^7; // Enable Interrupts EA is bit 7
```

Method 3: `int_constant`

This method uses an absolute bit address for the **sbit**. For example:

```
sbit OV = 0xD2; // here D0+2, offsets 2 from PSW to give the OV flag
sbit CY = 0xD7; // here D0+7, offsets 2 from PSW to give the CY flag
sbit EA = 0xAF; //bit 7 of the interrupt Enable register is A8+7=AF
```

Note however that not all SFRs are bit-addressable. Only those SFRs whose address is evenly divisible by 8 are bit-addressable. A quick test to see if the address is divisible by 8, the lower nibble of the SFR's address must be 0 or 8. For example, SFRs at 0xA8 and 0xD0 are bit-addressable, whereas SFRs at 0xC7 and 0xEB are not.

To calculate an SFR bit address, add the bit position to the SFR byte address. So, to access bit 6 in the SFR at 0xC8, the SFR bit address would be 0xCE (0xC8 + 6).

The sbit data type declaration can also be used to access individual bits of variables declared with the bdata memory type specifier. This example is covered in the Lab at the end of this chapter.

Example in C:

```
#include<reg51.h>
//reg.h contains sfr defs & sbit defs  for standard
8051.

sbit sign=P1^2; // bit 2 of P1 is defined for bit
operation as sign
void main(void)
{
bdata    char   evaluate_bit;//bit    data    variable
declaration

evaluate_bit=P1; // byte to test is on port 1
// Using the MASK 0x04 to isolate bit 2
if (evaluate_bit & 0x04) {
evaluate_bit=1;
}
// Alternatively, using bit operation sbit
if (sign ==1) {
evaluate_bit=1;
}
}
```

Special Function registers (SFRs)

In C programming SFRs are declared in the same fashion as other C variables. The only difference is that the data `type` specified is `SFR` rather than `char` or `int`. For example:

```
sfr P0 = 0x80;    /* Port-0, address 80h */
sfr P1 = 0x90;    /* Port-1, address 90h */
sfr P2 = 0xA0;    /* Port-2, address 0A0h */
sfr P3 = 0xB0;    /* Port-3, address 0B0h */
```

In this example, `P0`, `P1`, `P2`, and `P3` are the SFR name declarations given in hexadecimal numbers (hence the `x` in `0x80;`). Names for `SFR` variables are defined just like other C variable declarations. Any symbolic name may be used in an `SFR` declaration. All of the SFRs are declared in `reg51.h` and a separate declaration as above will not be necessary if the `reg51` header file is included. Nevertheless, it is worth mentioning how these are declared.

5.3. Setting the serial port

Setting the Mode

The serial port on the 8051 is a universal asynchronous receiver transmitter (UART). It is capable of full duplex serial I/O and it can be programmed in one of four modes. To programme the control modes we write specific bytes to the special function registers that correspond to the desired operation. The values of the bytes written are calculated on the basis of the control bits that need to be set or cleared in the SFR. The "Serial Control" (SCON) SFR bits are defined in the Table 5.2. [31] Here each of the register bits are addressable by location and the value that each bit takes determines the operation of the port. In order to control the operation of the peripheral, the microcontroller must be programmed to send the appropriate signals to this register. The programming is determined by the value of individual bits that are written to the register. If a '1' is written to a location this implies that the bit is set. If a '0' is written then this means that the bit is cleared. Thus for example if the byte `0101 0000` is written this would in turn mean that the register is configured to run as an 8-bit UART, controlled by Timer 1. Receive enable bit is set (i.e. bit 5).

Table 5.2

Bit	Name	Bit Address	Explanation of Function
7	SM0	9Fh	Serial port mode bit 0
6	SM1	9Eh	Serial port mode bit 1.
5	SM2	9Dh	Multiprocessor Communications Enable
4	REN	9Ch	Receiver Enable. This bit must be set in order to receive characters.
3	TB8	9Bh	Transmit bit 8. The 9th bit to transmit in mode 2 and 3.
2	RB8	9Ah	Receive bit 8. The 9th bit received in mode 2 and 3.
1	TI	99h	Transmit Flag. Set when a byte has been completely transmitted.
0	RI	98h	Receive Flag. Set when a byte has been completely received.

As mentioned earlier, there are four modes of operation and these are selected by two bits, namely SM0 and SM1. Their values correspond to the modes of operation shown in Table 5.3

Table 5.3

SM0	SM1	Serial Mode	Explanation	Baud Rate
0	0	0	8-bit Shift Register	Oscillator / 12
0	1	1	8-bit UART	Set by Timer 1 (*)
1	0	2	9-bit UART	Oscillator / 32 (*)
1	1	3	9-bit UART	Set by Timer 1 (*)

(*) Note: The baud rate indicated in this Table is doubled if PCON.7 (SMOD) is set.

Bits **SM0** and **SM1** let us set the serial mode to a value between 0 and 3. The four modes are either (8-bit/9-bit, UART or Shift Register) and they also differ in the way that the baud rate will be calculated. Namely, in modes 0 and 2 the baud rate is fixed based on the oscillator's frequency. On the other hand, in modes 1 and 3 the baud rate is variable based on how often Timer 1 overflows.

Looking at the next bit of the SCON SFR, the **SM2** is a flag for multiprocessor communication. This can be useful in certain advanced serial applications but it is beyond the scope of this course. For now it is safe to say that you will almost always want to clear this bit so that the flag is set upon reception of any character.

REN is "Receiver Enable". You will need to set this bit when you want to receive data via the serial port.

The last four bits (bits 0 through 3) are used when actually sending and receiving data. That is to say, they are not used to configure the serial port. The TB8 and RB8 bits are used in modes 2 and 3. Their use is beyond the scope of this course, and more information can be found in [31].

TI means is the "Transmit Interrupt" bit. It is used to tell the 8051 when the last byte sent to the serial port have been completed. In short, when a programme writes a value to the serial port, a certain amount of time will pass before the individual bits of the byte are "clocked out" the serial port. This is because in serial transmission bytes are sent one bit at time. If the programme were to write another byte to the serial port before the first byte was completely output, the data being sent would be corrupted. Thus, the 8051 signals the programme that it has "clocked out" the last byte by setting the TI bit. When the TI bit is set, the programme may assume that the serial port is "free" and ready to send the next byte.

RI bit means "Receive Interrupt" It is used to tell the 8051 when the last byte received from the serial port have been completed. That is to say, whenever the 8051 has received a complete byte it will trigger the **RI** bit to let the programme know that it needs to read the value quickly, before another byte is read.

Setting the baud rate

Once the Serial Port Mode has been configured, as explained above, the programme must configure the serial port's baud rate. [31] This only applies to Serial Port modes 1 and 3. The baud rate is determined based on the oscillator's frequency when in mode 0 and 2.

In mode 0, the baud rate is always the oscillator frequency divided by 12. This means that if your crystal is *11.059MHz*, mode 0 baud rate will always be *921,583* baud. In mode 2 the baud rate is always the oscillator frequency divided by *64*, so an *11.059MHz* crystal speed will yield a baud rate of *172,797*.

In modes 1 and 3, the baud rate is determined by how frequently timer 1 overflows. The more frequently timer 1 overflows, the higher the baud rate. There are many ways one can cause timer 1 to overflow at a rate that determines a baud rate, but the most common method is to put timer 1 in 8-bit auto-reload mode (timer mode 2) and set a reload value *(TH1)* that causes Timer 1 to overflow at a frequency appropriate to generate a baud rate.

To determine the value that must be placed in *TH1* to generate a given baud rate, we may use the following equation (assuming PCON.7 is clear).

$$TH1 = 256 - ((Crystal / 384) / Baud) \qquad (5.1)$$

If PCON.7 is set then the baud rate is effectively doubled, thus the equation becomes:

$$TH1 = 256 - ((Crystal / 192) / Baud) \qquad (5.2)$$

For example, if we have an *11.059MHz* crystal and we want to configure the serial port to *19,200* baud we try using this value in the first equation:

$$TH1 = 256 - ((Crystal / 384) / Baudrate)$$

$$TH1 = 256 - ((11059000 / 384) / 19200)$$

$$TH1 = 256 - ((28,799) / 19200)$$

$$TH1 = 256 - 1.5 = 254.5$$

We therefore calculate that in order to obtain 19,200 baud on an *11.059MHz* crystal we have to set *TH1* to *254.5*. We can only set integer values so if we set it to *254* we will have achieved *14,400* baud and if we set it to *255* we will have achieved 28,800 baud. Neither of these values is correct.

At this point we can resort to second equation, which uses PCON bit 7 (SMOD) to double the baud rate. Thus we have:

$$TH1 = 256 - ((Crystal / 192) / Baudrate)$$

$$TH1 = 256 - ((11059000 / 192) / 19200)$$

$$TH1 = 256 - ((57699) / 19200)$$

$$TH1 = 256 - 3 = 253$$

Here we are able to calculate a nice, even *TH1* value. Therefore, to obtain *19,200* baud with an *11.059MHz* crystal we must:

- Configure Serial Port mode 1 or 3.
- Configure Timer 1 to timer mode 2 (8-bit auto-reload).
- Set *TH1* to *253* to reflect the correct frequency for *19,200* baud.
- Set PCON.7 (SMOD) to double the baud rate.

At this stage it is suggested that we go through some C programming exercises. The reason that we covered the serial port is so that we can use it to display the results of our C programming effort. Programming other SFRs will be considered later.

At this point we will proceed to the laboratory exercises for this chapter. These exercises, first of all introduce the use of the serial port and conveniently we can use the serial port to print out results from other programs in Lab exercises. The other programs will serve to demonstrate some basic C programming examples to include:

- Variable declarations
- Writing to serial port
- `sbit` operation, working with individual bits
- Software loops, controlled iterations.
- Decisions with the if statement
- Break and Continue statements
- Switch statement
- Using C variable types
- Using logical operators

5.4.   Lab A: Some more C programming examples

Objectives: After completing this lab you will be able to programme in C to include the following:

- Use the correct language syntax to programme in C language for data manipulation.
- Use `sbit` feature to isolate individual bits of Special Function Registers
- Use programming statements such as While, Form If-Else, Break, Continue Switch
- Use functions to pass parameters and return values

Introduction

The following exercises use the C language in general terms, and they will also apply for embedded applications in the KEIL IDE. The emphasis here is to learn how to use C. More detailed explanation of the routines used is available in text reference. [35] As we have seen during dScope debug sessions in Chapter 3, a programme executes a sequence of actions that are described by the programme code. Usually a programme will perform some action on data and this data is normally held in variables. A variable has a unique name within the scope of the programme, which is given by the programmer. And a named variable is used to hold a value that is permitted to change as the programme executes.

In C programming, before you can use a variable you have to declare it and this involves stating what `type` of variable it is. The variable `type` can be defined as `int` (integer), `float` (floating-point), `char` (character) and others. The variable definitions are always given before any executable statements in any programme block. In the examples given below it is suggested that you type in the code, save it in a project and build it within µVision. Then you can execute the programme in debug and in this manner confirm that you understand how the programme works.

Exercise 1: Working with data in the C language [35]

Task	Detail
Log onto Windows	Log onto windows and start μVision IDE as described in Lab A of Chapter3.
Writing to the serial port	The first programme for this exercise will be to write to the serial port. This involves programming the various SFRs to set the baud rate and other options that support serial communications. The main reason for doing this exercise at this stage is so that we can write the outputs from our programs in the serial window. Note that the serial window is selected as one of the view option on the main menu of dScope. Write the following programme in μVision and build it so that it has no errors. Do not include the line numbers as I have only used them to aid my explanation below.

Task: **Code for writing to serial port**	<pre>1. #include <reg51.h>
	2. #include <stdio.h>
	
	3. main()
	4. {
	5. TCON =0x50;
	6. TMOD = 0x20;
	7. TH1 = 0xFA;
	8. TR1 = 1;
	9. TI = 1;
	10. PCON = 0x80
	11. printf ("\n Serial port write example\n"); }</pre>

Explain each line of this programme	**Line 1:** Header file congaing SFRs **Line 2:** `stdio.h` is the header file that contains the function `printf` **Line 3:** `main()` programme start **Line 4:** Opening brace of `main()` **Line 5:** Programme TCON, control register with 0000 0101, this corresponds to counter operation bits 0 and 2 set. Interrupt 0 and 1 Type control bits **Line 6:** Programme TMOD with 0000 0010, select timer 1 **Line 7:** Programme Timer high byte with 1111 1010 **Line 8:** This sets the Timer 1 Run Control bit. It is cleared by software **Line 9:** This sets the transmit interrupt flag. Allowing

	programme to know when byte sending is complete. It is set by the hardware when byte is transmitted, and cleared by software after servicing. **Line 10:** This sets the SMOD bit of the PCON SFR so that the baud rate is doubled. (As per calculations in chapter 5) **Line 11:** Print function, in this case printing to the serial port. When executed this programme should print the words, "Serial port write example" to the serial port.
	Now that we can write to the serial port, retain the above code as a component of each of your programs so that you can use the `printf` function to send any results of your programme to the serial port. Let us now consider some basic programming exercises in C. As mentioned earlier these are sourced from [34] with author's permission.
Assigning values to variables	Assignment is a term used to describe the action of giving a value to a variable. In the example below, three variables are defined for use in the programme and the rest of the programme is merely a series of illustrations of various assignments. Most of the statements are self-explanatory.

Task write programme to demonstrate assignment statements	Type the following programme and run it in dScope so that you can be sure that you understand how it works.

```
/* This programme gives examples of assignment statements
*/
# include <reg51.h>
# include <stdio.h>
void main(void)
{
int x,y,z; //declare variables
x = 12;
y = 5;
z = x + y;
z = x - y;   /* simple subtraction */
z = x * y;   /* simple multiplication */
z = x / y;   /* simple division */
z = x % y; /* simple modulo (remainder) */
z = 12*x + y/2 - x*y*2/(x*z + y*2);
z = z/4+13*(x + y)/3 - x*y + 2*x*x;
x = x + 1;   /* incrementing a variable */
y = y * 5;
x = y = z = 50;   /* multiple assignment //all variables
assigned the same value*/
x = y = z = 2*30/4;
}
```

| Use debug to run the above programme | On the set-up menu in dScope arrange to watch variables x, y and z. It would be useful to watch their values in decimal. Just to remind you how this is done I have a screen shot below.

Set up watches on variables x, y, z and see how their values change as you go through the programme. Step through the programme to confirm that you have understood the assignment operations. |

File View Setup Peripherals Help

8051.dll

Module: EX2_MOD5

Commands Go! GoTilCurs! StepOut! StepInto! StepOver! Stop!

hll

```
 29:   //printf ("
+30:   z = z/4+13*
 31:   //printf ("
+32:   x = x + 1;
 33:   //printf ("
+34:   y = y * 5;
 35:   //printf ("
+36:   x = y = z =
 37:   //printf ("
+38:   x = y = z =
 39:   //printf ("
 40:   }
```

Watchpoints

current watch defintions:

```
00:  x
01:  y
02:  z
```

Kill selected

Expr.:

Define watch   Show symbols...

Number output base: Output line Mode:
○ 10   ○ 0xnn   ○ Single   ○ Multiple

Close   Help

Watch

```
x:  15
y:  15
z:  15
```

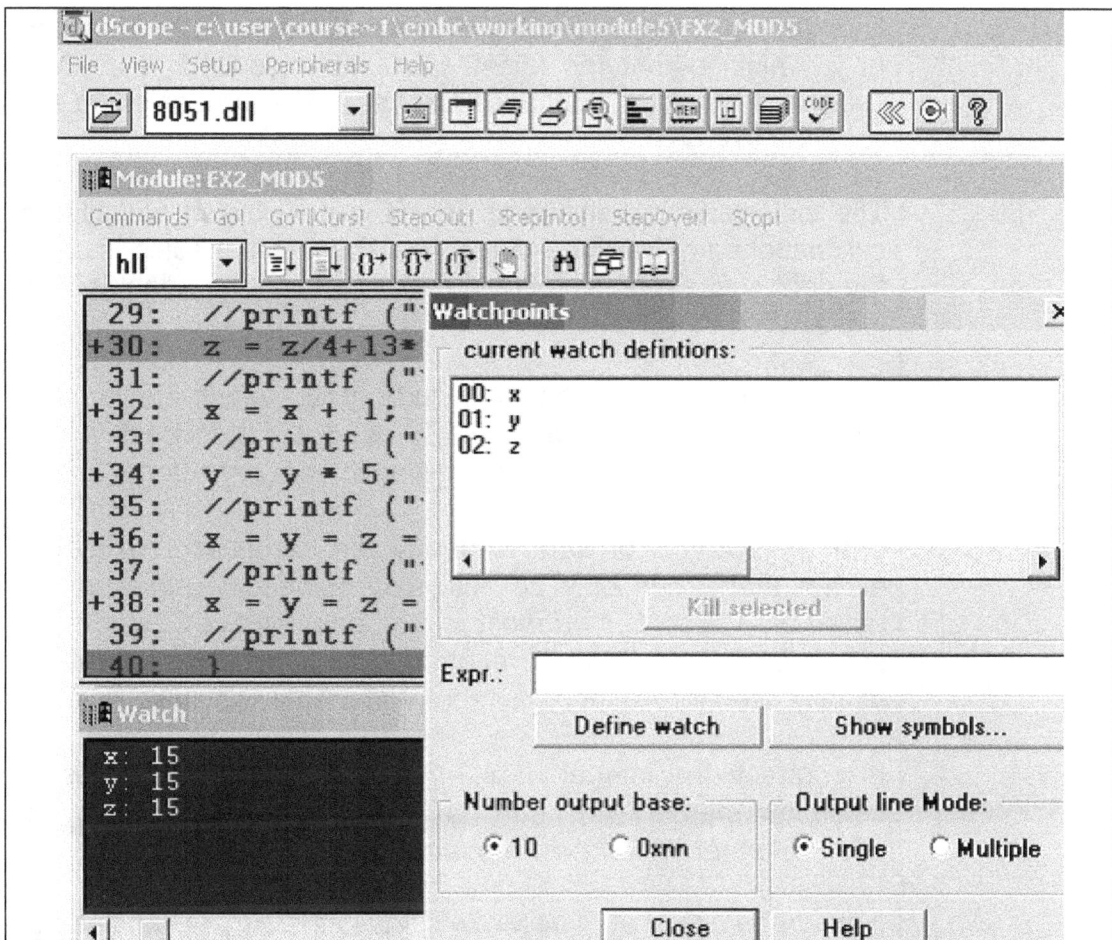

Explain the programme execution	Looking at the example assignments that are given in the above programme we find that the first two lines of the assignment statements assign numerical values to the variables named x and y.
	The next five lines illustrate the five basic arithmetic functions and how to use them.
	The fifth is the modulo operator and gives the remainder when the two variables are divided. By definition this operator can only be applied to `int` or `char type` variables, as these do not support floating-point arithmetic.
	The last two lines depict the use of multiple assignments, which are scanned by the compiler, in the order from right to left. The result is a very useful construct, namely,

```
x = y = z = 50;/* multiple assignment */
x = y = z = 2*30/4;
```

In the first of the above multiple assignments, the compiler uses the value 50, to assign to z, then continues to the left and finds that this, latest result of a calculation should be assigned to y. Thinking that the latest calculation resulted in a 50, it assigns it to y, and continues the leftward scan assigning the value 50 to x also.

The last statement illustrates that it is possible to actually do calculations and assign the result to multiple variables. In fact, the rightmost expression could even contain the variables x, y, and z.

Other common data types include float, which declares a floating-point number and `char` used for declaring single character variables (i.e. not strings which are considered later).

The `char type` of data is nearly the same as the integer except that it can only be assigned numerical values in the range of -128 to 127 on most implementations of C, since it is stored in only one byte of memory. The `char type` of data is usually used for ASCII data, more commonly known as text.

In contrast, the integer data `type` is stored in two bytes of computer memory on nearly all microcomputers. Two bytes offer 16-bit representation with a range −32k to + 32K.

It would be useful at this time to discuss the way C handles the two types `char` and `int`. Most functions in C that are designed to operate with integer `type` variables will work equally well with character `type` variables because they are a form of an integer variable. Those functions, when called on to use a `char type` variable, will actually promote the `char` data into integer data before using it. For this reason, it is possible to mix `char` and `int type` variables in your programme.

If only positive values are going to be used the `unsigned data type` is used. i.e. `unsigned int` count;

Exercise 2: Printing to serial port on the 8051

Let us briefly look at how functions are used in C. All functions in C have the same structure. This is shown in the Figure below.

Functions are defined by writing a function prototype, which is just like a first call to a function. After the function has been declared with a prototype, it can be used within the main or other functions.

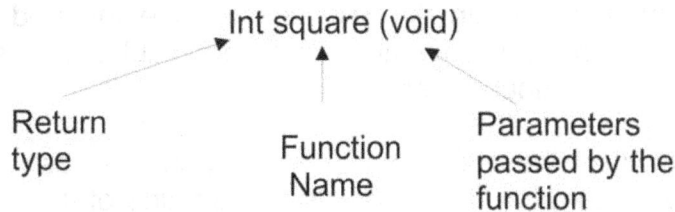

Int square (void)

| Return type | Function Name | Parameters passed by the function |

{ these braces signal the start of the function
This the Body of action statements and these terminate with a semicolon (;)
return (whatever the return value or variable is);
} These are the end braces

As we have already seen in earlier chapters, the call to the function main is `main()`, and the empty braces indicate that the function is expected to return a value, which is not defined. We will see later that putting the word void in front of the main() will indicate to the compiler that the function returns nothing (i.e. void).

To illustrate the use of the `printf` function type in the following example, and runt it in dScope. Remember that you are using `printf` to write to the serial port. In conventional C programming on the PC (i.e. Borland C) `printf` will print to the screen. This will not happen in KEIL, and we have to initialise the serial port to act as the destination for `printf` data. (This was the first exercise in this chapter)

```
#include "stdio.h"
void main()
{
   printf ("This is a line of text to output.\n");
   printf("And this is another ");
   printf("line of text.\n\n");
   printf("This is a third line.\n");
}
```

| **Programme explanation** [34] | In this example there are four programme statements, each one being a call to the function `printf()`. The top line will be executed first, then the next, and so on, until the fourth line is |

complete. The statements are executed in order from top to bottom.

Notice the backlash symbol (\n) near the end of the first line. The backslash is used in the `printf()` statement to indicate that a special control character is following. In this case, the \n indicates that a new line is requested. There are others as for example a \t would result in a tab being generated at that point in the text.

Also note that these symbols are text manipulation operators and are used within the text field (inside inverted commas), which means that they are not recognisable, by the compiler outside these boundaries.

Thus, when the statement containing \n executes, this is an indication to return the cursor to the left side of the monitor and move down one line.

A complete description of this programme is now possible. The first `printf()` outputs a line of text and returns the carriage. The second `printf()` outputs a line but does not return the carriage so that the third line is appended to the second, then followed by two carriage returns, resulting in a blank line. Finally the fourth `printf ()` outputs a line followed by a carriage return and the programme is complete.

Evidently the above programme is quite trivial but it serves to demonstrate some basic principles of programming in C.

Now that you can use `printf` to write to the serial port let us consider some more programming examples.

Exercise 3: `sbit` operation

Using the bitwise operator `sbit`	The programme below illustrates the use of the `sbit` operator that was discussed earlier in the chapter. You should be able to follow what is happening by now. Write the code and set-up watch points on PSW, overflow, sign and carry. Step trough the code using dScope and ensure that you have understood the use of the `sbit` operator.

```c
/* This programme works with the sbit operator that we use to MASK
selected bits in a byte */

# include <reg51.h>
# include <stdio.h>

sbit sign = P1^2; //  sign is bit two of port 1  has to be declared
before main()
sbit overflow = PSW^2; // identifies bit 2 as the Overflow flag in
PSW
sbit carry = PSW^7; // identifies bit 7 as the Carry flag in PSW
                //see chapter 2 for PSW bit allocation

void main()
{
bdata char evaluate_bit;
unsigned int sign_test;

// initialising the serial port for printf command
TCON = 0x50;
TMOD = 0x20;
TH1 = 0xFA;
TR1 = 1;
TI = 1;
PCON = 0x80;

evaluate_bit=P1; // byte to test is on port 1
// Using the MASK 0x04 to isolate bit 2 if it is true the
evaluate_bit is set to 1
if (evaluate_bit & 0x04) {
     sign_test=1;
     }
// Alternatively, using bit operation sbit, This is more elegant
if (sign ==1) {
     sign_test=1;
     printf("\n\nBit two of Port 1 is currently %d\n",sign_test);
     }
//Example of sbit to read the flag register PSW
     PSW=0x04; // let us cause an overflow PSW bit 2
     P0=PSW;  // show this on port P0
if (overflow ==1)
     printf("The result caused an overflow in the high byte\n");
     PSW=0x80; // let us cause an a carry PSW bit 7
     P0=PSW;  // show this on port P0
if (carry ==1)
     printf("The carry flag has been set\n");
}
```

Exercise 4: Using loops in C

The following exercises are designed to show you some basic programming techniques in C. For a more detailed reference please look at [34,35].

The WHILE Loop [34]

The while loop basically states that while a certain condition is True, the statements that are contained in the braces following a loop will continue executing.

Thus, the while loop continues to loop for as long as the condition is True and when the condition becomes False, the looping is discontinued. It is evident that the decision statement has to be part of the loop.

An example is given below;

```
/* This programme gives examples the use of the While Loop */
/* normally printf function prints to the screen (terminal) */ /* not
in KEIL so we */
/* configure serial port to receive data */

# include <reg51.h>
# include <stdio.h>

void main()
{
int count;
// initialising the serial port for printf command
TCON = 0x50;
TMOD = 0x20;
TH1 = 0xFA;
TR1 = 1;
TI = 1;
PCON = 0x80;
// example programme of while loop
count = 0;
while (count < 6) {
        count = count + 1;
        printf("The value of count is %d\n",count);
        }
}
```

Explaining the programme	This example programme begins with function main (), which is the programme entry point. In the next step we define an integer variable count, which we then set to zero. Before we enter the while loop we set up the serial port to print from the `printf` command. Next we enter the while loop itself.

The syntax of a while loop begins with the keyword while, which is followed by an expression of a condition. In this case the condition is (count < 6).

There follows a compound statement enclosed in braces. The word compounded refers to a collection of statements enclosed by braces, and as such they are executed as a single statement. The basic structure is shown in Figure below.

```
while (condition) {
compounded statements;
i++ /*incrementer*/
}
```

The while statement determines that as long as the condition tested in parenthesis is True, all statements within the braces will be executed. In this case, since the variable count begins with a value 0, the first time that the programme runs, condition (count < 6) will be True and the statements in braces will be executed. These statements are,

```
printf("The value of count is %d\n",count);
count = count + 1;
```

The first of these printf is a function which prints out the values of the variable count on the screen. In our case, we have programmed the serial port to receive this printout. The %d tells the compiler that the value printed is a decimal integer, \n writes it to a new line and count is the name of the variable to print.

The next line ensures that the variable count is incremented every time the compounded statements are executed. The increments will eventually cause the variable count to reach 6, at which point the condition in the while loop will not be True and the statements that follow this condition will not be executed.

We have used the while loop and the for loop in earlier exercises, but have not really explained how it works. This is why in the above example a little more emphasis is placed on explaining the code. We will not cover other looping options and the reader can refer to [34] for examples and explanation of the for and do-while loops.

Exercise 5: The IF Statement

Describing the If statement	If statements are used to determine test conditions, in a manner quite similar to that discussed earlier for loops. [34] The basic structure of an If statement is shown in Figure below;

	/*The basic If Statement*/
	
	 if(condition) {
	 compounded statements;
	 }
	
	 The rules for evaluating the statement are as follows:
	
	 1. The logical expression ahead of the question mark is evaluated.
	 2. If it is True, the expression between the question mark and the colon is evaluated.
	 3. If it is not True, the expression following the colon is evaluated.
	 The result of the evaluation is used for the assignment.
	
	 An example of a programme using the conditional If statement is shown below.

```
#include "stdio.h"
# include <reg51.h>
void main()
{
int testdata;
// initialising the serial port for printf command
TCON = 0x50;
TMOD = 0x20;
TH1 = 0xFA;
TR1 = 1;
TI = 1;
PCON = 0x80;

for(testdata = 0;testdata < 10;testdata = testdata + 1) {
    if (testdata == 2) // if statement 1
       printf("testdata is now equal to %d\n",testdata);
       }
 }
```

Explanation of the programme	The above example programme uses a `for` loop to increment the variable data after each iteration of the loop. In the loop data is started at zero, and incremented for as long as it is less than 10. When this point is reached (i.e., data=10) the loop terminates. The If statement checks if data is equal to two and since this is False, the loop bypasses the `printf` command that follows the If statement. This is repeated until data is incremented to the value of two at which point the If statement returns a True and the `printf` command is allowed to execute.

	If statements have a further option to combine an Else statement. An Else statement allows us to specify the exact action to execute when the If condition returns a False.
	
	That is to say, a plain If tells the programme what to execute when the result is True. If the result is False this execution is not performed.
	At this point it is possible to put an Else to specifically address the issue of what needs to be done when the If condition returns a False.
	Thus, the statement has the structure as shown in Figure below. [34]
	
	/*The If-Else Statement*/
	
	if(condition) {
	compounded statements; /* Executed if True*/
	}
	else {
	compounded statement; /* Executed if False*/
	}
	    Just to illustrate this flexibility the following example has an If statement followed by an If-Else statement both of which are compounded through the `for` loop. Thus, if the first If returns a False the second If is executed. When the second If returns a True, this part is executed and when it returns a False, the Else is executed.
	
	A little difficult to explain, but if you step through the code it should be quite clear to you what is going on. Here is the code that you need to consider;

```
#include "stdio.h"
#include <reg51.h>
void main()
{
int testdata;
// initialising the serial port for printf command
TCON = 0x50;
TMOD = 0x20;
TH1 = 0xFA;
TR1 = 1;
TI = 1;
PCON = 0x80;

for(testdata = 0;testdata < 10;testdata = testdata + 1)
    if (testdata == 2) // if statement 1
printf("testdata is now equal to %d\n",testdata);

    else // else if statement is not is satisfied
printf("testdata is now %d, which is not equal to 2 \n",testdata);
}
```

The above programme is only slightly modified version of the first if programme. If you build the programme and run it in dScope you can see the difference that the else makes to the programme. (i.e. it actually does something when the If result is False). Make sure that you do this in order to confirm that you have understood the structure If-Else.

Exercise 6: The BREAK and CONTINUE keywords

If statements are use widely in programming, and at times the programme structure can become difficult to follow when deep nesting is used. To enable a more elegant means of dealing with nested conditional structures, C offers the Switch and the `Continue` and `Break` statements.

Keywords break and continue offer us the opportunity of controlling programme flow. After an If statement has been tested a `break` or a `continue` command will result in subtle differences in programme behaviour.

When the condition tested returns a True, the break will exit the programme segment. Conversely, when the condition returns a False, the `continue` will skip that value and proceed with other values of the variable. An example is given below.

```c
#include "stdio.h"
# include <reg51.h>
void main()
{
int window;

// initialising the serial port for printf command
TCON = 0x50;
TMOD = 0x20;
TH1 = 0xFA;
TR1 = 1;
TI = 1;
PCON = 0x80;


for(window = 5;window < 15;window = window + 1){
        if (window == 8)
        break;
        printf("In the break loop, window is now %d\n",window);
        }
for(window = 5;window < 15;window = window + 1){
        if (window == 8)
    continue;
printf("In the continue loop, window is now %d\n",window);
        }
}
```

Notice that in the first for loop of the programme, there is an `if` statement that calls a break if window equals 8. If this is `True`, the `break` will jump out of the loop and begin executing statements following the loop, effectively terminating the loop.

Note that with the break statement, once you break out of the loop there is no return path even if the condition is later satisfied.

If you require the loop to be re-entered the `continue` command can be used. This is shown in the second `for` loop of the above example.

This is the essential use of `break` and `continue` commands and re explanations of this can be found in [34].

Exercise 7: Using the Switch Statement

The `switch` statement enables us to implement a nested `If` structure more elegantly.

The `switch` (variable `name`) statement precedes a series of conditions that are tested. These conditions are labelled `case x`. Here the `case` indicates a condition and the `x` the value to be used in the testing. Thus, the variable name takes on the value of `x`, and the test condition determines which particular value of the variable `name` is current.

As with the If statement considered earlier, the `break` statement performs the exit from `switch` when a particular case evaluates to `True`. It is worth pointing out at this stage that when none of the case conditions is satisfied we use a `default` option to enable the programme to terminate.

We will now introduce an example of a programme segment using the `switch` operator. Let us consider the following example programme, which makes use of the `switch` statement;

The programme given below begins with the keyword `switch` followed by a variable in parentheses, which is the switching variable, in this case named `something`.

Considering the example programme, if the variable named `something` contains the value 3 during this pass of the `switch` statement, the `printf` will cause `"The value is three"` to be displayed, and the `break` statement will jump out of the `switch`.

If on the other hand the variable has the value 5, the statements will begin executing at the line in the programme where `"case 5:"` is found. However, in the above example, there are no statements to execute for cases 5,6,7 and the first statements found are for the case 8 statements.

Therefore the switch for `cases 5,6,7` are executed as `null` and the `break` statement will direct the execution out the bottom of the `switch`. In other words even if there are no statement to execute, the `case` will still complete provided that a `break` is configured properly.

```
#include <stdio.h>
#include <reg51.h>
void main()
{
int something;

// initialising the serial port for printf command
TCON = 0x50;
TMOD = 0x20;
TH1 = 0xFA;
TR1 = 1;
TI = 1;
PCON = 0x80;
```

```
for (something = 3;something < 13;something = something + 1) {
  switch (something) {
    case 3 : printf("The value is three\n");
       break;
    case 4 : printf("The value is four\n");
        break;
      case 5 :
      case 6 :
      case 7 :
      case 8 : printf("The value is between 5 and 8\n");
            break;
      case 11 : printf("The value is eleven\n");
            break;
      default : printf("an undefined value\n");
        break;
   } /* end of switch */
} /* end of for loop */
}
```

Exercise 8: C variable types

The following programme is included to give you examples of defining the various variable types.

Please note that C51 does not support all the types that are available in C. This is because the 8051 is not expected to work with floating-point numbers and double precision arithmetic.

The programme given below programme contains nearly every standard simple data type available in the programming language C for the 8051.

There are other types, but they are the compound types (i.e. - arrays and structures) that we will cover later.

The programme below also shows how the various types are used with the printf() function. These are given here as much for demonstration purpose as for reference in case you need to remind yourself how to assign and print variables.

```
#include "stdio.h"
# include <reg51.h>
void main()
{
int var_a;    /* simple integer type */
long int var_b;    /* long integer type */
short int var_c;   /* short integer type */
unsigned int var_d;  /* unsigned integer type */
char var_e;          /* character type */
        var_a= 3201;
        var_b= 3333;
        var_c = 321;
        var_d = 4321;
        var_e = 'X';
// initialising the serial port for printf command
TCON = 0x50;
TMOD = 0x20;
TH1 = 0xFA;
TR1 = 1;
TI = 1;
PCON = 0x80;
printf("var_a %d\n",var_a); /* decimal output */
printf("var_a %o\n",var_a); /* octal output   */
printf("var_a %x\n",var_a); /* hexadecimal output */
printf("var_b %ld\n",var_b); /* decimal long output */
printf("var_c %d\n",var_c); /* decimal short output*/
printf("var_d %u\n",var_d);/* unsigned output    */
printf("var_e %c\n",var_e); /* character output   */
printf( "\n");
printf("var_a %d\n",var_a); /* simple int output  */
printf("var_a %7d\n",var_a); /* use var_a field width of 7 */
printf("var_a %-7d\n",var_a);/*left justify in field of 7*/
var_c = 5;
var_d = 8;
printf("var_a %*d\n",var_c);/* use var_a field width of 5 */
printf("var_a %*d\n",var_d);/* use var_a field width of 8 */
printf("\n");

}
```

The above example is intended to be used as a reference for type
declarations. More explanation about each statement in the above code can be
found in [34].
Execute the above programme in dScope and ensure that you results are as
expected.

Exercise 9: Using Logical operators

Logical operations evaluate to either True or False and these invariably rely on a decision statement where a decision is made based on the result of a comparison. Logical term implies that the result of the comparison is either a True or a False. No other value is acceptable.

In logical compares a False is defined as a value of zero, and True is defined as a non-zero value. Any integer or character `type` of variable can be used for the result of a True/False test, or the result can be an implied integer or character.

Before you can understand the statements you must be familiar with the operators used in the logical comparison statements. These are;

```
== equal to
> greater than
< less than
!= not equal to
<= less than or equal to
>= greater than or equal to
```

Note that when used with `char type` data the comparisons have the following meanings;

```
X > y means x comes alphabetically after y
X < y means x comes alphabetically before y
```

And the logical operators;

```
&& means logical AND operation
|| means logical OR operation
! means logical NOT operation
```

Here are some examples that should be fairly intuitive. Detailed explanations are available in [34].

Run this code in dScope and confirm that you understand the logical operators. Since the programme is not printing, I suggest you use watch points to monitor variables `a,b,c,x,y,z,r,s,k`.

```
main()
{
int x = 11,y = 11,z = 11;
char a = 40,b = 40,c = 40;
long int r = 12,s = 12,k = 12;
/* First group of compare statements */
   if (x == y) z = 1; /* This will set z = -13 because the condition
that x==y is True*/
   if (b <= c) r = 0;   /* This will set r = 0.0 because b=c and
the condition evaluates to True */
   if (r = s) k = c/2;   /* This will set t = 20 because r is
equal to s and the condition evaluates to True. The resulting
operation divides 40/2, which is 20 and assigned to c */
/* Second group of compare statements */
   if (x = (r != s)) z = 1000;
/* This will set x = 0 and z = 1000, note that the x
is assigned the value and it is not a condition tested ( i.e. ==).
Thus, the test is r!=s, which is True giving a logical 1 value,
this is then assigned to x. Since the test condition is True, z is
assigned 1000 */
   if (x = y) z = 222; /* This sets x = y, and z = 222 there is no
condition being tested so the simple assignment is performed*/
   if (x != 0) z = 333; /* This sets z = 333 because the condition
tested is True, that is x is not equal to 0 */
   if (x) z = 444;     /* This sets z = 444 once again no
condition is tested so a simple assignment takes place*/
/* Third group of compare statements */
   x = y = z = 77;
   if ((x == y) && (x == 77)) z = 33; /* set z = 33 because
the Boolean expression evaluate to True*/
   if ((x > y) || (z > 12))  z = 22; /* set z = 22 because
z>12 is True and it is an OR operation and either True will be
sufficient*/
   if (x && y && z) z = 11;        /* set z = 11 a simple
assignment occurs since no condition is tested so a simple assignment
occurs*/
   if ((x = 1) && (y = 2) && (z = 3)) r = 12;
/* This sets  x = 1, y = 2, z = 3, r = 12 because,
as before there is no test condition and the simple assignment takes
place*/
   if ((x == 2) && (y = 3) && (z = 4)) r = 14;
/* This does not change anything because x is not
equal to 2 and so the condition evaluates to False */
/* Fourth group of compares */
   if (x == x); z = 27; /* z always gets changed
because the condition will always evaluate to True*/
   if (x != x) z = 27; /* Nothing gets changed
because the condition will always evaluate to False */
   if (x == 0)  z = 27;
/* This sets x = 0, z is unchanged since there is no
condition tested it will always perform the assignment */
}
```

Additional operators	When you begin looking at other C programs you will come across some statements that we have not mentioned so far. These are cryptic constructs that simplify programme writing, but unless you are familiar with them, they are likely to make it impossible for you to understand the code. The following programme segments illustrate the use of these operators.

```
    /* incrementing */
x = x + 1;     /* This increments x */
x++;          /* This increments x */
++x;          /* This increments x */
z = y++;       /* z = 2, y = 3 */
z = ++y;       /* z = 4, y = 4 */

    /* decrementing */
y = y - 1;     /* This decrements y */
y--;          /* This decrements y */
--y;          /* This decrements y */
y = 3;
z = y--;       /* z = 3, y = 2 */
z = --y;       /* z = 1, y = 1 */
```

You can simply add the code before the ending brace of `main()` in the above example. You can run it in dScope and see how the operators modify variables.

The above statements all increment or decrement x, that is they all simply add 1 to the value of x, or subtract 1 from the value of x. The first statement in each group is quite obvious but others need a bit of clarification. Namely, a double plus sign either before or after variable increments that variable by 1.

Additionally, if the plus signs are before the variable, the variable is incremented before it is used, and if the plus signs are after the variable, the variable is first used, then incremented.

Similar logic applies to the decrementing, except that the double minus signs are used.

157

Next, we examine arithmetic operators. Once again the assignment is simplified by combining the operators so that += which in simple terms means add the number (+ part) to what we already have (= part)

Any of the four basic functions of arithmetic, +, -, *, or /, can be handled in this way, by putting the desired in front of the equal sign and eliminating the second reference to the variable name.

Here are some example of these;

```
/* arithmetic operations */
a = a + 12;    /* This adds 12 to a */
a += 12;       /* This adds 12 more to a */
a *= 6;      /* This multiplies a by 6 */
a -= b;       /* This subtracts b from a */
a /= 2;      /* This divides a by 2 */
```

Once again you can simply add the code before the ending brace of `main()` in the above example. You can run it in dScope and see how the above statements modify variables.

Exercise 10: C functions

Functions in C are a collection of programme statements, which are used to perform some task that may need to be done a number of times. It is generally considered good practice to design your programme so that the function main calls other functions in the order that they are needed.

A function will contain variables that are needed to perform the tasks within. If a variable is required in the main programme and in the function that is called from main then this variable is a global variable. A global variable needs to be declared before `main()`. A variable that is only used by a function is declared within the braces of that function and is referred to as a local variable. There are other points to note regarding functions, and considering an example programme as shown below best covers these;

```c
# include <reg51.h>
# include <stdio.h>
int sum_total; /* This is a global variable available to all
functions*/
main()
{
void  primary();   /* This is a function prototype */
int  square(int);  /* This is a function prototype */
void  ending();    /* This is a function prototype */
int counter;
// initialising the serial port
TCON = 0x50;
TMOD = 0x20;
TH1 = 0xFA;
TR1 = 1;
TI = 1;
PCON = 0x80;
   for (counter = 1;counter <= 7;counter++)
    square(counter); /* This calls the square function */
    ending();       /* This calls the ending function */
}
void primary()     /* This is the function named primary */
{
   sum_total = 0; /* Initialise the variable "sum_total" */
   printf("This is the start of the square programme\n\n");
}
int square(int number)   /* This is the square function */
int number;
{
int n_squared;
   n_squared = number * number; /* This produces the square */
   sum_total += n_squared;
   printf("The square of %d is %d\n",number,n_squared);
}

void ending()   /* This is the ending function */
{
   printf("\n The sum of the squares is %d\n",sum_total);
}
```

Detailed analysis of the above programme is available in reference [34]. Here I will only discuss the basic programme flow.

Notice that we have a variable declaration before `main()`. i.e.

```
int sum_total;
```

When we declare a variable in this way we are saying that it is available to all functions that are used in the programme.

In essence a variable is declared in the function that it is used in. Quite often it is not required to declare it anywhere else, since it will not be used there.

From the above programme following main, the executable part of this programme begins with three function prototypes. In C every function needs to be defined before it is used, and this is done by the prototype.

The function primary() does not do much except that it sets the starting value of the variable sum_total to zero and display a message on the screen.

This variable is set to zero because we plan to use it to accumulate a sum of squares.

When the end brace of the function is reached control of the programme returns to the statement following this call.

In the above programme this is the for loop statement which will be executed seven times and each time it will call another function named square().

Finally a function named ending() will be called and executed. The structure of this programme is shown in Figure shown below.

Figure showing the structure of the function-calling programme

Note that each time that the function `square()` is called a variable called counter is passed onto the function so that it can be used in the calculation. That is why this variable is enclosed in brackets in the function call as follows;

```
square(counter);
```

The variable 'counter' is part of the 'for' loop which is part of the function `main`.

This informs the compiler that when you go to the function, you wish to take along the value of counter to use in the execution of that function. The term used to describe this is to say that the variable is passed with the function. You can pass more than one variable with a function provided that it is suitably declared.

Looking ahead at the actual programme statements, rather than the function call, for the function named `square()`, we find that another variable enclosed in its parentheses, that is the variable `number`. That is,

```
square(number)   /* This is the square function */
```

So we note here that when the function is called the variable passed is called counter, and within the function itself, the variable passed is called `number`.

In other words when the function square is used, the variable that is passed to this function, from the calling function does not have to have the same name in both functions. Even with a different name, the variable will still contain the correct value.

Be sure to execute this code and step through it using dScope. Your output should be the squares of numbers and their sum_total.

The next programme demonstrates how a function can return a value to the calling programme. The code is very similar to the example used above. Run the code in dScope and step through it to confirm that you have understood the principle of returning a value.

```c
# include <reg51.h>
# include <stdio.h>

main() /* This is the main programme */
{
int x,y;
int  squ(int);  /* This is a function prototype */
// initialising the serial port
TCON = 0x50;
TMOD = 0x20;
TH1 = 0xFA;
TR1 = 1;
TI = 1;
PCON = 0x80;

  for(x = 0;x <= 5;x++) {
   y = squ(x); /* function call to get the value of x*x */
   printf("The square of %d is %d\n",x,y);
   }
  for (x = 0;x <= 5;++x)
   printf("The value of %d is %d\n",x,squ(x));
}

int squ(in) /* function to get the value of in squared */
int in;
{
int square;
  square = in * in;
  return(square); /* This sets squ() = square and returns this value
to main as the square of variable x */
}
```

As mentioned earlier, one way to get a value back to the main programme after a call to a function, was to declare a global variable by defining it ahead of main(). There is nothing wrong with this approach, but sometimes the variable does not need to be available to all functions, which is the feature of a global variable. Instead it is possible to return the variable to the calling function using the return() from the function.

CHAPTER 6 DISCRETE MODELLING

6.1   Introduction

Discrete time representation of systems refers to sampled systems, where values of functions are not continuous in time; rather they are taken at discrete sampling instants. If the choice of sampling interval is appropriate, then any continuous function can be represented by a series of sampled values. In computer control systems discrete representation is needed because computers are digital processors. Before the introduction of computers to control processes, analogue control systems were used in all areas of engineering. Analogue controllers that processed analogue inputs and produced analogue outputs controlled analogue devices. In the field of general engineering, the control systems area is absolutely huge and a vast amount of literature has been published on the subject of control.

At the same time, devices such as relays and switches were used to control the sequence of operations. For example, early telephone exchanges used relays to switch in the correct lines. This sequential control was in fact discrete but it bore no significant relationship to the classical control theory. With the advent of computers these two areas became integrated and digital computers are now used to control processes in feedback control as well as sequential mode.

In this text I do not wish to address the details of control systems theory because it is outside my intended scope. Instead I am only going to introduce those concepts of control that are relevant to explain how an embedded computer control system can be implemented.

6.2   Software control

In order to implement control functions in computer software it is necessary to develop system models that are in discrete form. i.e. based on information about the system that is obtained by sampling at regular, discrete time intervals. [35]. In discrete time the values of all the variables that participate in the control system must be synchronised. This is to say that discrete time gives a snapshot of the system at specific sampling points. If you were able to freeze the system at a sampling instant you could monitor and record all the variables. You could then release the freeze button and the system would move to the next sampling instant. During this move period, you would not know what happens to the system variables, and you would have to assume that they remain constant during the sample period. In reality the variables would change, and it is known that 'discretising' always introduces what is normally called a quantisation error. Nevertheless, this error is not always significant, and control systems can be designed to take these into account. These aspects are beyond the scope of this text but an excellent treatment of discrete control can be found in other texts. [36]

In general, when discrete models are developed it is therefore necessary to assume that the system being modelled does not experience a change between sampling instants, and by the same token, that all control signals remain constant during this interval (i.e. between samples). This assumption is justified on account of the information that we have on the process that we are trying to control (i.e. moment of inertia J etc). Figure 6.1 shows a possible input and output signals in discrete time domain. The input variable is assumed constant between samples. The output variable on the other hand is not constant between samples, which should make sense, as it is usually the variable that is used in control systems.

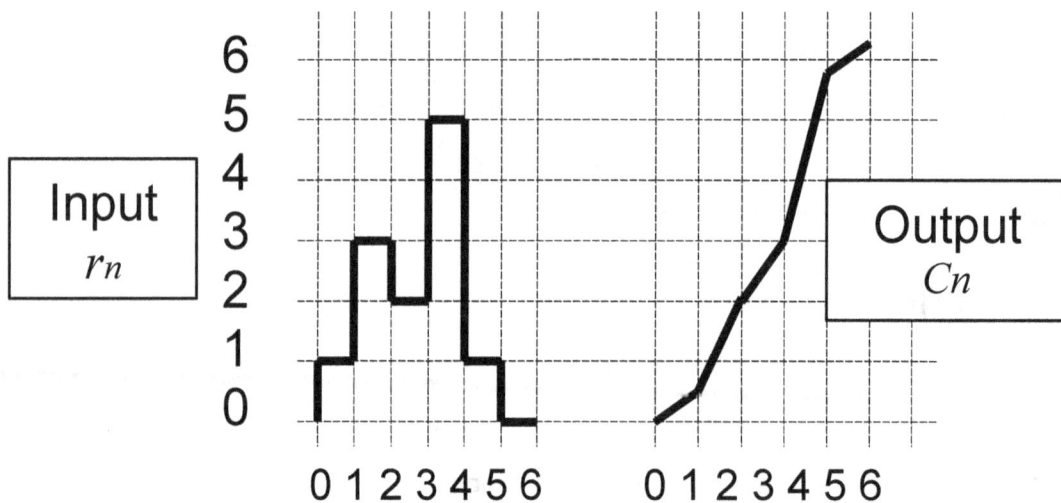

Figure 6.1 Discrete process input (r_n) and output (c_n)

Modelling in the time domain is describing the variation of a particular variable with time. In discrete systems this variation is obtained by comparing the measurements of the particular variable taken at the sampling instants. For example the sequence of values shown in the input signal in Figure 6.1 could be represented as discrete values at sampling instants n=1,2,3,4,5,6. The values at these sampling instants form an array of numbers, which are the discrete approximation of the continuous function. Since this array of numbers represents actual values (coefficients) of the function at discrete time instants, it describes the vector,

$$V_t = (1,3,2,4,1,0)$$

Another way to represent this input signal is to use a polynomial, where the coefficients of the polynomial represent the value of vector V_t at successive sampling instants. For example,

$$V(Z) = 1 + 3Z + 2Z^2 + 4Z^3 + 1Z^4 + 0Z^5 \qquad (6.1)$$

Here the polynomial is in Z. But Z is NOT a variable it is simply a unit-delay operator and the power to which Z is raised simply determines how much delay is in this particular coefficient. For example in equation 6.1 the value $1Z^4$ means that the value after the fourth sampling instants is 1. Therefore, it is seen that the Z-operator can be used to shift samples forward one unit delay at a time. For example, multiplying equation 6.1 by Z gives,

$$ZV(Z) = Z + 3Z^2 + 2Z^3 + 4Z^4 + 1Z^5 + 0Z^6$$

To illustrate this, the coefficients of this vector are plotted in Figure 6.2 where it is seen that the whole vector is delayed or shifted forward by one unit of sample time. Figure 6.2 shows the same waveform as Figure 6.1, but now the waveform has been delayed. Each of the coefficients now occurs one sample later. Thus it is seen that when the function $B(Z)$ is multiplied by Z^n the signal V_t is delayed by n time units. In this example $n=1$ but in practice it can take on other integer values depending on by how many sampling intervals, the signal needs to be delayed. Additionally n can be either positive or negative. The negative powers of Z simply mean that that the data is defined before $t = 0$.

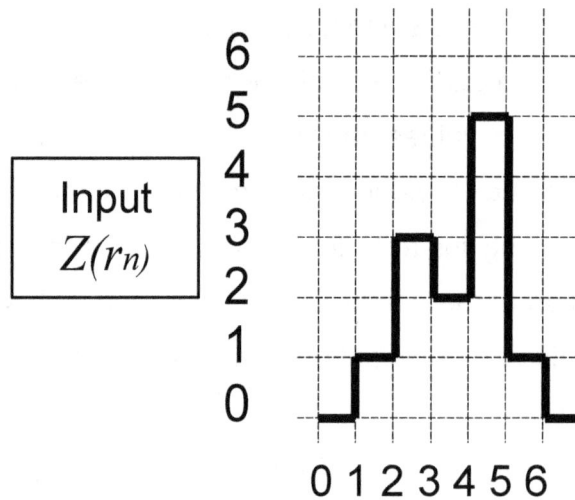

Figure 6.2 Applying the Z-Operator to the original input vector (r_n)

Thus, using the Z operator as a polynomial with positive values of n means that we are shifting the samples forward by n sample values. Conversely, using negative values of n means that we are shifting the samples backwards by n sample values. Rather than having negative values of Z it may be useful to define a backward shift operator such that B=Z-1 Thus, the B operator is used to shift back the variable to a value that it had one sample for every power of B. i.e.,

$$B y_n = y_{n-1}$$

$$B^2 y_n = y_{n-2}$$

$$B^m y_n = y_{n-m}$$

This form of representation is useful in discrete control systems because it enables discrete models to be described as difference equations. Namely, if samples (n) of a variable V are taken at regular time intervals ΔT (i.e., the sampling interval), the difference in the value of the variable between samples is given by the difference equation,

$$\Delta V = (V_{n+1} - V_n)$$

In this equation ΔV is the first derivative of the $V(t)$ and since we know the sampling period T, the differential can be calculated.

In continuous time systems, processes are modelled using differential equations. In discrete form these systems can be modelled using difference equations. More details about difference equations can be found elsewhere. [37,38]

6.3   Controller design

In order to design a controller in discrete time domain it is necessary to obtain discrete models for the following,

- **Process**: this is usually known or can be obtained by measurement.
- **Desired output:** this is also known and can be chosen by the control systems designer.
- **Controller**: this needs to be designed so that the combination of the controller and the process in the control loop provides the desired response.

In control systems it is normally required that a certain process behaves in a prescribed manner. For this to happen a controller needs to be designed. Thus, in order to make design possible all three of the above models must be considered. All three can be represented in continuous as well as in discrete time domain. For embedded computer control however it is necessary that these be in discrete time domain. Next we consider some simple models of processes in discrete form.

1st order process

Mathematical modelling is widely used in control systems and in the continuous time domain models are described by differential equations. Some physical models such as the charging of capacitance in a d.c resistance network can be described adequately by a 1st order differential equation. Other, more complicated systems are described using higher order equations. For example, a 1st order process relates the output variable $c(t)$ to the input variable $r(t)$ by a first order differential equation of the form,

$$\frac{dc(t)}{dt} = r(t) \qquad (6.2)$$

Figure 6.3 illustrates an example of a 1st order system containing an amplifier and a motor in an open-loop system. Open-loop here means that the input has no feedback about what the output is doing. In Figure 6.3, we wish to control the output variable c (t); by the application of an input reference variable r (t), which is in fact, a d.c input voltage to the amplifier. The process shown in Figure 6.3, can be described in continuous time domain by a 1st order differential equation relating the output variable c (t) to the input variable r (t) as follows,

$$\frac{dc(t)}{dt} = K \times r(t) \quad (6.3)$$

Where: $c\ (t)$-controlled variable (output-position),

$r\ (t)$- control parameter (input),

K - Gain constant of the amplifier.

If we assume that the input is constant (applied as a step-input) then the behaviour of the output can be calculated by integrating equation 6.3.

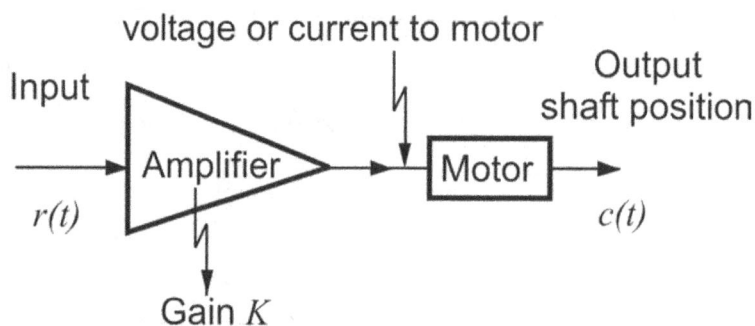

Figure 6.3 Control of position using a voltage to the motor

In order to obtain a mathematical model for this system we need to describe how the output varies with time, in response to the input. This means that we need to integrate equation 6.3 with respect to time. To do this we must establish the initial conditions. Thus the initial conditions are assumed as follows: At t=0,

Initial output $= c\ (t)=c\ (0)$

Initial input = $r(t) = r(0) = r_0$ for $0 \leq t < T$.

Given the initial conditions we can replace r (t) in equation 6.3 by r0=constant. By integrating the resulting equation we obtain an expression of the output variable at a time T.

$$c(t) = \int_0^T K \times r_0 dt$$
$$c(t) = [K \times r_0 T]_0^T + c(0) \qquad (6.4)$$
$$c(t) = K \times r_0 T + c(0)$$
$$c(t) = c(0) + K \times r_0 T$$

Equation 6.4 can be used to obtain the position at any time in the range given by the initial conditions. (i.e. in the range $0 \leq t < T$). Therefore if we choose to apply this equation systematically as we are increasing the time interval by a constant sample time increment then we will obtain values of the position at discrete time increments. (i.e. cn, cn-1, cn-2 etc). Each of these positions have been calculated by applying equation 6.4 and so the difference between positions at two consecutive sampling instants, namely sample instant n and $n-1$, can be obtained as an equation, namely,

$$c_n = c_{n-1} + KTr_{n-1} \qquad (6.5)$$

Equation 6.5 is the same as equation 6.4 but expressed in terms of sampling instants n rather than the time (t). The initial condition for any sampling instant n is that given in the previous sampling instant n-1. Thus, equation 6.5 is the difference equation, which is the discrete model for the system. Making the necessary adjustment to the input variable can perform controlling a first order process like this. The difference equation can then be used to determine the output variable.

Controlling processes implies that we are able to respond to a disturbance by an appropriate action. For example, if we are driving a car and a disturbance occurs in the shape of another vehicle entering our path, we apply control action to avoid an accident. In mathematical models a disturbance can be incorporated as an external input to the system. Thus for example, if an external disturbance is modelled as a function D (t), it can be included in equation 6.3 describing a 1st order process as follows,

$$\frac{dc(t)}{dt} = Kr(t) + D(t) \quad (6.6)$$

Notice that equations 6.3 and 6.6 identical except for the effect of the disturbance D (t). In other words, were D $(t)=0$ then the two equations would have the same effect. Integrating as before we obtain the discrete process model in the presence of a disturbance. Once again assuming that at $t=0$;

Initial output $= c$ $(t)=c$ (0)

Initial input $= r$ $(t)=r$ $(0)= r_0 for$ $0 \leq t < T.$

And additionally that the initial disturbance $=D$ (t) $=D$ $(0)= D_0 for$ $0 \leq t < T.$

Given these initial conditions for the disturbance and considering the input initial conditions as before, integrating equation 6.6 gives the position at time T in the presence of a disturbance D.

$$c(t) = \int_0^T Kr(t) + D(t)dt$$
$$c(t) = Kr_0 T + D_0 T + c(0)$$
$$c(t) = c(0) + (Kr\ T) + (D_0 T)$$

This gives the difference equation in discrete form,

$$c_n - c_{n-1} = KTr_{n-1} + TD_{n-1} \quad (6.7)$$

In control systems we need to determine the present output condition c_n. In order to be able to do this we need to know the values for the input and also the disturbance if indeed it is present. We also need to know the initial condition of the output. Thus, equations 6.5 and 6.7 allow us to determine the present value of the variable c_n, on the basis of the information available from the previous sampling instant $(n-1)$.

6.4   Transfer Functions

In control systems engineering we use the Transfer Function (TF) to describe the relationship between the output variable c (t) or c_n to the input variable r (t) or r_n. An example of an open loop control system is shown in Figure 6.4.

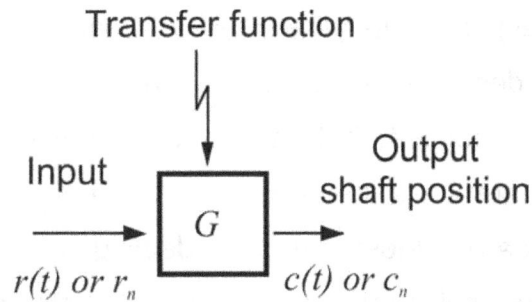

Figure 6.4 Open loop system TF

Strictly speaking the T.F is defined as the Laplace transform of the output variable to the Laplace transform of the input variable under the assumption of all initial conditions being zero. [39] It is worth recalling at this point that in continuous time domain the TF is described as a function of time (t) whereas in discrete time domain the TF is described in terms of sampling instants n. When analysing the behaviour of control systems the control engineers attempt to design a controller with a transfer function G_c so that it controls the process with a transfer function G_p in the desired manner. This control process involves quite a lot of algebraic manipulation and this can be difficult when the equations describing relationships are differential equations.

Frequency domain

In the analysis of control systems most relationships can be described as partial differential equations. Consequently, when the coefficients of these differential equations are constant in time and space, the solutions to these equations have exponential and sinusoidal terms. [40] Solving partial DEs by hand can be difficult and so control engineers have devised a method of converting these equations from the time domain into the frequency domain. This in turns simplifies the solution to these equations.

In the continuous time domain, equations are converted by using Laplace transforms into the frequency domain, where the manipulation of these equations is done by expressing the order of the differential equations in terms of powers of S. [39, 41, 42]

As a result equations in the S plane (i.e. frequency domain) are expressed in the powers of S and as a result their manipulation is relatively easy using simple algebra. After the algebraic manipulation is complete, in order to once again describe the relationship in the time domain, the inverse Laplace transform is applied. Tables of Laplace transforms and inverse Laplace transforms are used to make this conversion between time and frequency domains easier. Most textbooks dealing with control systems will describe the details of Laplace transform usage in control systems and we will not cover this here. It is sufficient tot say that Laplace Transform (L.T) of a function f (t) is defined as follows,

$$\text{L.T of } \left[f(t) \right] = F(S) = \int_0^{\infty} f(t).e^{-st} \qquad (6.8)$$

Where S is a complex variable in the frequency domain. It can be shown that the L.T of a differential is as follows,

$$\text{L.T of } \left[\frac{df(t)}{dt} \right] = sF(S) = s \int_0^{\infty} f(t).e^{-st} \qquad (6.9)$$

And that this extends to any n^{th} order differential namely,

$$\text{L.T of } \left[\frac{df^n(t)}{dt^n} \right] = s^n F(S) = s^n \int_0^{\infty} f(t).e^{-st} \qquad (6.10)$$

This means that any relationship, which can be described using linear differential equations in the nth order, can be represented as a polynomial in S.

For example, let the output c (t) be related to the input r (t) by the following equation,

$$\frac{dc(t)}{dt} = kr(t) \qquad (6.11)$$

Taking L.T of both sides and using equation 6.9 we convert this to the frequency domain as follows,

$$sC(S) = kR(S)$$

Therefore the relationship between the output and the input variables in the S-plane is described as follows,

$$\frac{C(S)}{R(S)} = \frac{1}{s} \qquad (6.12)$$

If we assume zero initial conditions then equation 6.12 is the transfer function for the system described by equation 6.11.

For discrete time domain systems a similar process is applied but instead of using the Laplace transform, the equivalent in discrete time domain is the z-transform. Tables of z-Transforms and inverse z-transforms are used to convert between the time and frequency domains.

There is in fact a relationship between the L.T and the z transforms. Namely, in sampled systems each sample instant can be considered as having been delayed from its predecessor by constant time duration (i.e. sample time T). This means that equation 6.8 can be applied for a time-delayed function, namely, a function that has been delayed by a delay time T. Recall the Z-operator earlier that was used to delay a unit sample. Thus the function can be described as having two distinct values namely,

$$\left\{ \begin{array}{ll} 0 & for \quad t < T \\ \\ f(t-T) & for \quad t \geq T \end{array} \right\}$$

Where T is the time delay between $f(t)$ and $f(t\text{-}T)$ and in this case it is also the sample time. Applying equation 6.8 it can be shown that, [36]

$$\text{The L.T of } \left[f(t-T) = e^{sT} \int_{0}^{\infty} f(t)e^{-st} \right] \quad (6.13)$$

Consequently, if we define a new complex variable $z = e^{sT}$ then the transformation from the L.T to the z domain can be performed by replacing e^{sT} with z. In fact by definition, [39, 41] the z-Transform of a number sequence e (k) is defined as a power series in z^{-k} with coefficients equal to the values of e (k), i.e.

$$E(z) = \zeta[\{e(k)\}] = e(0) + e(1)z^{-1} + e(2)z^{-2} + .. \ (6.14)$$

Where $\zeta[\{e(k)\}]$ indicates the z-Transform. In a general form equation 6.14 can be written as

$$E(z) = \zeta[\{e(k)\}] = \sum_{=0}^{\infty} e(k)z^{-k}$$

This transform is a very powerful tool in designing discrete control system. It allows the designer to describe any number sequence and it can be used in the analysis of any type of system that is described by a difference equation. In these applications the sampling time T is constant and theoretically the number sequence is a function of T. Thus the sequence would theoretically be as follows,

$$E(z) = \zeta[\{e(kT)\}] = e(0)T + e(1)Tz^{-1} + e(2)Tz^{-2} + ..$$

In practice however the T is dropped for convenience so that the form given in equation 6.8 is used instead. There are a large number of textbooks on control systems that describe this process in great detail. [36, 39, 41, 42]

In summary therefore it can be said that the z-transform is useful for the formulation and analysis of discrete-time systems. Using the z-transform discrete models can be solved with difference equations in a manner that is analogous to solving continuous models with differential equations. The role played by the z-transform in the solution of difference equations corresponds to that played by the Laplace transforms in the solution of differential equations.

Within this text I shall concentrate on defining the system in the simplest form possible that will enable a controller to be designed. That is to say, as far as possible we shall avoid the frequency domain analysis and instead we describe the system in terms of how the variables change with sampling instants n.

6.5   Discrete Transfer Function

With reference to Figure 6.5, and in order to make it easier to obtain a closed-loop transfer functions in discrete form, we will use the Backward Shift

Operator B that was mentioned earlier. This is used for convenience because it simplifies the equation, for example assume that the output c_n can be described in terms of the input variable r_n by the following equation,

$$C_n = K_1 r_n + K_2 r_{n-1} + K_3 r_{n-3} \quad (6.15)$$

With the B operator the equation is much simpler, i.e.

$$C_n = K_1 r_n + K_2 B r_n + K_3 B^2 r_n = y_n (K_1 + K_2 B + K_3 B^2) (6.16)$$

Once again, it has to be noted that B is not a variable; it is simply an operator that can be used to make the manipulation of difference equations easier so that we don't make a mistake with subscripts. Returning to the example of the previous section and using the B operator, the difference equation 6.5 becomes,

$$c_n = B c_n + KTB r_n$$

Which means that the transfer function would be:

$$\frac{c_n}{r_n} = \frac{KTB}{(1-B)} \quad (6.17)$$

Thus, equation 6.17 gives the open-loop transfer function for the first order system described in the previous section. Once again we note that an open loop system is one where the output variable provides no information about its value to the input, which is to say there is no feedback information. As a result, the input has no way of knowing if the output is in fact correct. This can be a limitation as far as automatic control goes so a closed-loop system is introduced that provides feedback about the output value to the input value. For a closed-loop system shown in Figure 6.5, the output is fed back so that it can be subtracted from the input. As mentioned earlier this is called negative feedback and the difference between the input and the output value is the error between them e_n.

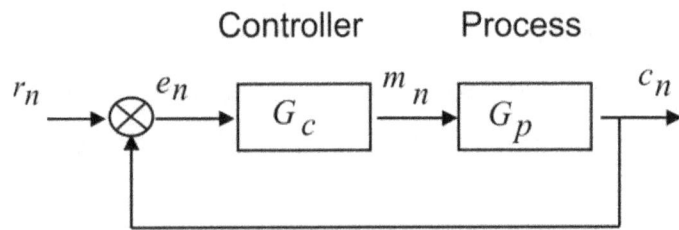

Controller   Process

m - manipulated process input   Gp - process gain
c - process output   Gc- controller gain
r - reference input   n - sample number
e - error signal

Figure 6.5 Block diagram of a closed loop control system

The principle of operation of the system in Figure 6.5 is that the input r_n is supplied as a reference control signal. This input is such that it should produce the desired output in an open-loop system. This is fed into a summing point where the actual value of the output c_n us subtracted from the input and producing the error e_n. The controller gain G_c acts on the error signal e_n to produce the manipulation output m_n, which is used to feed the process. Normally the controller gain G_c is what we need to design in order to control the process described by the process gain G_p. This process gain is established by analysing the performance of a process. For example,

$$Process\ Gain \Rightarrow G_p(B) = \frac{c_n}{m_n} \quad (6.18)$$

The process gain G_p acts on the manipulation output m_n to produce the output c_n.

$$Controller\ Gain \Rightarrow G_c(B) = \frac{m_n}{e_n} \quad (6.19)$$

Closed-loop Transfer Function (CLTF)

Closing the loop in control systems means that the output signal is returned or fed back so that it can be compared to the input signal. In negative feedback systems the output signal is subtracted from the input and this results in the error signal. In positive feedback systems the output signal is added to the input and in this manner the control action is enhanced. By far the most common is the negative feedback control system. The use of positive feedback is useful for producing oscillators. All feedback control systems are closed-loop and the feedback path can have a unity gain as shown in Figure 6.5. In other cases this gain can take on different values depending on hoe the signal is prepared for feedback. For example, if the output is a speed signal and the input is a position then a gain in the feedback path is required which can convert speed into position. With reference to Figure 6.5 the overall closed-loop TF $G(B)$ can be obtained as follows,

$$G(B) = \frac{c_n}{r_n}$$

But we know that the output c_n is given by the following expression,

$$c_n = e_n G_c(B) G_p(B)$$

We also know that $\qquad\qquad e_n = r_n - c_n$

Giving $\qquad\qquad c_n = (r_n - c_n) G_c(B) G_p(B) \qquad (6.20)$

The CLTF is therefore

$$G(B) = \frac{c_n}{r_n} = \frac{G_c(B) G_p(B)}{1 + G_c(B) G_p(B)} \qquad (6.21)$$

The need to describe both the process and the controller arises from the fact that the process must be controlled in a certain manner. The process is generally a physical system that offers some means of control. The controller transfer function therefore determines how the process output behaves.

In general the process gain can be obtained and it is the controller gain that needs to be designed in order to achieve the desired behaviour of the complete system.

6.6   Controller design considerations

If it is necessary to design a digital controller to provide the behaviour of the control system then a control strategy needs to be selected. There are a large number of different approaches to control systems design. In this text we will concentrate only on the strategy that is based on linear systems with feedback control for desired closed-loop response. Other types of systems that are based on feed-forward control, predictive control and other strategies are beyond the scope of this text.

In order that a suitable controller is designed it is necessary to have an accurate model for the process. If the controller is digital then the process needs to de modelled in discrete form. This usually takes the form of a discrete transfer function, which was presented earlier. To design a suitable controller for a desired closed-loop response in linear systems with feedback control it is necessary to make some assumptions regarding the process, these are as follows,

- Process can be modelled adequately by a linear transfer function.
- The constants in these transfer functions are readily available by computation or measurement.

If these assumptions are valid then the design of the controller can be obtained by knowing the desired response as well as the process model, and from these the controller model can be derived. An example of this is given next.

6.7   Feedback control for desired closed-loop response

If the process model is available or can be obtained and the overall behaviour is described by a CLTF as in equation 6.15 then we can isolate the controller gain G_c by algebraic manipulation. For example, if the desired CLTF is given by equation 6.21, which is reproduced here for convenience.

$$G_{desired}(B) = \frac{c_n}{r_n} = \frac{G_c(B)G_p(B)}{1 + G_c(B)G_p(B)}$$

And if it is further assumed that G_p is available, and then the controller gain G_c is the only unknown. Therefore the expression for G_c can be obtained as follows,

$$G_{desired}(B)(1 + G_c(B)G_p(B)) = G_c(B)G_p(B)$$

$$G_{desired}(B) + G_{desired}(B)G_c(B)G_p(B) = G_c(B)G_p(B)$$

$$G_{desired}(B) + G_c(B)(G_{desired}(B)G_p(B)) = G_c(B)G_p(B)$$

$$G_{desired}(B) = G_c(B)(G_p(B) - G_{desired}(B)G_p(B))$$

$$\frac{G_{desired}(B)}{(G_p(B) - G_{desired}(B)G_p(B))} = G_c(B)$$

Which gives

$$G_c(B) = \frac{1}{G_p(B)} \frac{G_{desired}(B)}{(1 - G_{desired}(B))} \quad (6.22)$$

Thus, it seen how by algebraic manipulation the equation describing the controller can be obtained. Now that we have the equation describing the controller we need to select the type of the response that we want form the overall system. This is to say that equation 6.22 describes the relationship between the process, the desired output and the controller, but it does not describe that how the output response should track the input signal. This is up to the designer to select and there are a number of choices some of which are given next.

6.8   Response considerations

When designing a controller the desired response can be selected by the designer to take on a number of forms. In order to illustrate this we consider the diagram shown in Figure 6.6 that defines some terms in the response of a second-order linear system. The diagram shows a unit step-input which is a dashed line and the response, which is seen as a series of, damped oscillations at a constant frequency called the undamped natural frequency. More details can be obtained in control systems textbooks, but for our purposes we define a few important characteristics, which are as follows,

- **Rise time:** This is the time that the response takes to reach the value of the step input, which is the reference value. In over-damped systems this changes to represent the time it takes to rise from 10%-90% of the reference input.

- **Overshoot:** For a step input, the percentage overshoot (PO) is the maximum value minus the step value divided by the step value. In the case of the unit step, the overshoot is just the maximum value of the step response minus one.
- **Settling time:** Settling time is the time required for an output to reach and remain within a given error band following some input stimulus.
- **Steady state error:** This represents the absolute value of the error after the system has settled to a steady state.

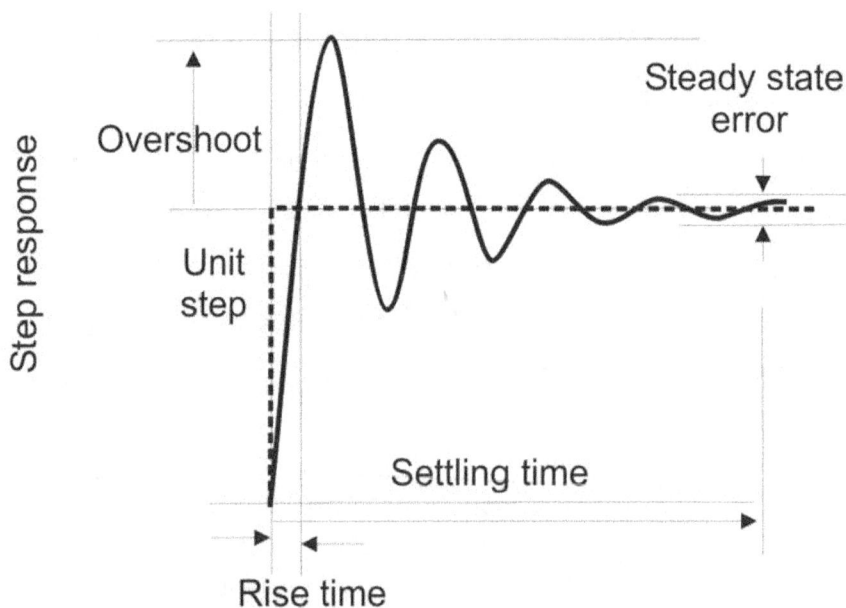

Figure 6.6. Response of a second order system to a unit step input

With these definitions in mind, the following response characteristics can be designed,

- **Dead-beat response** – Here the desired value is reached one sample period later than possible. The deadbeat response has the following characteristics: Zero steady-state error, Minimum rise time, and Minimum settling time, Less than 2% overshoot/overshoot.
- **First-order response** - The output is an exponential one with a time constant τ and the desired value is reached at rise time.

- **Minimum-error** - For example, minimum error to be reached in shortest time.

- **Disturbance rejection** - These are also called regulators since they attempt to maintain the response at a desired level in the presence of disturbances.

An alternative is to implement a variant of the three-term controller PID, or P+I, since the response of many systems is adequately controlled using this type of controller. A proportional–integral–derivative controller (PID controller) is a generic control loop feedback mechanism widely used in industrial control systems. Chapter 7 will look at the PID, also called the three-term controller, and how it can be implemented in discrete form.

Obtaining a system response

Before the controller is built the final design task is to determine the response of the overall system. When the overall TF in discrete form is available we can define an input function that can be used in this control system. The input must also be in discrete form and also it must be synchronised with the system.

Control systems designers have a variety of inputs that they can use in order to determine the output response. So far in this text we have only mentioned the unit step input. Other inputs can be used in order to analyse system response and make the necessary adjustments to obtain the desired response. These details are beyond the scope of this text and for more details on these design methods the reader can refer to numerous texts on automatic control systems. [39, 41, 42]

Exercises

6.1 Explain the difference between continuous time and discrete time representation of systems.

6.2 How does the choice of sampling time influence the accuracy of the system model?

6.3 Give examples of possible sampling frequencies for the following discrete control systems; Speed control system in a car (trip control system), Anti-Lock braking system in a motor car, head position control system on a hard-disk drive system.

6.4 What is the B operator used for in discrete models? How does it relate to a difference equation?

6.5 What are the 3 components needed to implement a functional discrete control system?

6.6 Describe the general approach to designing a closed-loop discrete control system.

6.7 Show how a first order process can be modelled in discrete form.

6.8 Show how you can take into account the effects of a disturbance in a discrete first order system model.

6.9 What is a Transfer Function?

6.10 Distinguish between open loop and closed-loop TFs.

6.11 What is the purpose of Laplace Transforms and z-Transforms, as well as their respective inverse transforms, in the design of control systems?

6.12 For a closed-loop control system with unity feedback, develop a closed-loop T.F in discrete form (use the b operator).

6.13 Given the CLTF developed in 6.15 above, show how you can design a controller for a desired closed-loop response.

6.14 Discuss the various options available to a designer for selecting the response types form a control system.

6.15 Describe the essential features of a typical response form a second-order linear system to a unit step-input.

6.16 What is the significance of using different input functions in order to obtain a system response?

CHAPTER 7 COMPUTER CONTROL

The following considerations will discuss elements of computer control, which pertain to embedded and real-time process control systems. In this context the term 'process' can refer to machine or plant, which may itself involve a number of internal subsystems. All the process and controller models are considered to be in discrete form as presented in chapter 6.

Definitions for real-time are numerous but within this text a real-time system is such that the action of the control system is performed in a timely fashion giving the process sufficient time to respond in order to interact with its environment.

7.1. Introduction

Figure 7.1 shows the typical tasks that computer control systems may be required to perform. Usually in computer control systems the physical process at the bottom of Figure 7.1 needs to be controlled in some way by the computer system.

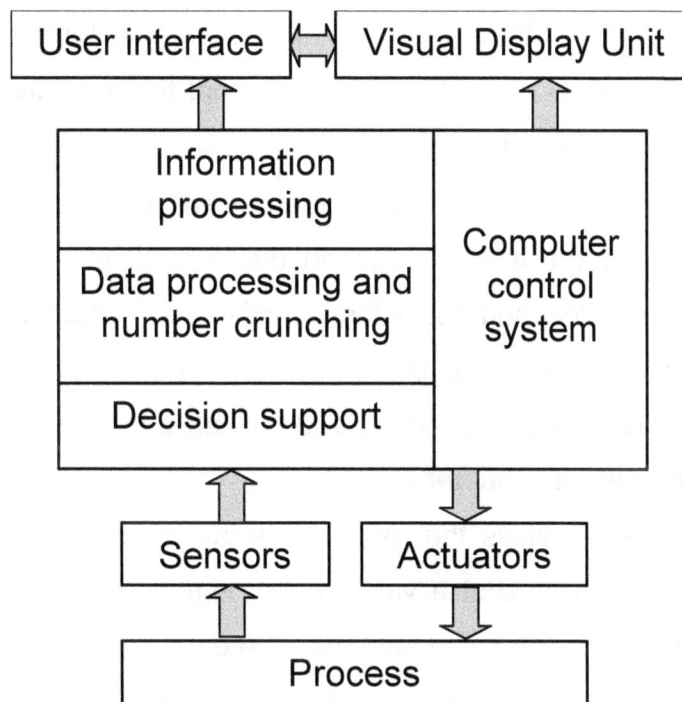

Figure 7.1 Schematic of a computer control system

The results of this control can be displayed on the display unit and any interaction with the user can be performed and this is at the top of Figure 7.1. Between the top and bottom of Figure 7.1 are the various components that make this control possible. Sensors and actuators form the first level interface to the process. Transducers or sensors pick up the values of the process variables, which are considered to be important for control purposes. Sensors are devices that generate an electrical signal whose current or voltage is proportional to the physical quantity being measured. For example sensors are used to measure, speed, temperature, acceleration, force, torque etc. For this reason the arrow in Figure 7.1 indicates that sensor information is sent to the computer control system.

A more detailed description of sensors is provided in chapter 9 of this text, however a brief overview is given here in order to help with explaining the principles of computer control.

The transducer signals are connected to the measurement interface of a computer system, which is usually configured to accept signals of a particular type. A widely adopted standard for interfacing to computer control systems is that the $0 \rightarrow 100\%$ range of any particular measurement converts to $4 \rightarrow 20$mA current or to $1 \rightarrow 5$V voltage. In order that the transducer information is processed in real-time it is necessary to measure these variables with sufficient frequency. This 'sampling frequency' will depend on the variable being monitored and will also depend on the amount of on-line processing required to convert, filter, and scale these variables. Typical devices that are used as interfaces between the computer and sensors are A-D converters. These devices take an analogue value and convert it to a digital value. These will be described briefly in Chapter 8.

Actuators are devices that perform certain action. For example, they can be motors to open or shut a valve, alarm signals to warn of a situation, hydraulic devices to move heavy loads etc. The direction arrow shows that the control system sends signals to the actuators, which in turn affect the process. These actuators will receive a control signal that will enable them to perform corrective action on the overall process.

Typically a computer control system is used to read the transducer inputs and perform some processing on these so that it can then send signals to the actuators to perform some corrective action. In this manner signals are monitored from the process and are analysed by the computer control system. This analysis is performed at various levels and is used to provide adjustments to the automatic control section or to provide information for users. It is also possible to include artificial intelligence and decision support in the software of the computer control system.

Interfacing

Interfacing the process to the controller requires that the I/O signals be suitably prepared for processing. For example, sensor information going to the computer control has to be in the form of digital data. It is not possible to send an analogue signal directly to the input port of a computer. At the same time the low power signal coming out of a computer output port, is not able to drive a physical motor. Interfacing the computer to I/O devices requires suitable electronic circuits that perform signal conditioning. A more detailed description of the basic components are described in Chapter 8 of this text such as,

- **Amplifiers**: Amplify signals so that they can be used to drive high power devices.
- **Opto-isolators:** Provide electrical isolation between the controller and process.
- **A-D and D-A converters:** These devices translate between analogue and digital signals.
- **Schmitt Triggers:** electronic circuit to shape the signal so that it has sharp rising and falling edges.
- **Buffers**: Used to protect the low voltage electronics from transients.
- **EMI screens:** screens to protect the control electronics form electromagnetic interference (EMI).

7.2. Embedded computer control systems

Control systems can be either open loop or closed-loop. In open loop systems there is no feedback and the control action assumes that the output is at the value that it is supposed to be. For example, a stepper motor is controlled by sending control pulses to the coils of the motor. There is no information as to whether the motor has actually reached the desired destination. On the other hand a position control servomechanism must be closed-loop because we want to know whether the desired position has been reached. The combination of transducer input and actuator output along with the associated computer processing is the essence of closed-loop computer control (feedback control). This is shown in Figure 7.2, which depicts a computer placed in a control loop. The fact that a computer is placed in the control loop gives these systems the name 'Embedded Computer Control Systems' or embedded controllers. There are a vast number of different types of algorithms that a control system engineer can use in the control loop. Some very sophisticated algorithms utilise machine learning and other types of intelligent. The PID controller is a very commonly used algorithm and it provides a useful example in many publications. Most control systems textbook that have digital control section will cover the PID controller in discrete form. [36, 40, 44]

Operator

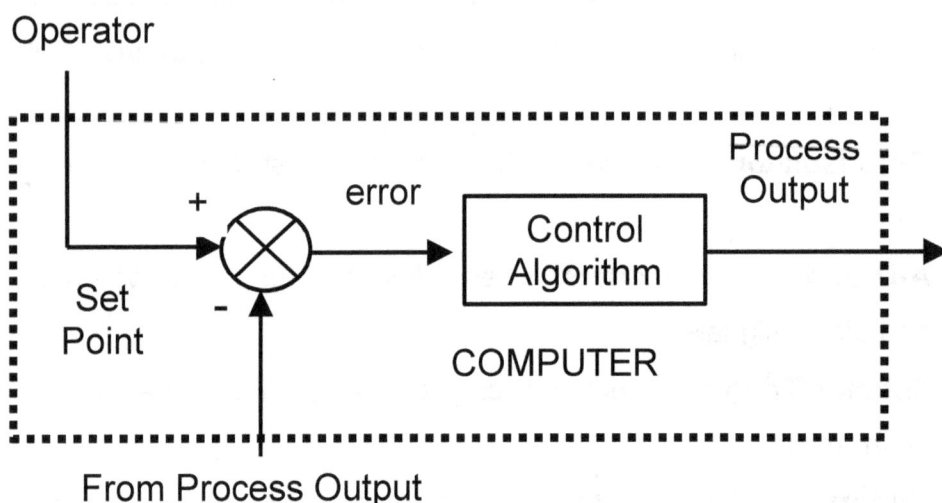

Figure 7.2 Block diagram of a computer control system in closed-loop

From Figure 7.2 the computer receives the set points from the operator, which define the desired output conditions. Additionally a measure of the actual output is fed back and subtracted from the set point in order to calculate any error. It is this error signal that is used to determine how much control is needed to make the output reach the desired value. For example, if at any instant in time the error=0 then there will be no control action. The control action is implemented using a control algorithm, which is coded in the computer software. This algorithm will provide the outputs to the actuators issuing to them the commands that control the process outputs. Typically, within the control algorithm two distinct functions are performed.

- The difference or error between the operating point and its reference value is calculated.

- Corrective action is determined by solving an equation or sets of equations that describe desired means of controlling the system. (i.e. proportional control etc)

In real-time applications the performance of a computer control system is largely influenced by the by the amount of on-line data processing that it is required to perform. Performance will also be affected by the microprocessor architecture and other characteristics such as CPU speed, memory access times etc. This on-line processing requirement includes the numerical calculations that are used to implement the control algorithms. Clearly the complexity of any algorithm implemented will also affect the speed and the accuracy of the computer control system.

A significant factor influencing the execution of computer instructions is the programming language used. High-level computer languages such as 'C', C++, Java etc. are well established and relatively easy to learn and are therefore convenient to programmers. On the other hand the low level assembly language programming is more difficult to work with, because it does not support the high-level programming features, such as classes, constructs etc. However programs written in assembly language produce very efficient code, which is often needed in real-time applications. Nevertheless, with improving processor speeds, and the time constraint on the actual development time there is increasing use of high level programming for embedded and real-time systems. [43]

As mentioned previously an embedded computer controller utilises a computer inside the control loop. This computer will perform the functions required of a controller but because it is a digital as opposed to an analogue controller it will have to perform its actions in discrete as opposed to continuous time domain. Discrete time systems were covered briefly in Chapter 6 and only a brief consideration will be given here as pertaining to computer applications in control systems. Recalling from Chapter 6 the diagram of a closed-loop control system as repeated here in Figure 7.3

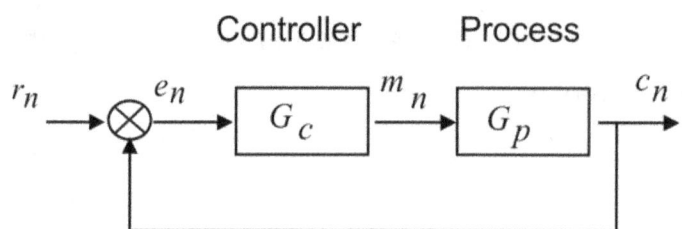

m - manipulated process input   Gp - process gain
c - process output   Gc- controller gain
r - reference input   n - sample number
e - error signal

Figure 7.3 Block diagram of a close loop control system

The subscript n used in Figure 7.3 indicates that the system is characterised by discrete samples taken at constant sampling period (T). For each sample n one iteration of the control loop is performed. This is done by incrementing n and applying the control algorithm for each increment. If the process model is known and if the desired behaviour of the process is established, (i.e. constant speed, constant torque, position control etc), then a controller can be designed to produce the desired output. (See Chapter 6, equation 6.22) By arranging the process output to feed back into the reference set point as shown in Figure 7.3, after n computations a discrete approximation of the continuous time domain system can be obtained.

This discrete model approach to control is particularly well suited to embedded computer control systems. In order to implement a digital controller on a computer the essential components of the control system have to be converted to the discrete time domain and the relevant process variables have to be converted to digital values. The core of the computer-based controller is the control algorithm. And therefore this too has to be represented in discrete form.

Based on the understanding that most continuous processes can be modelled with sufficient accuracy in the discrete time domain it follows that a discrete controller can accomplish the functions of an analogue controller. With reference to Figure 7.3 therefore, a control computer can be programmed to perform the following steps,

- Obtain a sample of the process output cn (i.e. Analogue to Digital converter interface ADC)
- Calculate the difference between the reference value rn and process output cn and store this as the error signal en.
- Perform the necessary computation of the manipulated process input signal m_n according to a prescribed control law (control Algorithm) (i.e. PID controller)
- Outputs the control signal m_n to the control element (Digital to Analogue interface)
- Continues with the next control variable
- Repeats the loop for next discrete time interval.

7.3. Control algorithm

In most cases a control system will use a set of variables that can directly influence system behaviour. For example, Figure 7.4 shows a valve that can be used to control the flow of water through a pipe. A rotation of the valve about the pivot point can regulate the valve opening from fully closed i.e. $\theta=0$ to fully open when $\theta=180$ degrees. If the valve-opening angle is controlled by an electric motor that can rotate the valve through 180 degrees, then the voltage that is supplied to the motor can be used to control the flow rate. Let us therefore assume that a voltage is used to control the opening of the valve.

Assuming that the closed-loop control system shown in Figure 7.3 is used to represent this control system. In this case the output variable is subtracted (i.e. negative feedback) from the set point value. This output variable is the flow rate, since that is what we want to control. When we calculate the error signal we must use the same units in the calculation. For example, if it is voltage that we are supplying as the set-point reference, then we must subtract voltage from it. We must therefore obtain feedback of the flow rate as a voltage that is suitably adjusted to the set-point value. For example, if a voltage range of 0-5V represents fully closed to fully opened, than the feedback must also use this range. It is for this reason that the various gains need to be included in the block diagram of a control system.

But Figure 7.3 shows a unity feedback gain system, and this means that there is no gain in the feedback path. This is an unlikely situation in control systems and typically the feedback transducer would exhibit a gain that would be included in the feedback path. If there were a gain in the feedback path of Figure 7.3, then it would need to be included in the calculation of the overall closed-loop transfer function. (See Chapter 6 CLTF)

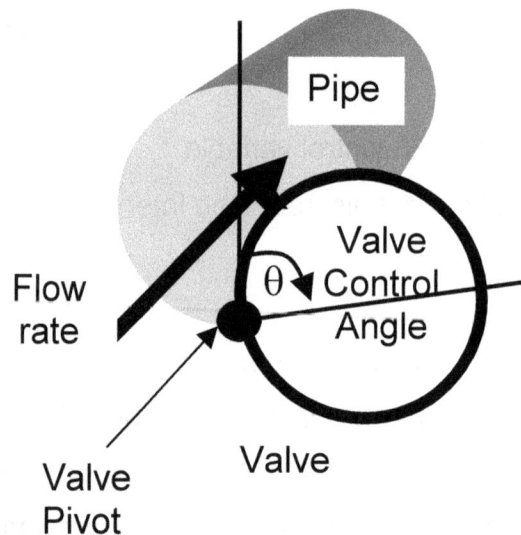

Figure 7.4 Example flow control valve

For a given control system the control algorithm defines how the variables that control the desired performance will be calculated. In the example of Figure 7.4, the control algorithm will be used to calculate the required adjustment to the valve motor voltage on the basis of the information it has about the process. The information about the process is the value of the error signal over the number of samples taken. If the present error value is e_n then the control algorithm will also have access to the error during the previous discrete time intervals e_{n-1}, e_{n-2} etc. This information will enable the controller to monitor the error over a number of discrete time samples and take appropriate action. On the basis of this information a useful form for control algorithms is as follows, [36, 44]

$$m_n - m_{n-1} = k_0 e_n + k_1 e_{n-1} + k_2 e_{n-2} + ...$$

(7.1)

In equation 7.1 the change in the manipulation variable (m_n) between samples is determined by coefficients of the present sample, and the previous two samples. If we assume that the error signal has been measured, this equation can be used to describe a control algorithm that will calculate the present value of the manipulation variable, which is needed so that equation 7.1 is balanced. All the other elements in equation 7.1 are known.

By maintaining a record of the variables at each sampling instant the past information about system behaviour can be analysed. Computer control systems can therefore be made to use artificial intelligence, because knowledge of past behaviour can be used to predict any future actions. Neural networks and Fuzzy logic controllers fall into this category, but these are beyond the scope of this text.

In this text, we will be using the discrete form of the Proportional Integral Derivative (PID) controller. This is the most common type of controller in industrial applications and can be implemented with relative ease both in its analogue as well as digital forms.

Proportional control action

When a control system feeds back a signal that generates an error between the desired and the measured value of the variable being controlled, then the logical approach would be to apply control, which is proportional to the error. For example, if you are driving a car, and are approaching an uphill slope, if you want to maintain speed, you will push the accelerator pedal in proportion to how fast you want to be going. Therefore, with proportional control, correction is made in direct proportion to the error. This can be shown by using to a number of equations as follows. For example in the continuous time domain the proportional compensation can de described as follows,

$$m(t) = k_p e(t)$$ (7.2)

Where k_p is the gain of the proportional controller.

If it is assumed that the discrete time domain has a sampling interval *(T)* such that it can be assumed that during this interval the error is constant, then the discrete form of equation 7.2 becomes,

$$m_n = k_p e_n$$ (7.3)

And, since the same control law governs the present and previous sampling instants, then the value of *m* for the previous sample (discrete time interval) is,

$$m_{n-1} = k_p e_{n-1}$$

Returning to equation 7.1, the incremental adjustment to the manipulated process input is given by the numerical difference between the present and the previous discrete time values i.e. (subtracting equation 7.3 from equation 7.2) which gives, the required change in the manipulation variable as follows,

$$\Delta m_n = m_n - m_{n-1} = k_p(e_n - e_{n-1})$$ (7.4)

Equation 7.4 represents the proportional control that is required to bring the output in line with the input. In many control applications this in itself is not sufficient because of the steady state error and therefore integral control is needed to compensate for this.

Integral control action

In closed-loop control, every time that a control action is applied there is a small error. This error is insignificant on the basis of a single control action, but when the control is repeated many times the error accumulates. Integral control is designed to correct for accumulation of small errors over time. This is done by integrating the error over a period of time, and applying an integral control gain to correct for this. Accordingly in continuous time domain, integral control action is given by equation 7.5.

$$m(t) = k_i \int_0^t e(\tau)d\tau \qquad (7.5)$$

Where k_i is the gain of the integral controller.

In discrete time domain, integration can be done numerically. There are many ways that this can be done but perhaps the simplest form is to consider that the integral can be approximated by summation of the areas under the discrete time intervals. This is known as Euler's method for numerical integration and it is shown Figure 7.5. The discrete error e_n at each sampling period is given by the amplitude of the error at that discrete point. The areas shaded are the product of the sampling time T and e_j. Thus,

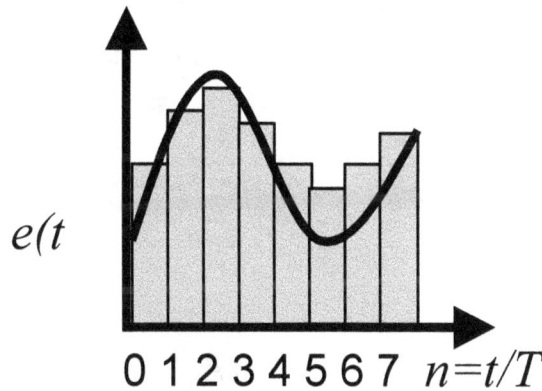

$$e(t$$

$$0\ 1\ 2\ 3\ 4\ 5\ 6\ 7 \quad n=t/T$$

Figure 7.5 Euler's method for numerical Integration

Thus, over the total number of samples the integral control action that is required to correct for the accumulated error can be represented by equation 7.6.

$$m_n = k_i \sum_{j=1}^n Te_j \quad (7.6)$$

In order to calculate the change in the manipulation variable m_n as given in equation 7.1, this equation can be rewritten as comprising the present value added to all the previous values, which is as follows,

$$m_n = k_i \sum_{j=1}^{n-1} Te_j + k_i Te_n \quad (7.7)$$

Equation 7.7 distinguishes the manipulation variable due to the present value of the error from the effects of all the previous samples excluding the present. By the same token from equations 7.6 and 7.7 it is implicit that the previous value of the manipulation variable, that is m_{n-1} is given by taking away from equation 7.7, the component of the manipulation variable, which is due to the present value of the error. Which is to say, take away the present value and whatever is left is from previous samples. This is shown in equation 7.8

$$m_{n-1} = k_i \sum_{j=1}^{n-1} Te_j \qquad (7.8)$$

According to equation 7.1, the incremental adjustment to the manipulated process input is given by the numerical difference between the present and the previous discrete time values i.e. (take away equation 7.8 from equation 7.7)

$$\Delta m_n = m_n - m_{n-1} = k_i [(\sum_{n=1}^{n-1} Te_j + Te_n) - (\sum_{n=1}^{n-1} Te_j)]$$

Therefore,

$$\Delta m_n = k_i Te_n \qquad (7.9)$$

Which is the discrete approximation of the integral control action that is needed to correct for the accumulate error.

Derivative control

With derivative action, the controller output is proportional to the rate of change of the error. In high inertia loads, this may not be necessary, since the rate of change of error will be governed by the inertia of the system. As a result, for example many variable speed drive (VSD) motor speed control systems only use P+I control. Nevertheless, where it is necessary to control the rate of change of the error, the derivative control action is used. In discrete form calculating the ratio of the change in the y-axis variable to the change in the x variable over the selected time interval can perform numerical differentiation. This is done in the same way that we would use to find the gradient of a function. This is shown in Figure 7.6 where the difference in the error at sample times n and $n-1$ are used to determine the y-axis variable change. The x-axis variable change is determined by the choice of sample time T.

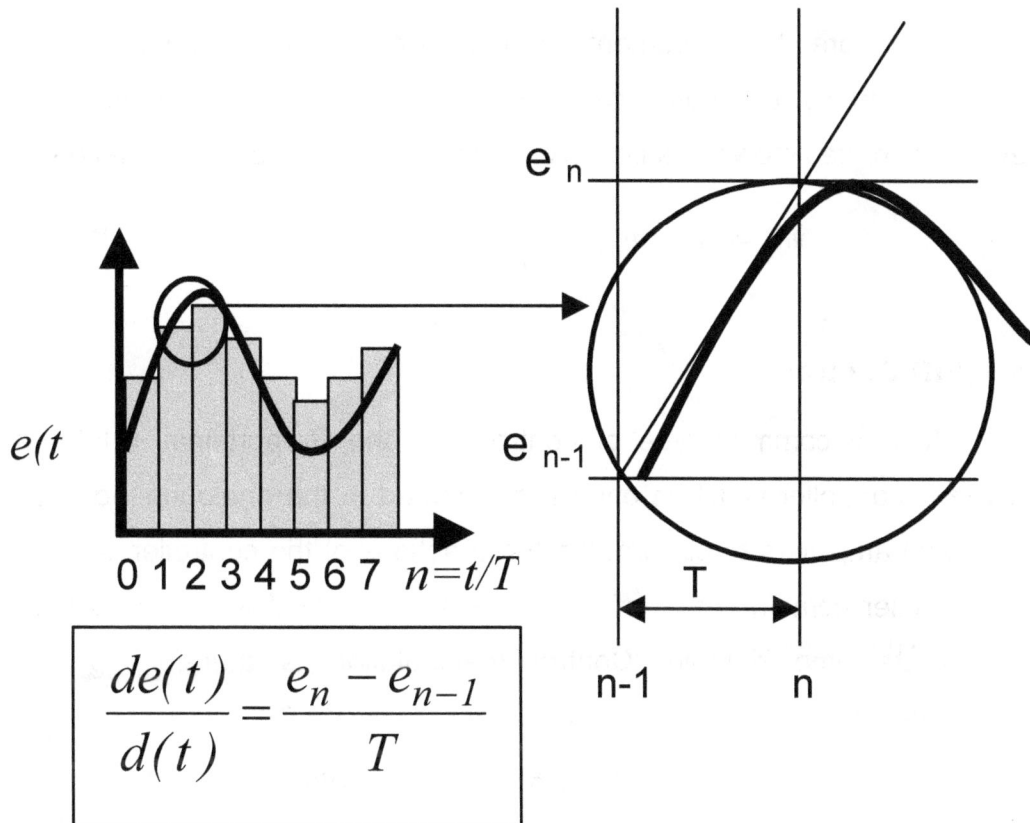

$$\frac{de(t)}{d(t)} = \frac{e_n - e_{n-1}}{T}$$

Figure 7.6 Discrete differentiation

Derivative control action in continuous time domain provides a correction to the manipulated process input, which is proportional to the derivative of the error, i.e.

$$m(t) = k_d \frac{de(t)}{dt} \qquad (7.10)$$

Where k_d is the gain of the derivative controller.

As illustrated in Figure 7.6 the derivative can be represented by backward difference approximation in order to obtain a discrete equation for the controller. i.e.

$$m_n = k_d \left(\frac{e_n - e_{n-1}}{T} \right) \qquad (7.11)$$

Similarly,

$$m_{n-1} = k_d \left(\frac{e_{n-1} - e_{n-2}}{T} \right) \qquad (7.12)$$

Therefore, the incremental adjustment to the manipulated process input is given by the numerical difference between the present and the previous discrete time values i.e. (take away equation 7.12 from equation 7.11)

$$\Delta m_n = m_n - m_{n-1} = \frac{k_d}{T} (e_n - 2e_{n-1} + e_{n-2}) \qquad (7.13)$$

7.4. PID Control

A very common type of controller is the Proportional + Integral + Derivative controller which is often implemented in the analogue world using operational amplifiers to perform the three actions of the controller. A discrete PID controller combines the effects of the three distinctive control actions in the discrete time domain. Control manipulation is therefore given by synthesising the corrective action of each term. i.e., [36, 44]

$$\Delta m_n = (\Delta m_n)_p + (\Delta m_n)_i + (\Delta m_n)_d \qquad (7.14)$$

Which from equations (7.4, 7.9 and 7.13) gives,

$$\Delta m_n = k_p(e_n - e_{n-1}) + k_i T e_n + \frac{k_d}{T} (e_n - 2e_{n-1} + e_{n-2}) \qquad (7.15)$$

Another way of representing this is to group all like error terms to give,

$$\Delta m_n = m_n - m_{n-1} = k_0 e_n + k_1 e_{n-1} + k_2 e_{n-2} \qquad (7.16)$$

Which is of the form of equation (7.1) and where,

$$k_0 = k_p + k_i T + \frac{k_d}{T} \qquad (7.17)$$

$$k_1 = -k_p - 2 \frac{k_d}{T} \qquad (7.18)$$

$$k_2 = \frac{k_d}{T} \qquad (7.19)$$

Algorithm:

Given k_p, k_i and k_d and error values at n, $n-1$ and $n-2$ a PID algorithm can be implemented. This is shown in Figure 7.7, which it should be fairly self-explanatory.

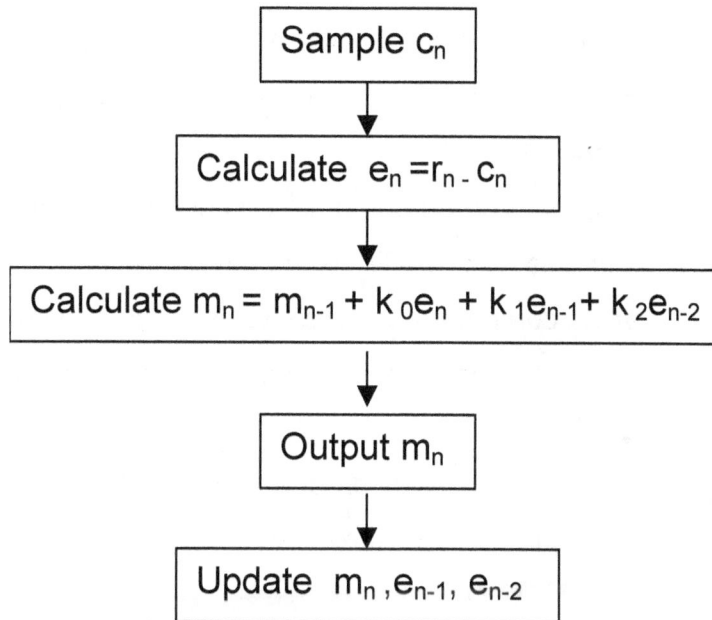

Sample c_n

Calculate $e_n = r_n - c_n$

Calculate $m_n = m_{n-1} + k_0 e_n + k_1 e_{n-1} + k_2 e_{n-2}$

Output m_n

Update m_n, e_{n-1}, e_{n-2}

Figure 7.7 PID control algorithm flowchart

Exercises

7.1. Describe the main components of an embedded computer control system.

7.2. Why is it necessary to have interface circuits for sensors and actuators that need to be connected to a computer control system?

7.3. Distinguish between open loop and closed-loop control systems and give a few examples of each.

7.4. What do you need in order to implement a control system?

7.5. Give some examples and briefly discus the operation of typical devices used in interfacing computer control systems to the outside world.

7.6. What do you need to consider when choosing a processor to implement a digital control algorithm?

7.7. Discuss the use of high level programming languages in embedded systems, and explain how they compare to low-level assembly programming.

7.8. Explain the actions that a computer control system is required to perform in order to implement a controller in discrete form.

7.9. What is a control algorithm and where in the control loop does it reside?

7.10. Can you have a control system without a control algorithm?

7.11. Explain how the error signal is calculated in feedback control systems.

7.12. Explain how sampling intervals enable the process to be modelled in discrete form.

7.13. Explain the principle of proportional control and show how it can be implemented in discrete form.

7.14. Why do we need integral control action and how is it implemented in discrete form?

7.15. Why do we need differential control action and how is it implemented in discrete form?

7.16. How would you implement a PID controller on an embedded computer?

CHAPTER 8 INTERFACING TECHNIQUES

This chapter introduces some electronic components that are used when interfacing computer control devices to the external input-output (I/O) devices. The detail is only brief and it is only provided as an overview. The reader is encouraged to use this as a starting point to research further literature on the subject. The content in this chapter should be sufficient to enable the reader to implement the required interface, after undertaking some research and literature survey for the appropriate devices.

8.1. Introduction

When signals have to be passed between the computer system and peripheral devices there is a need for dedicated circuit components, which perform the interfacing. Although the nature of the interface will depend on the application two general points need to be satisfied,

- The two sides of the interface must be compatible so that the signals are not distorted during transmission across the interface.
- The system interconnections should be free from any undue noise sensitivity and the timing constraints on both sides of the interface must be satisfied.

There area large numbed of devices that are commonly used to interface I/O peripherals to computer control systems. Therese vary with the type of the interface that is required, for example, a printer and a network interface card will require a different type of interface. Additionally, some control systems are used to supply control signals to high-power devices such as power transistors and Thyristors, which in turn drive large machinery. Some common interfacing component devices are as follows and will be briefly covered next,

- **Amplifiers**: Amplify signals so that they can be used to drive high power devices.
- **Opto-isolators:** Provide electrical isolation between the controller and process.

- **A-D and D-A converters:** These devices translate between analogue and digital signals.
- **Schmitt Triggers:** electronic circuit to shape the signal so that it has sharp rising and falling edges.
- **Buffers**: Used to protect the low voltage electronics from transients.
- **EMI screens:** screens to protect the control electronics form electromagnetic interference (EMI).

8.2.   Interfacing devices

Amplifiers

In embedded applications amplifiers are electronic devices that amplify signals so that they can be used to drive high power loads. The operational amplifier (Op-amp) is a very common device in the realm of analogue electronics. Other ICs are specifically made to suit an application. For example a H-bridge circuit is commonly used to drive d.c motors. The principle is to connect the motor in the so-called H-bridge configuration so that the direction of rotation can be controlled. The opening and closing of switches in the H-bridge can determine the direction of rotation. Speed of rotation can be controlled by the amount of applied voltage to the terminals. A typical configuration is shown in Figure 8.1

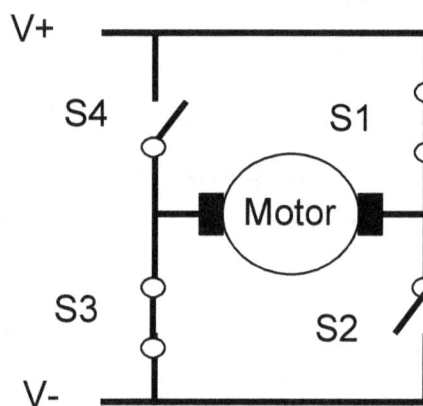

Figure 8.1 H-bridge motor drive circuits

For example, a common H-bridge IC is the L293D. The characteristics of this device are given in the datasheet. [45]

This is an example of a dedicated IC that is designed to provide bi-directional drive currents of up to 1 A at voltages from 4.5 V to 36 V. It is designed to drive active loads such as relays, solenoids, dc and bipolar stepping motors, as well as other high-current/high-voltage loads in positive-supply applications. All inputs are TTL compatible.

In digital control, the switches can be driven from a pulse width modulated (PWM) source, and this can be used to control the average d.c voltage applied to the terminals. This is beyond the scope of this text but the general term for these types of devices are switch-mode power converters.

The H-bridge as well as a PWM drive chip is readily available as building blocks in digital control. Other amplifier circuits include signal conditioning op-amps, comparators and a variety of electronic devices that can be used to condition signals so that they can be interfaced to a computer. For example op-amps are used in ADC and DAC as well as Schmitt trigger circuits described later.

Opto-isolators

These are used to isolate the computer port from the high voltage side that is needed to drive the actuator. This is to say that, if there is an electrical fault on the actuator side, the computer is protected by the isolator. A simplified diagram is shown in Figure 8.2, which shows that Opto-isolators, or Opto-couplers, are made up of a light emitting device, and a light sensitive device. These are packaged in a single IC but the two components are electrically isolated, i.e., there is no electrical connection between them, just a beam of light. The light emitter is nearly always an LED. The light sensitive device may be a photodiode, phototransistor, or even devices such as Thyristors, triacs etc. In normal operation the Opto-isolator passes the entire signal between the high power and the low power ends. From a design perspective it has to be said that Opto-isolators will only work up to a certain frequency. Some are much faster than others. Make sure that the Opto-isolator you use is fast enough for the signals you are putting through it. Opto-couplers are inexpensive and can be sources from most electronic catalogues.

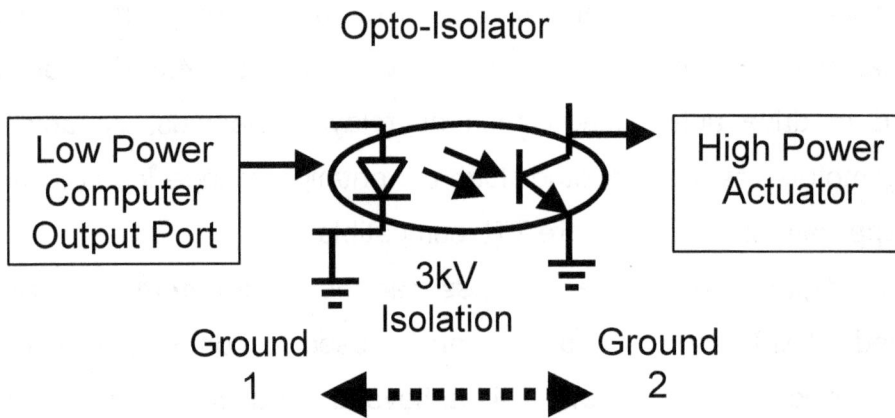

Opto-Isolator

| Low Power Computer Output Port | | High Power Actuator |

3kV Isolation

Ground 1 ◄·······► Ground 2

Figure 8.2 Typical use of an Opto-isolator

Digital to Analogue conversion (DAC)

From real-time control viewpoint perhaps the most common interface to the microcomputer would be through the measurement of process variables obtained by sensors and through issuing of control signal to actuators. Since a lot of the measurement and actuation devices operate on analogue signals these actions are performed by the computer after the appropriate analogue-to-digital (ADC) and digital-to-analogue converters (DAC) have been done.

The DAC converts numbers derived from a digital output signal into a physical quantity, usually an electrical voltage. Usually these numbers are updated at uniform sampling intervals and the DAC will be synchronised with the digital source. This synchronisation is done by the programmer who decides when to write in the instruction to trigger the DAC sample and hold circuit. Normally the output voltage is a linear function of the input number and the signal resolution depends on the number of bits used to represent the digital signal. For example, Figure 8.3 shows an analogue signal represented by a digital number with 4 bits. This is done for convenience since it gives 16 possible numbers in the range of 0-15. 8-bit resolution would be more accurate but the diagram would need to show 256 values.

It is seen from Figure 8.3 that the analogue voltage at each sampling instant can be described as a number in the range of 0-15. A signal envelope is shown to show how the analogue signal could look like.

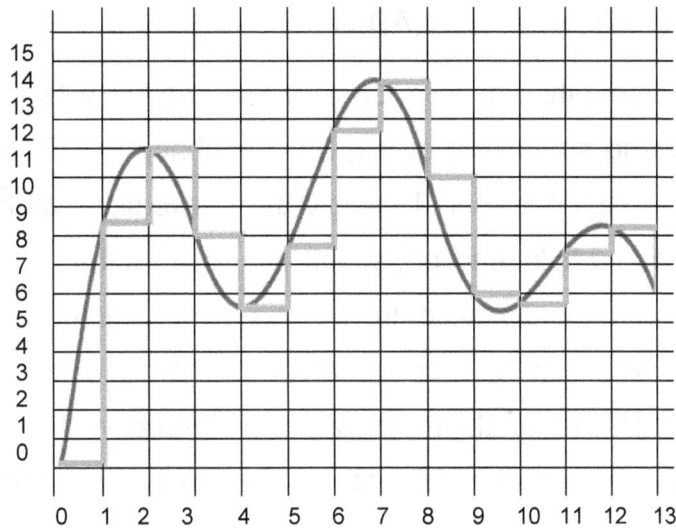

Figure 8.3 DAC using 4-bit resolution

Perhaps the best approach to learning about DACs is to read a typical data sheet. For example, the data sheet for the DAC number AD7568 from Analogue Devices describes a DAC IC that contains eight 12-bit DACs in one monolithic device. [46] The AD7568 is a serial input device, which supports direct interfacing with RS232 compatible devices, such as for example the 80x51 microcontroller.

A typical interface to the 8051 microcontroller is shown in Figure 8.4. The data sheet also gives timing waveforms and the typical applications include, process control, automatic test equipment and general-purpose instrumentation.

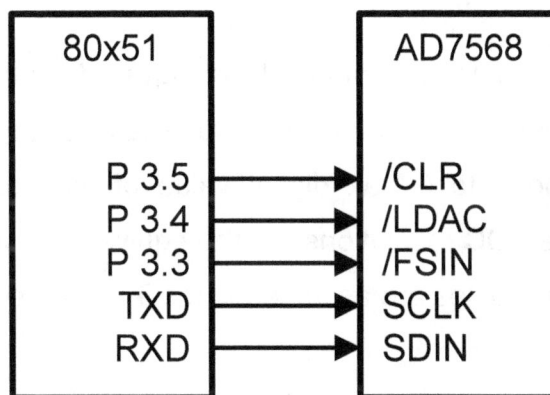

Figure 8.4 Typical interface between a DAC and the 80x51 [46]

Analogue to Digital Conversion (ADC)

ADC performs the opposite function from the DAC. Namely it takes an analogue signal and samples it at a given frequency to produce a series of discrete values in digital format. Typically the conversion will happen on the basis of a sample and hold function, so that the value of the digitised value can be synchronised with the digital controller. The most common type of ADC is a successive approximation type converter. This method uses an operational amplifier to compare the analogue input to a reference value. The reference value is passed through a DAC, stored in an internal register and the comparison is clocked to occur at a pre-set frequency. Figure 8.5 shows an analogue signal that is sampled at given instants to provide discrete amplitudes at these sampling instants.

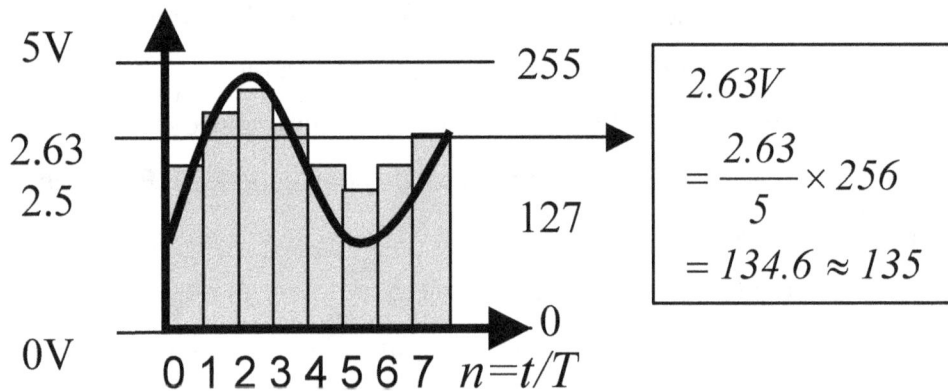

Figure 8.5 ADC function

$$2.63V$$
$$= \frac{2.63}{5} \times 256$$
$$= 134.6 \approx 135$$

Typically the analogue signal will be adjusted so that it is compatible with the analogue input of the ADC. Thus, for example, an analogue scale of 0-5V would correspond to 0-Max digital value of the converter. Table 8.1 summarises possible ADC resolutions ant the equivalent number ranges. Note that here all analogue values are assumed in the TTL range of 0-5V.

Table 8.1

Resolution in bits	Decimal resolution	Range in Hex	Accuracy V/bit	Average Error %
8	256	00-FF	0.019531	4.88%
12	4096	000-FFF	0.001221	0.31%
16	65536	0000-FFFF	7.63E-05	0.02%

Taking an example data sheet the Texas instruments ADS8344 is an 8-channel, 16-bit, sampling Analogue-to-Digital (A/D) converter with a synchronous serial interface. Typical power dissipation is *10mW* at a *100kHz* throughput rate and a +5V supply. The reference voltage (VREF) can be varied between 500mV and VCC, providing a corresponding input voltage range of 0V to VREF. The device includes a shutdown mode, which reduces power dissipation to under 15µW. Figure 8.6 shows a block diagram for this ADC.

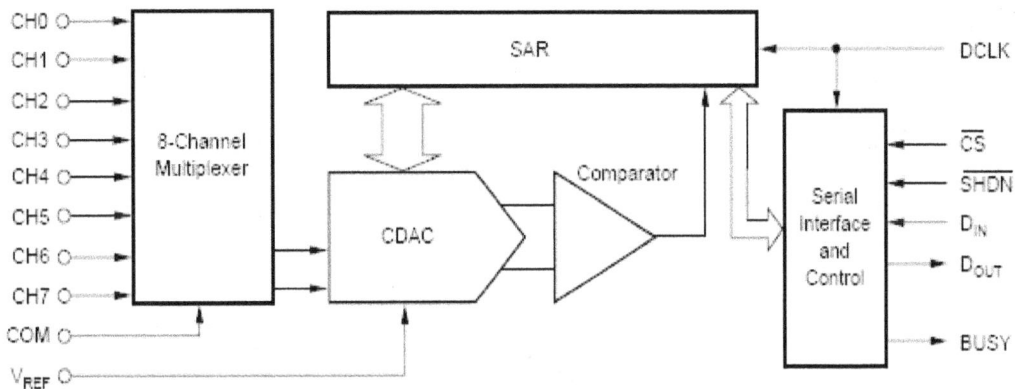

Figure 8.6. Texas instruments 16-bit serial ADC

The data sheet provides all the information that is needed to interface this ADC to a microcontroller, including timing waveforms and pin layouts. The reader is encouraged to read these data sheets since they include very detailed application and interfacing notes. [47] It is seen from the datasheets considered here that standard ADC and DAC chips are available for interfacing to microprocessor based systems. The above examples considered serial devices, but similar approach would be used to interface parallel devices. It is worth noting that parallel devices are faster but they do need parallel ports to interface to. This can use up a large number of the available port pins on a microcontroller. The decision to use serial or parallel AD/DA converter is made on the basis of the application and any real-time performance constraints.

AD/DA resolution

During the design process of an embedded controller it is important to consider the resolution of the ADC and DAC. The number of bits used to represent the analogue signal governs resolution. If for example an analogue signal with amplitude of 20V were to be represented by an 8-bit ADC the resolution per bit of the converted signal would be,

$$\frac{20V}{2^8} = \frac{20}{256} = 0.078 \, V/bit$$

This means that the accuracy is limited to within 78mV. If inside the computer software this voltage is represented by an 8-bit byte the hexadecimal (or binary) word used to represent 13V can be calculated from equation 8.1. Namely,

$$\frac{13}{20} \times 256 = 166.4$$

Since we can only work with integers we select 166, which means that the error is,

$$\frac{0.4}{256} \times 20 = 0.031$$

Which correspond to an error of 32 mV. The binary equivalent of 166d=101000110b. In this case it is up to the designer to decide if this accuracy is suitable for the application. If it is not then a higher resolution converter may be needed. For example, similar calculations using a converter with 12-bit resolution would yield an error as follows,

$$\frac{20V}{2^{12}} = \frac{20}{4096} = 0.0048 \, V/bit$$

$$\frac{13}{20} \times 4096 = 2662.4$$

$$\frac{0.4}{4096} \times 20 = 0.002$$

Which corresponds to an error of 2 mV. The binary equivalent of 2662d=1010001100110b. These calculation show that the error is significantly smaller when using a 12-bit converter

Schmitt Triggers

These are integrated circuits based on op-amps that are used to shape the signal so that it has sharp rising and falling edges. These are particularly useful in waveforms that are distorted due to stray capacitance and other electromagnetic interference. Once again a datasheet can be used to describe the characteristic features.[48] Typically, a Schmitt trigger is based on an op-amp comparator circuit, which switches the output negative when the input is on the rising edge with respect to a positive reference voltage. It then uses negative feedback to prevent switching back to the other state until the input passes through a lower threshold voltage on the falling edge. Thus the circuit provides a waveform with fast rise and fall times, and eliminates noise and fussiness from the original signal. The Schmitt trigger switches at different voltages depending upon whether it is moving from low to high or high to low, employing what is termed hysteresis. Consequently, the circuit symbol for one of these circuits incorporates the hysteresis symbol into it as shown in Figure 8.7.

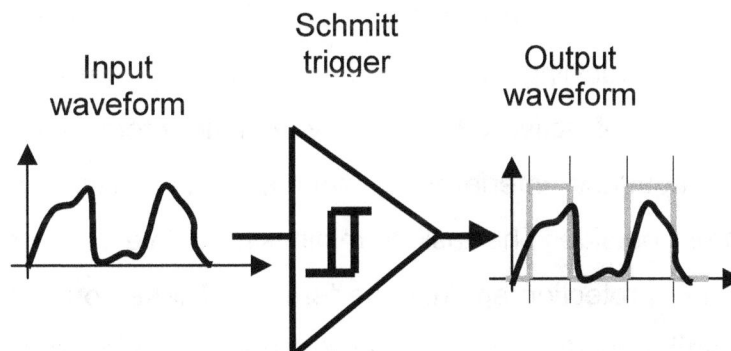

Figure 8.7 Schmitt trigger symbol and action [49]

Hex Buffers

Hex Buffers are inexpensive circuits that are used to change CMOS to TTL driver levels and also to protect the microprocessor I/O ports from transients. For example the data sheet for a Fairchild hex buffer type CD4049UBMS can be used as CMOS to DTL/TTL converters and can drive directly two DTL/TTL loads. [50] This is an inverting hex buffer and features logic level conversion using only one supply (voltage (VCC). The input signal high level (VIH) can exceed the VCC supply voltage when this device is used for logic level conversions.

EMI screens

Electromagnetic interference (EMI) is a major concern of digital circuit designers. We continue to develop higher level of integrated circuits that work at faster speeds and higher sensitivity as well as accuracy. By design therefore they are more susceptible to interference. There are two major concerns here namely,

- How susceptible our circuit is to EMI. Which is to say how often is it likely to fail in the presence of EMI.
- How much EMI does our circuit generate when it is working.

IC manufacturers are required by legislation to produce circuits that comply with regulations on EMI. This covers both the amount of interference that the circuits emit as well as how susceptible they are to interference. A very useful article on the design issues relating to EMI can be found form MAXIM IC manufacturer. [51] In this article details are given about design issues and methods adopted in tackling EMI. The design aim is to design an electronic circuit, which is free of active EMI (electromagnetic interference, also called RFI or radio frequency interference) sources and passively immune to disturbances from outside. The task of minimising active sources is probably easier than that of protection against interference. These sources of electrical disturbances can be conducted by the power lines or conveyed through the air by capacitive, magnetic, or electromagnetic radiation. In practice however, the most difficult interference to counteract is that conducted over physical signal lines connected to the equipment. In these cases common techniques are line filtering, power-supply design, proper layout, and shielding of the enclosure. In any case, one must distinguish between the need to protect against damage or malfunction, and the need to prevent signal or data distortion resulting from (for example) a disruption in the sequence of a microcontroller programme. The first problem is attacked via hardware design, the second via software algorithms. Before applying any protective elements, consider these basic rules:

- EMI protection should be considered while designing the circuit, not added afterwards.
- Block disturbances as near to the source as possible, preferably before they enter the equipment, and redirect them to ground.
- All sections that may be exposed to EMI disturbance, even electrically isolated sections, should be located as far as possible from sensitive circuitry.

Due to the fact that ICs cannot withstand kV-level voltages, such disturbances must be excluded from the input, converted to current, and then to heat. Ground-loop currents, which can enter an interface and run throughout the circuit, are often thwarted with galvanic isolation. Isolation is especially useful for the longer lines and high ground-loop currents that may occur in industrial systems.

Within this text we provide only a glimpse and the reader is encouraged to read through Maxim literature to gain a deeper understanding of the subject matter. [52]

8.3.   Address decoding

Address decoding is necessary whenever the CPU requires information from memory or I/O space. In the I/O space the information may come from a timer, interrupt controller or other peripheral whilst reading or writing to memory requires access to the selected memory location. Either way it is necessary to decode the address so that information can be accessed.

The practical decoding problem is concerned with causing the chip select (CS) pin or the chip enable (CE) pin of the device to go LOW and once this is done to proceed with reading or writing to this location. Note that some chips may be active High, and in this case the decoder needs to send logic '1' to select the chip. The essential principles of address decoding will apply to any type of processor although details will vary depending on the size of the address bus, I/O space or memory size and details of reserved locations etc.

Address decoding classification

Decoding of address space can be classified as follows,

- **Full decoding:** Uses all the available address lines to decode the address. This can be wasteful if the full 16K block is not being implemented. For example, if the address space is 16 bits wide, and only 2K-bytes (i.e. 2^{11} = 2048 = 2K-bytes) of memory is implemented, this means that we would need to decode nine lines even though there was nothing on these addresses. This would be wasteful in effort and cost of hardware for decoding. (i.e. logic gates)

- **Partial Decoding:** For smaller address blocks it is wasteful to perform full decoding as mentioned earlier. Instead partial decoding is implemented by simply ignoring some of the address lines. This technique is very often used in microcontroller applications where the microprocessor is embedded into the final product. Here the memory configuration is fixed and the ability to expand the memory is not required.

- **Block decoding:** Practical microcomputers use memory that comprises several blocks of memory chips (i.e. SIMMS). Each memory block will require a separate decoder unless a special block decoder is built.

- **Prom Decoders:** Replaces all combinational logic with high speed PROM. Thus a single 24 pin PROM replaces a number of TTL packages with the added facility that a new memory configuration can be programmed into a new PROM.

Address space and I/O port organisation

In order to provide an example of interfacing we will consider the Intel 80x86 family of processors. We will focus on the 16-bit version rather than the modern 32-bit and 64-bit processors. This is simply to reduce the number of bits that require decoding. Otherwise, the principle remains the same. The 8086 family provide an I/O space, which is separate from memory space. The I/O space can accommodate up to 64K 8-bit ports, or up to 32K 16-bit ports. Ports are addressed the same way as memory except that there are no segments in the port address space. It is worth noting that Intel reserves some of the available I/O space. Any I/O interface design should therefore take this into consideration. To access a port, the bus interface unit (BIU) places the port address (0-FFFFh) on the lower sixteen lines of the address bus. Different forms of the I/O instructions allow the address to be specified as fixed value or as a variable taken out of register DX. The IN and OUT instructions transfer the data between the accumulator and I/O space. Where this may be required, I/O devices can also be placed in the memory space. This memory-mapped I/O provides flexibility since any instruction that references a memory location can be used to access memory-mapped I/O space.

Example: Interfacing ROM to 8086 CPU.

This is shown in the Figure 8.8. Note that two chips are needed because the 80x86 family of microprocessors use separate addresses for Even and for Odd address locations. This is because they wanted to maintain compatibility with the 8-bit predecessor, the 8085. The 8086 uses the high byte and the low byte pair to represent 16-bit data. For 8-bit operation the Bus High Enable (BHE) pin signals when the high byte is used and when not. For 16-bit data access this is not required in the decoder circuit. The 8086 has 20-bit address bus providing 1MB of addresses.

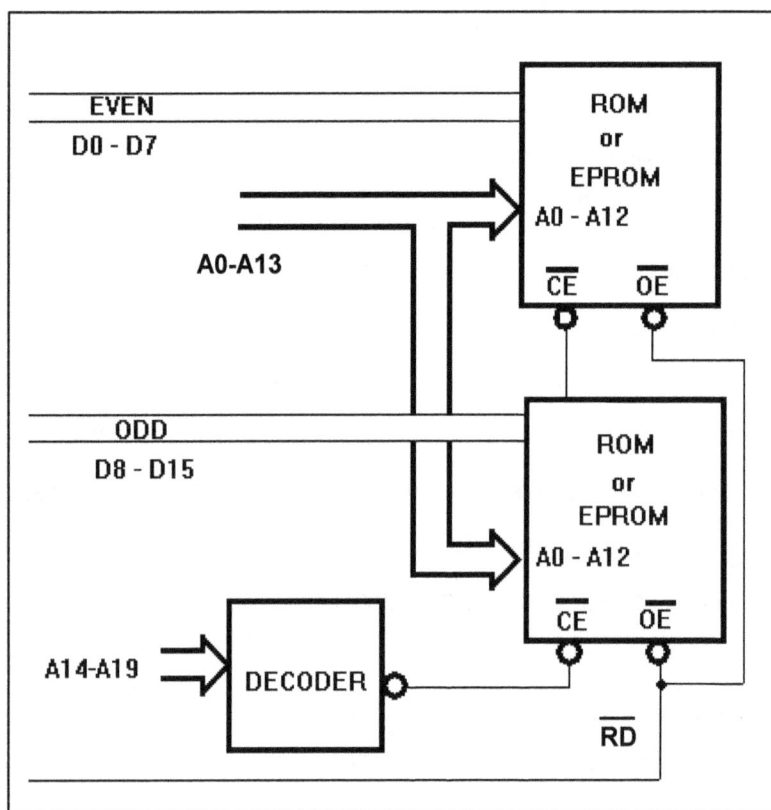

Figure 8.8. Interfacing the 2764 8K-Byte EPROM to the 8086 CPU

Figure 8.8 shows address lines A0-A13 used to select 2^{13}=8K-bytes. These address lines are used for both the EVEN and ODD bytes enabling access to 16K-bytes. The address decoder decodes the remaining unused lines A14-A19 causing the chip enable pin to go low for any address above FC000h i.e., => (2^{20} - 2^{14} = FFFFFh – 4000h=FC000h). Where 4000h = 16384d which is 16K addresses.

A possible address decoder for the above system could use an 8-input NAND gate as shown below.

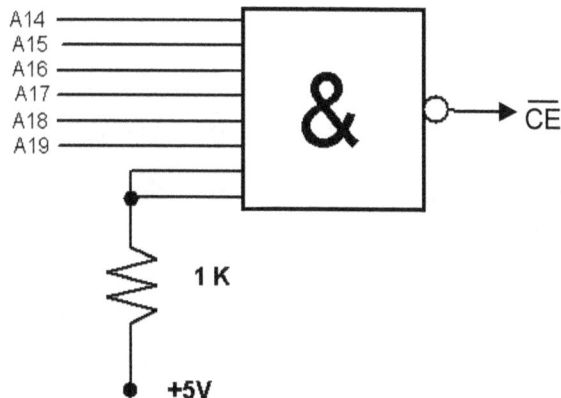

Figure 8.9. Address decoder for 16K ROM starting at address FC000h

From this example it can be seen that an address decoder is a circuit that examines the unused address lines and utilises these to enable a specified range of addresses to be implemented. This is important in view of the constraint that one memory block must not be allowed to overlap another.

Example of full decoding

Task: Design a detailed interface to the 8031 ROM-Less microcontroller to access the memory shown in the following memory map. The memory map starts at location 1000h and all the separate memory chips are stacked one on top of the one below, as shown in the diagram below.

Memory Map

Size 16K	ROM
Size 8K	RAM
Size 2K (Start at 1000h)	ROM

Solution

This is only an example and it has to be stressed that other ways of decoding memory are possible. Nevertheless, in order to emphasise the process we will design this as a full decoder using logic gates.

The way to design a decoder is to decide the Start and the End addresses for each memory chip. The start of the first chip is given as 1000h and all the other chips are aligned contiguously in memory. Simple calculation shows that,

For the first 2K ROM chip:

1000h + 4K of ROM.   Now 2K is 4*1024=2048d= 800h

Therefore Start address=**1000h** and the End address=1000h+7FF=**17FFh**

For the 8K RAM chip:

1800h + 8K of ROM   Now 8K is 8*1024=8192d=2000h

Therefore Start address=**1800h** and the End address=1800h+1FFF=**37FF**

For the 16K RAM chip:

3800h + 16K of ROM   Now 16K is 16*1024=16384=4000h

Therefore Start address=**3800h** and the End address=3800h+3FFF=**77FF**

In order to design the decoder these start and end numbers need to be converted to binary form. This is done and shown in Table 8.2

Table 8.2

Address Bits	$2^{15}2^{14}2^{13}2^{12}$	$2^{11}2^{10}2^{9}2^{8}$	$2^{7}2^{6}2^{5}2^{4}$	$2^{3}2^{2}2^{1}2^{0}$	Size	
1000h(Start)	0001	0000	0000	0000		
17FFh(End)	0001	0111	1111	1111	4k	ROM
1800h(Start)	0001	1000	0000	0000	8k	RAM
37FFh(End)	0011	0111	1111	1111		
3800h(Start)	0011	1000	0000	0000	16k	ROM
77FFh(End)	0111	0111	1111	1111		

Decoding the first 2K ROM chip:

As a rule when designing decoders, only the bits that do not change are put into the decoder. For example looking at Table 8.2 in the first 4K of RAM starting at 1000h the bits that are not changing between the Start and End addresses are address bits A12-A15. For convenience, these are highlighted in grey below. All the other bits are allowed to change as the addresses are selected within the chip in the range of 1000h to17FFh, inclusively.

Address Bits	$2^{15}2^{14}2^{13}2^{12}$	$2^{11}2^{10}2^{9}2^{8}$	$2^{7}2^{6}2^{5}2^{4}$	$2^{3}2^{2}2^{1}2^{0}$	Size	
1000h(Start)	0001	0000	0000	0000		
17FFh(End)	0001	0111	1111	1111	4k	ROM

Thus to decode this first chip, the address lines A15, A14, A13, A12 need to be taken into a NAND gate the output of which is fed into the Chip Select (CS) pin of the 4K ROM memory chip. This is shown in Figure 8.10, where the signals that need to be inverted are shown with the small circle at the input.

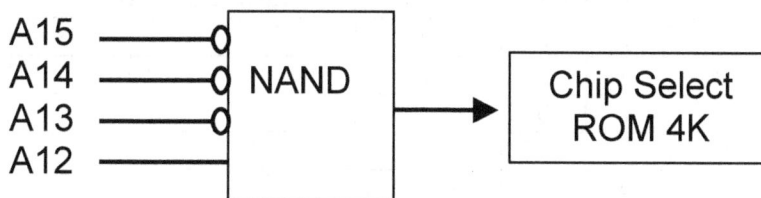

Figure 8.10. 4K ROM decoder circuit 1000h to 17FFh

Decoding the 8 K RAM chip

A similar approach is taken to decode the 8K. The only difference is in the starting address being rather unusual. Namely it is much easier to decode with addresses that start at hexadecimal numbers in the high order bits only, i.e. it is easier to decode starting at 1000h, 2000h, 3000h, then say at 1800h, 2800h, 3800h etc, as is the case here. Nevertheless, the procedure will be performed with these numbers.

Thus, looking at Table 8.2 (segment reproduced below) in the 8K of RAM starting at 1800h the bits that are not changing between the Start and End addresses are address bits A14-A15.

Close scrutiny of Table 8.2 shows that bits A11-A13 are changing but there may be some restrictions. In fact the only bits that are definitely allowed to change are A0-A10. For convenience, these are highlighted in grey below.

Address Bits	$2^{15}2^{14}2^{13}2^{12}$	$2^{11}2^{10}2^{9}2^{8}$	$2^{7}2^{6}2^{5}2^{4}$	$2^{3}2^{2}2^{1}2^{0}$	Size	
1800h(Start)	0001	1000	0000	0000	8k	RAM
37FFh(End)	0011	0111	1111	1111		

Thus to decode the second chip, the address lines A15, A14, A13, A12 and A11 need to be used in the decoder. A15 and A14 can go directly into a NAND gate, because they do not change at all.

Bits A11-A13 need to take only the values that are within the range shown in the table, that is any 3 bit binary value between 011 and 110 (inclusive). No other combination of these three bits is allowed. To illustrate this let us construct a truth table for a three input gate, in all there are 8 possible combinations as shown in Table 8.3.

Table 8.3

A13	A12	A11	Decimal	Address in ROM?
0	0	0	0	N
0	0	1	1	N
0	1	0	2	N
0	1	1	3	Y
1	0	0	4	Y
1	0	1	5	Y
1	1	0	6	Y
1	1	1	7	N

The above truth table shows that between 011 and 110 there are other values for which the address is inside the ROM chip. The four addresses that are shaded in table 8.3 are all inside the chip and must be decoded. This can be arranged by a combination of 4 AND gates and an OR gate. The complete diagram for the decoder is shown in Figure 8.11. Notice that only inputs in the range 011 to 110 into the AND gates will result in a '1' out of the OR gate. The actual 3 bit value that each gate is designed to decode is included in the diagram.

The simple rule for constructing a decoder such as this is to look at the inputs to the NAND gate and ensure that all inputs are logical '1' for the gate to provide a logic '0' output to the chip select pin. Those input bits that are logic '0' therefore need to have an inverter before the NAND gate processes them. Thus for example as seen in Figure 8.11, input 011 has the inverter on the first bit only. This makes the NAND gate process 111 giving logic '0' at the output. This output is fed into the chip select pin of the device that is located at this address.

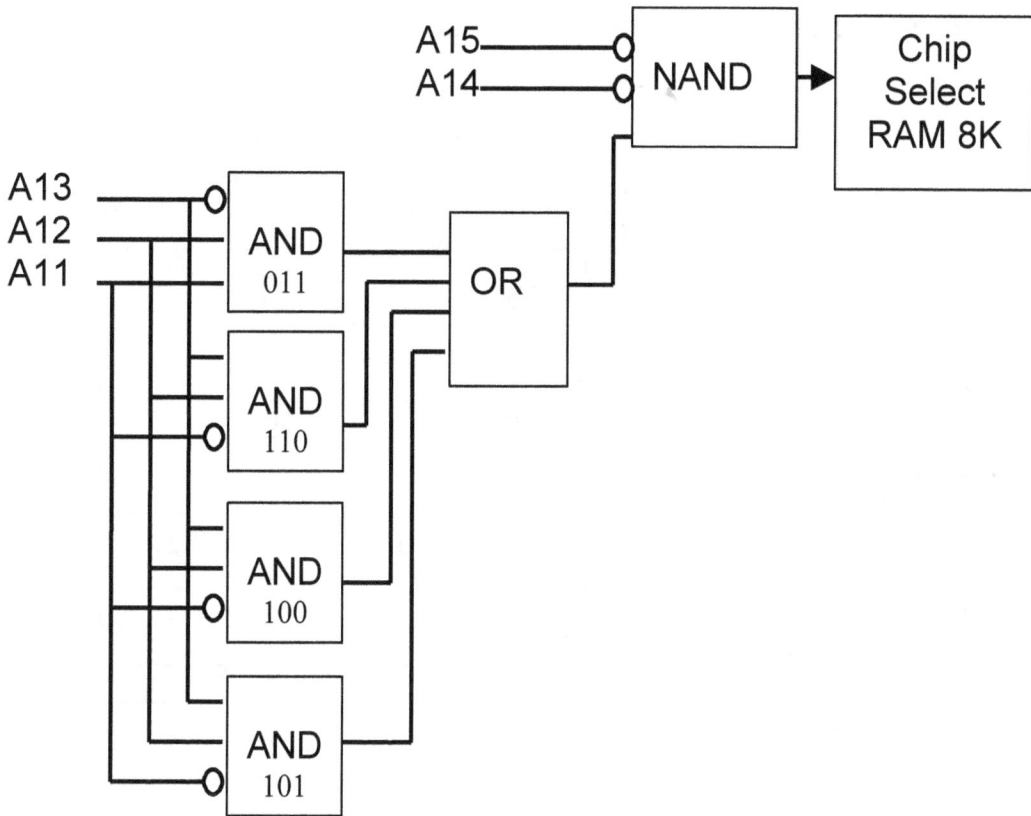

Figure 8.11. 8K RAM decoder circuit 1000h to 17FFh

Decoding the 16K ROM chip

A very similar approach is taken to decode the 16K. Thus, looking at Table 8.2 (segment reproduced below) in the 16K of RAM starting at 3800h the only bit that is not changing between the Start and End addresses is address bit A15. Close scrutiny of Table 8.2 shows that bits A11-A14 are changing but as before there may be some restrictions.

Address Bits	$2^{15}2^{14}2^{13}2^{12}$	$2^{11}2^{10}2^{9}2^{8}$	$2^{7}2^{6}2^{5}2^{4}$	$2^{3}2^{2}2^{1}2^{0}$	Size	
3800h(Start)	0011	1000	0000	0000	16k	ROM
77FFh(End)	0111	0111	1111	1111		

Thus to decode this chip, the address lines A15, A14, A13, A12 and A11 need to be used in the decoder. A15 can go directly into a NAND gate, because it does not change at all. Bits A11-A14 need to take only the values that are shown in the table that is any 4 bit binary value between 0111 and 1110 (inclusive). No other combination of these four bits is allowed. To illustrate this

217

let us construct a truth table for a four input gate, in all there are 16 possible combinations.

Table 8.4

A14	A13	A12	A11	Decimal	Address in ROM?
0	0	0	0	0	N
0	0	0	1	1	N
0	0	1	0	2	N
0	0	1	1	3	N
0	1	0	0	4	N
0	1	0	1	5	N
0	1	1	0	6	N
0	1	1	1	7	Y
1	0	0	0	8	Y
1	0	0	1	9	Y
1	0	1	0	10	Y
1	0	1	1	11	Y
1	1	0	0	12	Y
1	1	0	1	13	Y
1	1	1	0	14	Y
1	1	1	1	15	N

The truth table shows that between 0111 and 1110 there are other values for which the address is inside the ROM chip. The eight addresses that are shaded in Table 8.4 are all inside the chip and must be decoded. This can be arranged by a combination of 8 AND gates and an OR gate. The complete diagram for the decoder is shown in Figure 8.12. In this diagram each of the AND gates show the binary 4-bit configuration that they are set to allow.

The decoder arrangement of Figure 8.12 looks very cumbersome but it has to be said that is only used to illustrate the principle and it would not normally occur in practice. This is to say that the designer would normally choose starting addresses such that these single bit decoders are avoided.

To make the decoder easier to implement the designer could choose more suitable starting addresses for the chips. The choice would be constrained by the condition that there is no memory overlap. For example the choice of starting addresses of 1000h, 2000h and 4000h, for the 4K, 8K and 16K chips would be suitable. This is because the 4K would not extend into the 8K range starting at 2000h, because it would end at 17FFh. Similarly, the 8K starting at address 2000h, would end at address 3FFFh, which is outside the range of 4000h.

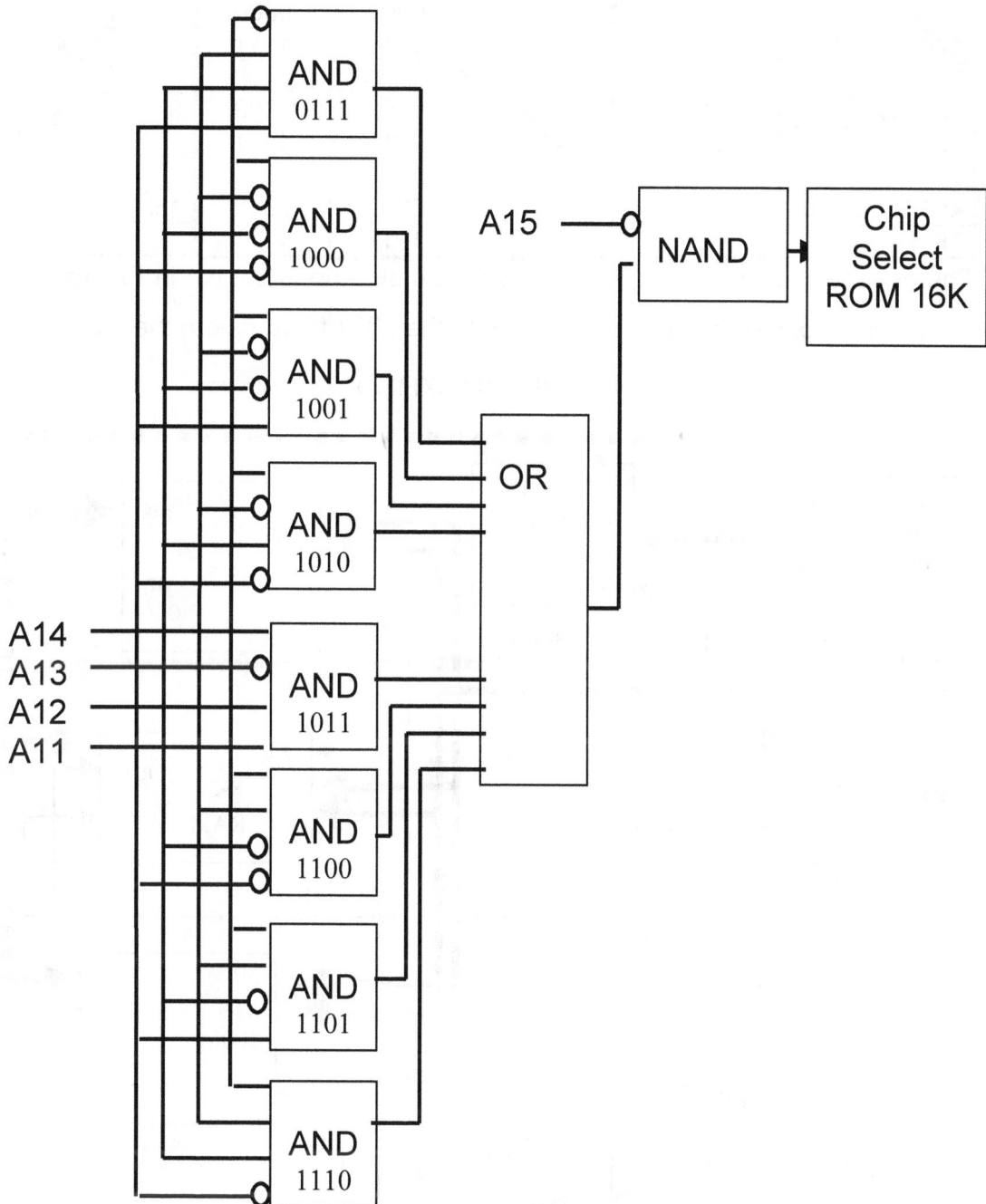

Figure 8.12. 16K ROM decoder circuit

Thus reworking the memory map given in this example with the new start addresses for the three of 1000h, 2000h and 4000h, the address range would be as given in Table 8.5

Table 8.5

Address Bits	$2^{15}2^{14}2^{13}2^{12}$	$2^{11}2^{10}2^{9}2^{8}$	$2^{7}2^{6}2^{5}2^{4}$	$2^{3}2^{2}2^{1}2^{0}$	Size	
1000h(Start)	0001	0000	0000	0000		
17FFh(End)	0001	0111	1111	1111	4k	ROM
2000(Start)	0010	0000	0000	0000	8k	RAM
3FFFh(End)	0011	1111	1111	1111		
4000(Start)	0100	0000	0000	0000	16k	ROM
7FFFh(End)	0111	1111	1111	1111		

The decoder for this arrangement is very simple and is shown in Figure 8.13, which also includes the interface details to the 8051 to complete the example.

MULTIPLEXED DATA BUS

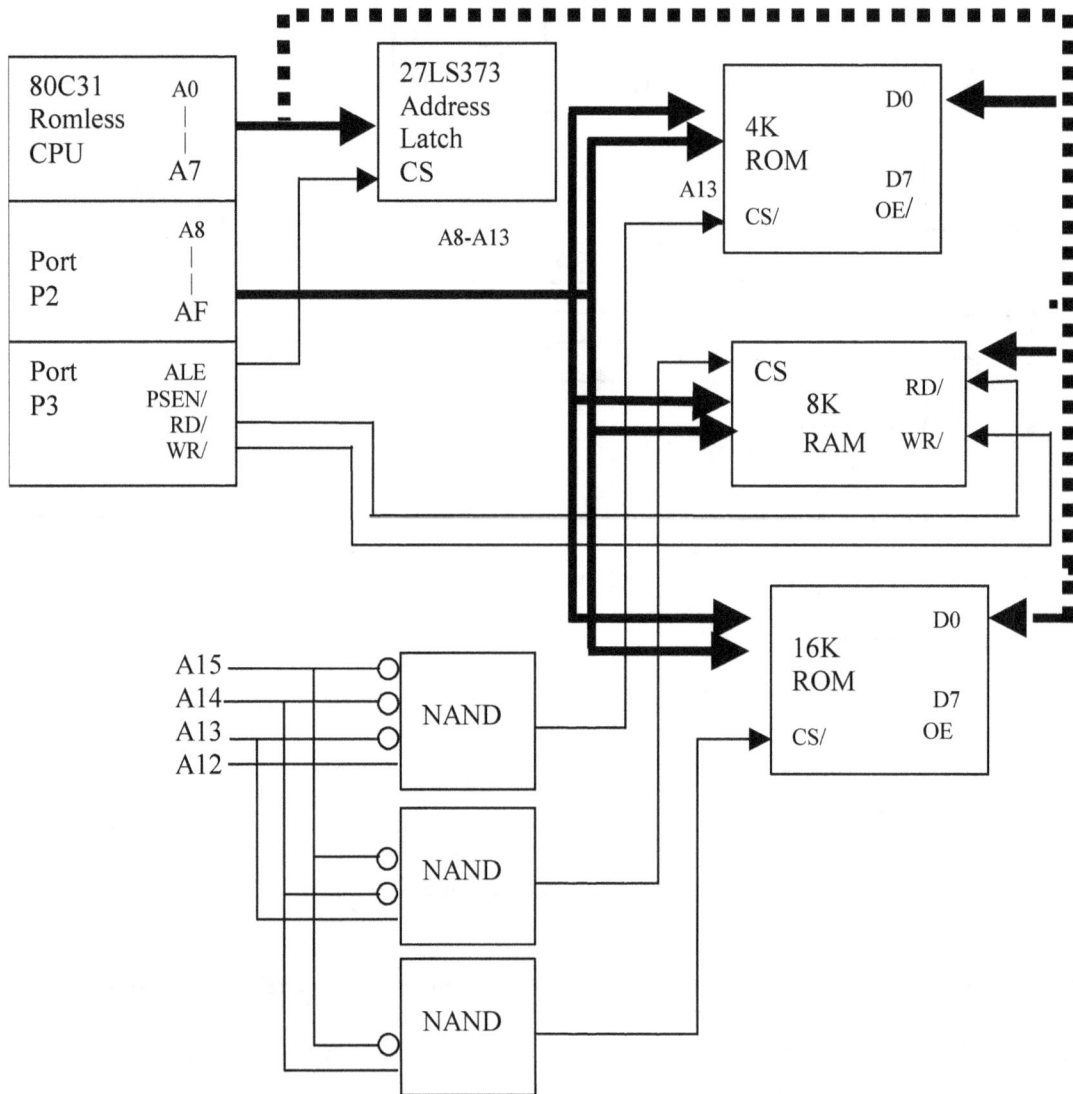

Figure 8.13 decoder with a suitable choice of start addresses

Examples

8.1 What are the two main points that need to be observed when designing an I/O interface to the computer?

8.2 Explain giving examples how the following electronic components are used when interfacing to computers. Amplifies, Opto-isolators, A-D and D-A converters, Schmitt Triggers, Hex-Buffers, EMI screens.

8.3 Within EMI compatibility considerations, distinguish between designs to limit the EMI emissions as opposed to design to control susceptibility to EMI.

8.4 How does the resolution of an A/D converter impact on accuracy? Provide example calculations.

8.5 You are measuring current in the range of 0-100mA. You need to be accurate to within 1 part-per-million. What resolution of the A/D converter would you need to use?

8.6 You have an 8-bit DAC and you are using it to convert a triangular waveform with amplitude of $5V$ peak at a frequency of $1KHz$. What is the maximum absolute accuracy of amplitude measurement in Volts? What would you consider to be a suitable sampling time?

8.7 You want to drive a dc motor from a microcontroller. You need to provide speed control and also motor reversal. The motor is permanent magnet device and has a rated current of $0.5A$. How would you go about interfacing the drive to the commuter?

8.8 You are using a 16-bit A/D converter to measure temperature in the range 0-100 degrees Celsius. What would be the binary value that represents a temperature of 87 degrees?

8.9 Distinguish between partial and full address decoding and compare their application areas.

8.10 What are PROM decoders and how are they used?

8.11 You need to design a decoder circuit to interface a Timer chip (8253) and a ROM chip with 32K of ROM. You have a 16-bit address bus. How would you deign a decoder to allocate the required memory space?

CHAPTER 9 SENSORS

9.1. Transducers

A transducer is a device that takes energy from the system that it measures to give an output signal that can be transformed to an electrical signal and that corresponds to the measured quantity. The trend in terminology is to use the term 'Sensor' for an input transducer and 'Actuator' for output transducers. A transducer whose output energy is supplied entirely by its input signal is termed 'passive' and one in which the energy is derived from an external source is termed 'active'. For example, sensors based on resistive, capacitive and inductive elements are passive because they do not require external power supply to manifest a response to the input signal. On the other hand, sensors based on semiconductors such as transistors, op-amts etc all require external power and are called active devices.

When designing systems, which rely on measurement, there are several important considerations, which need to be taken into account when choosing sensors for a particular application,

- Sensitivity
- Accuracy and linearity
- Repeatability
- Reliability
- Cost

Sensitivity

These can be explained by considering a typical transducer input /output system as shown in Figure 9.1. Here the inputs comprise three different components. The desired signal (Sd), the noise associated with the input (Sn) and the manipulation of the signal (Sm). All three combine to provide the output of the transducer system. The functions f (S_n, S_m) and g (S_d, S_m) describe the conversion process that transforms the input signal to the appropriate output.

- The noise input Sn represents any unwanted signals to which the sensor is responsive. (i.e. f (Sn..)
- The modifying stimulus Sm represents external signals that can cause the response of the transducer to alter. (i.e. f (Sm.)
- These signals affect both the true signal Sd and the noise signal Sn. (i.e. g (Sd..).
- The sensitivity of the transducer is defined as the rate of change of output signal So as the desired input signal varies. This is given by equation 9.1.

$$\frac{dS_o}{dS_d} = K + \frac{dS_n}{dS_d} + \frac{dS_m}{dS_d} \qquad (9.1)$$

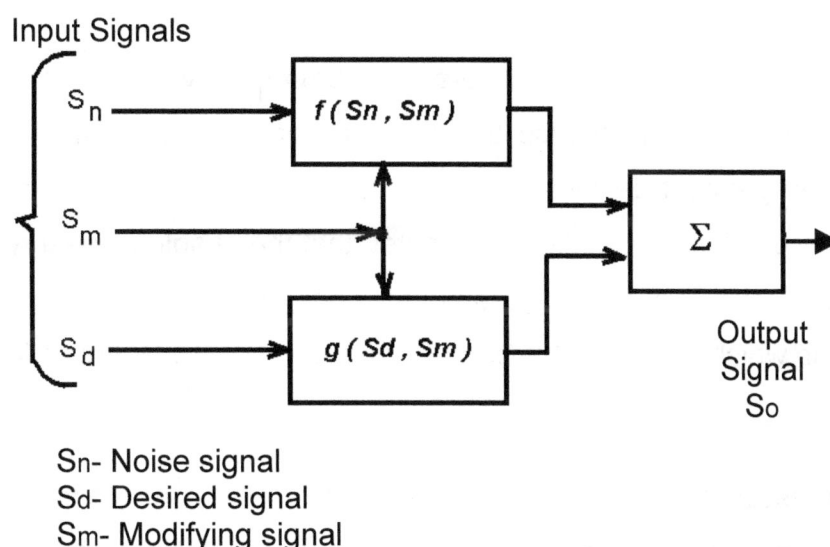

Figure 9.1 Sensor signal components

Accuracy and linearity

The ability to maintain accuracy over the entire measurement range is governed by the linearity of the system, that is to say, how nearly is the response directly proportional to the stimulus? A common method of specifying a linear transducer is by reference to an average calibration curve, which is taken as the best fit through the set of points relating input to output (see Figure 9.2)

223

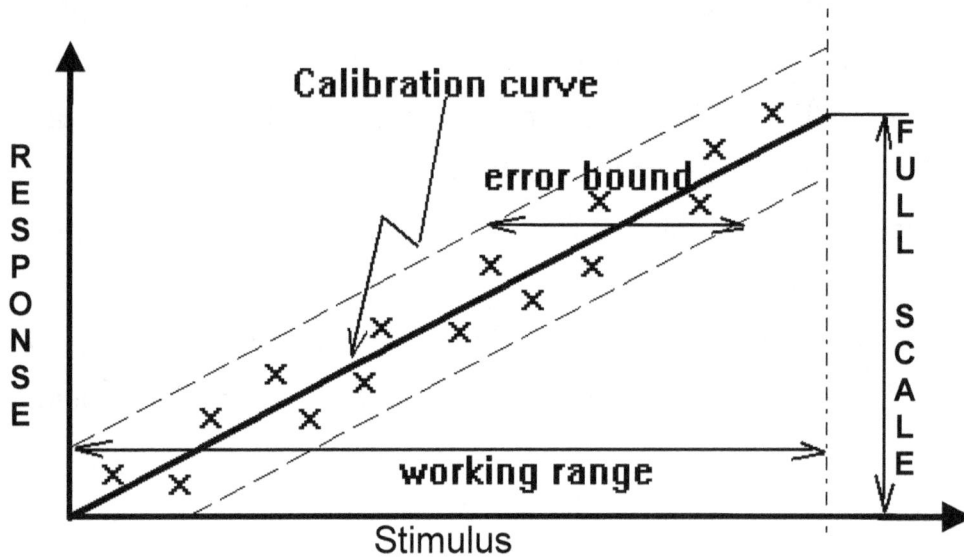

Figure 9.2 Average calibration curve

In engineering practice the accuracy of an instrument is defined in terms of the greatest deviation from the calibration line, which is quoted as a percentage of full-scale reading. In is noted that the absolute linearity of sensor response to stimulus is not paramount since at times a highly non-linear relationship which is predictable can be very useful. (i.e. hysteresis loop)

Repeatability

In essence repeatability is a measure of how consistent is the sensor data during a change in the operating conditions. It is defined as the error band expressing the ability of the transducer to reproduce an output signal, at specified values of the sensor variable (i.e. pressure, temperature etc), after exposure to any other pressure and temperature within the specified range.

Reliability

Reliability of a transducer is defined in terms of the period of time over which it continues to perform accurately. This assessment is normally quoted in statistical terms and is given as a confidence factor that the transducer will perform as required. This confidence factor is often given as 'mean time to failure' (MTTF) defined over total period of use. In design terminology this is considered to be a reliability metric and can be defined by equation 9.2.

$$MTTF = \frac{Sum\ of\ all\ failures + (number\ of\ survivors\ x\ period\ of\ use)}{Total\ number\ of\ failures}$$
$$(9.2)$$

Example

Consider the example of an industrial situation where a large number of pressure transducers of a given type A are installed. Fault reporting has found that over a 1000-hour period, 25 transducers work satisfactorily throughout, one failed after 600 hours, another after 15 hours and another failed after only 5 hours. Therefore for the Type A pressure sensor, the MTTF as given by equation (9.2) can be calculated as follows,

$$MTTF = \frac{(5)+(15)+(600)+(25000)}{3} = 8540\ hrs$$

This means that for the Type A pressure sensor, we can expect a failure rate of 1 in 8540 hrs of use. This needs to be built into the design when the sensor is planned for use. In some cases this failure may not be acceptable and an alternative needs to be selected. Another useful reliability metric is the mean time between failures (MTBF), which is given by equation 9.3.

$$MTBF = \frac{total\ period\ of\ use\ of\ the\ device}{Total\ number\ of\ failures}\ (9.3)$$

These serve to illustrate the general concept and the reader is directed to other literature on reliability metrics for additional information.

Cost and limits of accurate sensing

The cost of sensing equipment depends largely on the type of sensing that is required and also the accuracy that needs to be satisfied. For example a temperature sensor for a central heating system will not be as complex or as accurate as a temperature sensor measuring the change in temperature in a nuclear facility, where a fractional change in temperature needs to be detected. For example, a typical product on the market today is the air temperature sensor OMC-443 from Observator. [53]

This sensor provides an accurate measurement of temperature using a platinum Pt100 sensing element. It features a build-in amplifier that can feed a 4...20 mA output. This corresponds to a temperature range of −40 to +60 deg. C. The accuracy is given as < ± 0.3°C, repeatability < ± 0.1°C and at the time of writing the retail price of this sensor in the U.K. is £350. On the other end of the retail price scale at £2 in the UK, is the LM335Z sensor from Maplin electronics. This is a semiconductor device that has a breakdown voltage directly proportional to absolute ambient temperature and has a linear output equal to 10mV/ C. The device operates over a current range of 400µA to 5mA (1mA recommended) and even when not calibrated it has a typical temperature error of only 2° C over its operating range. When calibrated the error is 1° C. With suitable interfacing electronics, this device could be useful in many temperature measurement applications.

These are just examples, but it is evident that a wide range of accuracy and cost are available, but in general it can be said that, the more accurate the more expensive. In recent times embedded microcontrollers have been used to provide real-time control to sensing equipment. This in turn increases the capabilities of the sensor and also the cost.

9.2.   Sensor types

Resistance transducers

Resistance transducers are very common in industry since they can be adapted to a wide range of sensor applications. Typically, these devices rely on a potential divider circuit with a high quality wire-wound potentiometer, which have a linearity of ±0.25%. The most accurate types are based on a bridge circuit with resistance standards used to balance the bridge. These will not be considered here and instead only a simple potentiometer circuit will be considered. Table 9.1 shows some common application of resistance transducers.

Table 9.1

Device	Description	Application
Light Dependent Resistor	Resistance falls with increasing light level	Light operated controls, smoke detection,
Thermistor	Resistance falls with increased temperature	Electronic thermometers
Strain gauge	Resistance changes with force	Automotive sensing
Moisture detector	Resistance falls when wet	Moisture detection

A typical arrangement of a potential divider circuit is shown in Figure 9.3.

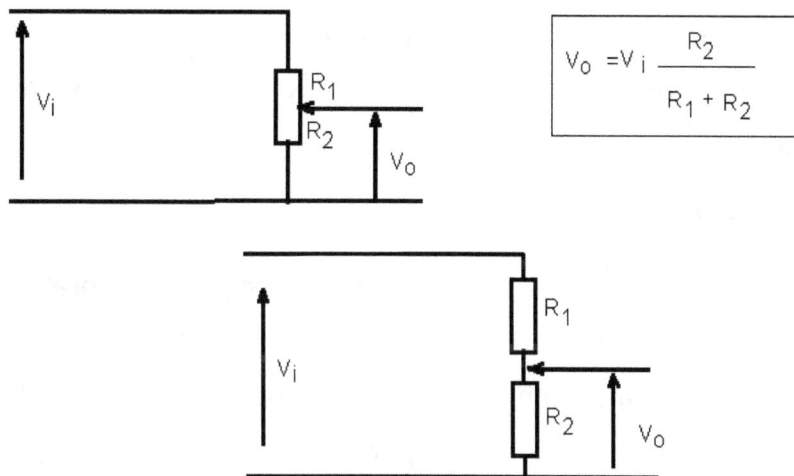

Figure 9.3. A simple potentiometer circuit

It is seen from Figure 9.3 that the output voltage is related to the input voltage by an equation involving resistances R_1 and R_2. Typically one of these will be the known resistance and the other would be the unknown sensor resistance value. In a measurement situation the unknown resistance can be calculated by measuring V_{in} and V_{out} and using equation 9.4

$$\frac{V_o}{Vi} = \frac{R_2}{R_1 + R_2} \quad (9.4)$$

Current sensors

Typical current sensors consist of a Hall-effect sensor mounted in an air gap of a magnetic core, a coil wound around the core and a current amplifier. [54] The current carrying conductor placed through the aperture of the sensor produces a magnetic field that is proportional to the current. The core concentrates the magnetic field, which is measured by the Hall sensor. The Hall sensor is connected to the input of the current amplifier, which drives the coil. The current through the coil produces an opposing field to that provided by the current through the aperture. The magnetic flux in the sensor core is constantly controlled at zero. The amount of current required to balance zero flux is the measure of the primary current flowing through the conductor, multiplied by the number of turns on the coil. This current can be expressed as a voltage by passing it through a resistor.

Current sensors are used in applications requiring high linearity and accuracy, fast response and low temperature drift such as variable speed drives, over current protection, current feedback control systems, robotics and welding power supplies.

Temperature sensing

In the present day the most common types of temperature-sensitive transducers are the Thermistor based devices. Thermistor devices are cheap and reasonably accurate with relatively fast response times. Thermistors provide an inexpensive means of temperature measurement and are widely used in control systems where a high degree of accuracy is not required. Because they have a non-linear characteristic they are often used in conjunction with a microprocessor controller, which is programmed to account for the non-linearity. Knowing the equation constants, accurate values can be obtained by means of a look-up table or on-line approximation algorithms.

Thermistors

The term Thermistor is derived from 'thermally sensitive resistor' and applies to temperature dependent resistors that are based on semiconductors. [55] Their operation is based on the variation in the number of charge carriers in a semiconductor with the change in temperature. This means that they normally have a negative temperature coefficient. (i.e., when temperature increases the number of charge carriers increases and resistance decreases).

This dependence varies with impurities and when the doping is very heavy, the semiconductor achieves metallic properties, which yields a positive temperature coefficient. Thus it is seen that Thermistors can have either a positive or a negative temperature coefficient, i.e., PTC and NTC respectively. The majority of Thermistors used in sensing have negative temperature coefficients of about 4%. Resistance values at 25° C range from about 100 Ω to 25 kΩ, although resistance of 500 kΩ are available.

One possible arrangement for connecting the Thermistor to a measurement circuit is to use a bridge as shown in Figure 9.4. The bridge component values determine the output voltage range and are in general, chosen to give good linearity with reasonable sensitivity. The equation relating the input voltage to the output voltage in terms of the residences in the bridge arms is given by equation 9.6.

$$V_o = V_i [\frac{1}{1 + \frac{R_t}{R_3}} - \frac{1}{1 + \frac{R_2}{R_1}}]$$

(9.6)

Equation 9.6 can be used to calculate the unknown R_t when the bridge is balanced and when all the other resistances are known.

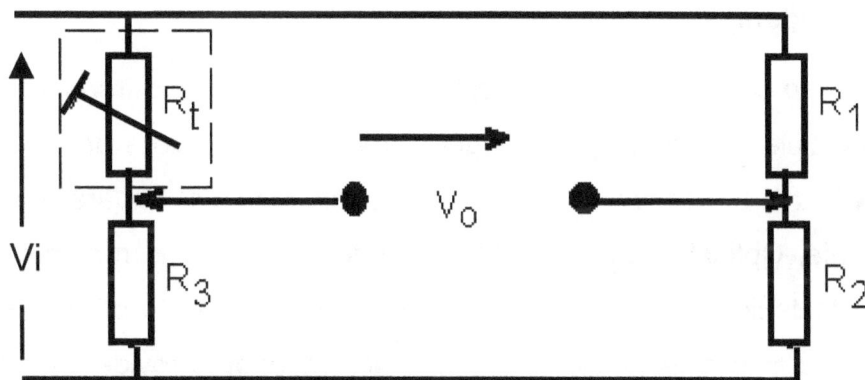

Figure 9.4 Simple bridge circuit to measure resistance

9.3. Sensor equipment examples

The sensor market in the industrial applications is huge by any standards. A large number of manufacturers provide a variety of sensing equipment and many companies provide bespoke sensor design. Very complex sensing equipment includes digital signal processing software and hardware so that the complete sensing solution is provided. The various categories and types are as follows.

Position	Speed	Temperature	Force
Potentiometer	Derivative of position	Thermocouple	Strain gauges
Rotary and Optical encoders	Range of differentiated position sensors	Resistance thermometer	Piezoelectric materials
Capacitive and inductive proximity sensors	Tacho-generators	Thermistors	Position sensors where
Phase and amplitude modulated sensors			Displacement is proportional to force

Example sensor products include pressure sensors, signal transmitters, submersible level sensors and customised pressure sensing systems from 1 mbar up to 1000 bar as well as liquid level switches, oxygen and other gas, colour sensors, flow and force sensors, torque sensors etc. Some examples of products on the market today are presented next.

Rotary encoders

These can be inductive or optical devices. Inductive transducers work on the principle of detecting a change in magnetic flux. Coils are arranged in such a way that the sensor is able to detect flux changes that are proportional to the angle. Optical encoders utilise a slotted disc that is rotating, and the sensor detects light passing through the slots. Compared to other systems of angle measurement, like inclinometers, rotary encoders provide a comparably high measuring frequency and a constant precision over the full measuring range, which extends beyond 360°. [56] Resolution Per Revolution up to 16 Bit (65536 Steps).

Air quality sensors

A very large number of air quality sensors are available on the market. These vary in cost and sensitivity as well as the gas that they are designed to sense. For example, the AMS gas sensor module is factory pre-calibrated for usage in conjunction with control microprocessors. [57]

This module is composed of gas sensor and a load resistor on a PCB, and three lead wires as shown in Figure 9.5. Because of its wide sensitivity spectrum and low power consumption, this sensor is ideal for the detection of indoor air pollution, which is caused by cigarette smoke, cooking fumes, etc. This module enables users to create a low cost indoor air monitor by eliminating the need for a sophisticated calibration process. Connections are simple and shown in Figure 9.5

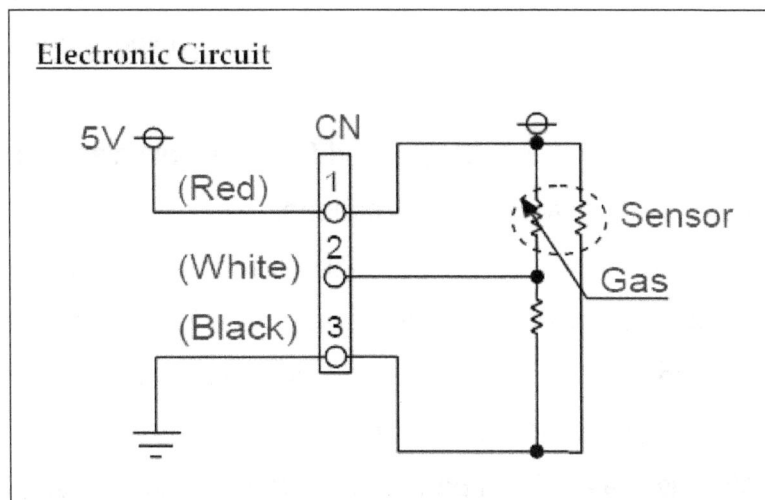

Figure 9.5 Air quality sensor circuit

Tachogenerators

These devices are used to measure speed because they generate a voltage that is proportional to their rotational speed. They can be d.c or a.c excited and come with a variety of characteristics. For example, Precilec offer a wide range of d.c and ac Tachogenerators. These sensors are arranged in a variety of enclosures and frame sizes and also with various electrical characteristics. For example, voltages between 2V and 6000V at rotating speeds ranging from 1000 rpm up to 12,000 rpm. [58]

Pressure sensing

A piezoelectric material generates an electric charge when mechanically deformed. Conversely, when an external electric field is applied to piezoelectric materials they mechanically deform. They are therefore used in sensing mechanical force and consequently pressure and torque depending on the application. Example piezoelectric material includes quartz, some ceramic materials, living bone, etc. In general, piezoelectric materials are classified into types ranging from Hard to Soft depending on how much excitation they produce in the presence of an external force. Four types are commonly identified, Type I to Type IV, namely,

Type I: These are hard material. High power or "hard" ceramics can withstand high levels of electrical excitation and mechanical stress. These materials are suited for high voltage or high power generators and transducers.

Type II: This material is ideally suited for ultrasonic cleaning, sonar, and other high power acoustic radiation applications.

Type III: This material is used in high power applications, even though its piezoelectric activity level is slightly lower than Type II devices. With an extremely high mechanical quality and extremely low loss factor, these materials have the ultimate power handling capability.

Type IV: This material is a barium titanate ceramic that is still used for a variety of sonar and specialized transducer applications. [59]

Board level, or PCB-mountable pressure sensors are available that use piezoelectric technology to produce an electrical signal that is proportional to the applied pressure. Applications of these sensors include pressure sensing in air and in non-corrosive gases for pressure ranges from 1 to 500 PSI. Board level sensors are used for medical applications, airflow, HVAC, leak detection and other test and industrial applications. [60]

Capacitive sensors

Capacitive sensors use the electrical property of "capacitance" to make measurements. These are no contact devices capable of high-resolution measurement of the position and/or change of position of any conductive target. The nanometre resolution of high-performance capacitive sensors makes them indispensable in today's nanotechnology world. They can also be used to measure the position or other properties of nonconductive targets.

Capacitive sensors use the electrical property of "capacitance" to make measurements. Capacitance is a property that exists between any two conductive surfaces within some reasonable proximity. A change in the distance between the surfaces changes the capacitance. It is this change of capacitance that capacitive sensors use to indicate changes in position of a target. High-performance displacement sensors use small sensing surfaces and as result are positioned close to the targets (0.25-2mm). [61] An example of a proximity sensor based on capacitance is available from Capacitec. [62]

Capacitive sensors detect the change in capacitance caused by the approach of an object in their electrostatic field. These sensors find broad use in sensing metals, plastics, or liquids and are used extensively in applications involving packaging, and liquid level sensing. Another example of capacitive sensor applications is the Humidity and Temperature Transmitters for use in air-conditioning systems. [63] Here capacitive humidity sensors are used to guarantee of high long-term stability, resistance to dew formation, small hysteresis and good dynamic performance.

Inductive sensors

An inductive sensor uses the magnetic field as the medium to detect metallic objects without touching them. A typical transducer would incorporate the electronics that set up an induction loop, which is very sensitive to the presence of metallic materials. That is to say, the inductance of the loop changes according to the material inside it and since metals are much more effective inductors than other materials the presence of metal increases the current flowing through the loop. This change can be detected by sensing circuitry, which can signal to some other device whenever metal is detected.

Common applications of inductive sensors include metal detectors, traffic lights, car washes, and a host of automated industrial processes. Because the sensor does not require physical contact it is particularly useful for applications where access presents challenges or where dirt is prevalent. The sensing range is rarely greater than 6cm, however, and it has no directionality. [64]

Exercises

9.1 Distinguish between Active and Passive transducers.

9.2 What characteristics need to be taken into consideration when using a transducer in embedded applications? Describe these characteristics and give some examples of where these characteristics may be very important.

9.3 Discuss how embedded controllers can be used with transducers to develop sophisticated sensing devices.

9.4 Explain the principle of operation of resistance transducers and discuss typical applications.

9.5 Explain how potential divider circuits can be used in resistance measurement. Show how you could use a temperature sensitive resistor in such a circuit to measure temperature. In this case, explain what sensor characteristic is necessary before you can use it.

9.6 What are Hall-effect transducers and how are they used?

9.7 Explain how Thermistors work and show a typical configuration of a temperature measurement application.

9.8 Explain how Thermistors can be used in bridge circuits to measure temperature.

9.9 Explain how a piezoelectric material is used in sensing devices.

9.10 What are the main types of piezoelectric materials and what are their typical applications?

9.11 Discuss the principle of operation of Tachogenerators and where they can be used as sensing devices.

9.12 Do a quick literature survey to find out more about sensors detecting air quality, including smoke detectors. Write a brief summary of the common sensor types.

9.13 Explain the principle of operation of capacitive sensors. Suggest possible applications.

9.14 Explain the principle of operation of inductive sensors. Suggest possible applications.

REFERENCES

Note: All websites accessed between Nov 2007 and Feb 2008.

[1] MIPS Technologies http://www.mips.com/company/about-us/
[2] Intel, www.intel.com
[3] Power Macintosh: L1 and L2 Cache Explained.
http://docs.info.apple.com/article.html?artnum=14750
[4] XDR™ Memory Architecture. http://www.rambus.com/us/products/xdr_xdr2/index.html
[5] Wikipedia, http://en.wikipedia.org/wiki/Compiler_optimisation
[6] [Idle Time Power Management for Personal Wireless Devices, Nevine AbouGhazaleh,
Robert N. Mayo, Parthasarathy Ranganathan, Mobile and Media Systems Laboratory, HP
Laboratories Palo Alto, HPL-2003-102, September 17th , 2003]
http://www.hpl.hp.com/techreports/2003/HPL-2003-102.pdf
[7] http://www.dspdesign.com/products/index_html?category_id=55
[8] http://www.embeddedstar.com/press/content/2003/5/embedded8849.html
[9] A 2000-MOPS embedded RISC processor with a Rambus DRAM controller
Suzuki, K.; Daito, M.; Inoue, T.; Nadehara, K.; Nomura, M.; Mizuno, M.; Iima, T.; Sato, S.;
Fukuda, T.; Arai, T.; Kuroda, I.; Yamashina, M.
IEEE Journal of Solid-State Circuits, Volume 34, Issue 7, Jul 1999 Page(s):1010 - 1021
Digital Object Identifier 10.1109/4.772417]
http://ieeexplore.ieee.org/Xplore/login.jsp?url=/iel5/4/16778/00772417.pdf
[10] Time-Based ISDN/Async (Legacy) DDR.
 http://www.embeddedintel.com/news.php?article=363
[11] www.hindawi.com/journals/ES/si/0022008003.pdf
[12] Basic concepts of real-time operating systems, by David Kalinsky (Nov. 18, 2003)
 http://linuxdevices.com/articles/AT4627965573.html
[13] www.keil.com
[14] www.tenasys.com
[15] SAP enterprise software.
http://www.sap.com
[16] Application programming definition.
http://en.wikipedia.org/wiki/Application_programming
[17] David Solomon, Mark Russinovich, Windows Internals and Advanced Troubleshooting
Tutorial.
[18] http://en.wikipedia.org/wiki/Joint_Test_Action_Group
[19]
http://www.goepel.com/content/html_en/index.php?site=bs_tutorial&level1=scan&level2=bs_tu
torial
[20] http://www.eembc.org/press/pressrelease/020513.htm
[21]
http://www.analog.com/processors/blackfin/?sourceid=goo_dsp+search_blackfin+processor_bl
ackfin_subcat_ptab
[22] Embedded RISC Processor Selection, February 1993 Benchmark,by Daniel Mann,
Advanced Micro Devices http://www.amd.com/epd/?9k/select_an/select_an.pdf
[23] http://www.arm.com/
[24] http://www.amd.com/gb-uk/
[25] http://www.freescale.com/
[26] http://www-306.ibm.com/chips/index.html
[27] www.sun.com
[28] http://focus.ti.com/docs/prod/folders/print/msp430c314.html
[29] http://www.transmeta.com/corporate/index.html
[30] http://www.atmel.com/products/AT91/]

[31] mcs51 user manual

[32] Kernighan and Richie C programming textbook

[33] http://www.ansi.org/

[34] LTL ltd Procedural programming in C

[35] C51 primer

[36]] R. Haggarty, Discrete mathematics for computing, Pearson Education Limited,, 2002

[37] G. Bollinger, N. A. Duffie, Computer Control of Machines and Processes,Addisin-Wesley, 1981

[38] http://people.revoledu.com/kardi/tutorial/DifferenceEquation/WhatIsDifferenceEquation.htm

[39] C. L. Phillips, R. D. Harbor Feedback Control Systems, Prentice Hall International, Inc, 4 edition, 10 April 2000.

[40] R. Aris, Mathematical Modelling Techniques, Dover Publications Inc.; New Ed edition, Oct 1994.]

[41] R.C. Dorf, R. H Bishop, Modern Control Systems, Pearson Education; 10 edition, 20 May 2004

[42] A.J. Stubberud, I. J. Williams, J. J. DiStefano, Feedback and Control Systems, Second Edition, Schaum's Outlines; 2 edition, 1 Sep 1995.

[43] http://www.embedded.com

[44] S. Bennet, Real-time Computer Control: An Introduction, Pearson Education Limited (April 1988)

[45] http://focus.ti.com/lit/ds/symlink/l293d.pdf

[46] http://www.analog.com/UploadedFiles/Data_Sheets/AD7568.pdf

[47] http://www.rovingnetworks.com/documents/ADS8344.pdf

[48] http://www.fairchildsemi.com/an/AN/AN-140.pdf

[49] http://www.fairchildsemi.com/ds/MM%2FMM74HC14.pdf

[50] http://www.intersil.com/cda/deviceinfo/0,0,CD4049UBMS,0.html

[51] http://www.maxim-ic.com/appnotes.cfm/appnote_number/1167/

[52] http://www.maxim-ic.com/appnotes.cfm/appnote_number/1167/

[53] http://www.seawatersolutions.com/temperature-sensor-170-p.asp]

[54] http://www.directindustry.com/prod/honeywell-sensing-and-control/closed-loop-current-sensor-12365-118644.html

[55] http://www.doctronics.co.uk/voltage.htm#temperature

[56] http://www.directindustry.com/prod/fraba-posital/absolute-rotary-encoder-15172-207044.html

[57] http://www.sensorsandtransmitters.com/pdfs/ams2600.pdf

[58] http://www.precilec.com

[59] http://www.morganelectroceramics.com/piezomaterials/pzmat2.html

[60] http://www.directindustry.com/cat/detectors-sensors-transducers/pressure-sensors-pressure-switches-AB-115.html

[61] http://www.lionprecision.com/tech-library/technotes/cap-0020-sensor-theory.html

[62] http://www.directindustry.com/prod/capacitec/capacitive-proximity-sensor-15734-210082.html

[63]http://www.directindustry.com/prod/galltec-mess-und-regeltechnik/capacitive-humidity-and-temperature-transmitter-28234-263565.html

[64] http://en.wikipedia.org/wiki/Inductive_sensor

APPENDIX

MCS-51   Assembly instructions

The tables that follow are assembled from the Intel user manual and they should be fairly self explanatory. For additional information you can access the instruction set on the KEIL website [13] for the Instruction Set as follows:

ACALL: Absolute Call

ADD, ADDC: Add Accumulator (With Carry)

AJMP: Absolute Jump

ANL: Bitwise AND

CJNE: Compare and Jump if Not Equal

CLR: Clear Register

CPL: Complement Register

DA: Decimal Adjust

DEC: Decrement Register

DIV: Divide Accumulator by B

DJNZ: Decrement Register and Jump if Not Zero

INC: Increment Register

JB: Jump if Bit Set

JBC: Jump if Bit Set and Clear Bit

JC: Jump if Carry Set

JMP: Jump to Address

JNB: Jump if Bit Not Set

JNC: Jump if Carry Not Set

JNZ: Jump if Accumulator Not Zero

JZ: Jump if Accumulator Zero

LCALL: Long Call

LJMP: Long Jump

MOV: Move Memory

MOVC: Move Code Memory

MOVX: Move Extended Memory

MUL: Multiply Accumulator by B

NOP: No Operation

ORL: Bitwise OR

POP: Pop Value From Stack

PUSH: Push Value Onto Stack

RET: Return From Subroutine

RETI: Return From Interrupt

RL: Rotate Accumulator Left

RLC: Rotate Accumulator Left Through Carry

RR: Rotate Accumulator Right

RRC: Rotate Accumulator Right Through Carry

SETB: Set Bit

SJMP: Short Jump

SUBB: Subtract From Accumulator With Borrow

SWAP: Swap Accumulator Nibbles

XCH: Exchange Bytes

XCHD: Exchange Digits

XRL: Bitwise Exclusive OR

Mnemonic ©Intel	Description	Bytes	Cycle
ADD A, R	Add register to A	1	1.
ADD A, @R	Add data memory to A	1	1
ADD A, #data	Add immediate to A	2	2
ADDC A, R	Add register with carry	1	1
ADDC A, @R	Add data memory with carry	1	1
ADDC A. #data	Add immediate with carry	2	2
ANL A, R	And register to A	1	1
ANL A, @R	And data memory to A	1	1
ANL A. #data	And immediate to A	2	2
ORL A, R	Or register to A	1	1
ORL A, @R	Or data memory to A	1	1
ORL A, #data	Or immediate to A	2	2
XRL A, R	Exclusive or register to A	1	1
XRL A, @R	Exclusive or data memory to A	1	1
XRL A. #data	Exclusive or immediate to A	2	2
INC A	Increment A	1	1
DEC A	Decrement A	1	1
CLR A	Clear A	1	1
CPL A	Complement A	1	1
DA A	Decimal adjust A	1	1
SWAP A	Swap nibbles of A	1	1
RL A	Rotate A left	1	1
RLC A	Rotate A left through carry	1	1
RR A	Rotate A right	1	1
RRC A	Rotate A right through carry	1	1
IN A, P	Input port to A	1	2
OUTL P, A	Output A to port	1	2
ANL P, #data	And immediate to port	2	2
ORL P, #data,	Or immediate to port	2	2
INS A, BUS	Input BUS to A	1	2
OUTL BUS, A	Output A to BUS	1	2
ANL BUS, #data	And immediate to BUS	2	2
ORL BUS, #data	Or immediate to BUS	2	2
MOVD A, P	Input expender port to A	1	2
MOVD P, A	Output A to expander port	1	2
ANLD P, A	And A to expander port	1	2
ORLD P, A	Or A to expander port	1	2
INC R	Increment register	1	1
INC @R	Increment data memory	1	1
DEC R	Decrement register	1	1
JMP addr	Jump unconditional	2	2
JMPP @A	Jump indirect	1	2
DJNZ R, addr	Decrement register and skip	2	2
JC addr	Jump on carry = 1	-	2
JNC addr	Jump on carry = 0	2	2
JZ addr	Jump on A zero	2	2
JNZ add,	Jump on A not zero	2	2
JT0 add,	Jump on TO = 1	2	2
JNT0 addr	Jump on TO = 0	2	2
JT1 addr	Jump on T1 = 1	2	2
JNT1 addr	Jump on T1 = 0 - -	2	2
JF0 addr	Jump on FO = 1	2	2
JF1 addr	Jump on F1 = 1	2	2

Mnemonic ©Intel	Description	Byte	Cycle
ADD A, R	Add register to A	1	1.
ADD A, @R	Add data memory to A	1	1
ADD A, #data	Add immediate to A	2	2
ADDC A, R	Add register with carry	1	1
ADDC A, @R	Add data memory with carry	1	1
ADDC A. #data	Add immediate with carry	2	2
ANL A, R	And register to A	1	1
ANL A, @R	And data memory to A	1	1
ANL A. #data	And immediate to A	2	2
ORL A, R	Or register to A	1	1
ORL A, @R	Or data memory to A	1	1
ORL A,#data	Or immediate to A	2	2
XRL A, R	Exclusive or register to A	1	1
XRL A, @R	Exclusive or data memory to A	1	1
XRL A. #data	Exclusive or immediate to A	2	2
INC A	Increment A	1	1
DEC A	Decrement A	1	1
CLR A	Clear A	1	1
CPL A	Complement A	1	1
DA A	Decimal adjust A	1	1
SWAP A	Swap nibbles of A	1	ˉ1
RL A	Rotate A left	1	1
RLC A	Rotate A left through carry	1	1
RR A	Rotate A right	1	1
RRC A	Rotate A right through carry	1	1
IN A, P	Input port to A	1	2
OUTL P, A	Output A to port	1	2
ANL P, #data	And immediate to port	2	2
ORL P, #data,	Or immediate to port	2	2
INS A, BUS	Input BUS to A	1	2
OUTL BUS, A	Output A to BUS	1	2
ANL BUS, #data	And immediate to BUS	2	2
ORL BUS,#data	Or immediate to BUS	2	2
MOVD A, P	Input expender port to A	1	2
MOVD P, A	Output A to expander port	1	2
ANLD P, A	And A to expander port	1	2
ORLD P, A	Or A to expander port	1	2
INC R	Increment register	1	1
INC @R	Increment data memory	1	1
DEC R	Decrement register	1	1
JMP addr	Jump unconditional	2	2
JMPP @A	Jump indirect	1	2
DJNZ R, addr	Decrement register and skip	2	2
JC addr	Jump on carry = 1	2	2

Mnemonic	Description	Bytes	Cycle
JTF addr	Jump on timer flag	2	2
JNI addr	Jump on FN -T = 0	2	2
JBb addr	Jump on accumulator bif	2	2
CALL addr	Jump to subroutine	2	2.
RET	Return	1	1
RETR	Return and restore status	1	2
CLR C	Clear carry	1	1
CPL C	Complement carry	1	2
CLR FO	Clear flag 0	1	1
CPL FO	Complement flag 0	1	1
CLR F1	Clear flag 1 -	1	2
CPL F1	Complement flag 1	1	1
MOV A, R	Move register to A..,..	1	1
MOV A, @R	Move data memory to A	1	1
MOV A, #data	Move immediate to A	2	2
MOV R, A	Move A to register	1	1
MOV @R, A	Move A to data memory	1	1
MOV R, #data	Move immediate to register	2	2
MOV @R, #data	Move immediate to data memory	2	2
MOV A, PSW	Move PSW to A	1	1
MOV PSW. A	Move A to PSW	1	1
XCH A. R	Exchange A and register	1	1
XCHA,@R	Exchange A and data memory	1	¯1
XCHD A, @R	Exchange nibble of A and register	1	1
MOVX A, @R	Move external data memory to A	1	1
MOVX @R. A	Move A to external date memory	1	1
MOVP A, @A	Move to A from current page	1	1
MOVP3 A, @A	Move to A from page 3	1	2
MOV A. T	Read timer/counter	1	1
MOV T, A	Load timer/counter	1	1
START T	Start timer	1	1
STRT CNT	Start counter	1	1
STOP TCNT	Stop timer/counter	1	1
EN TCNTI	Enable timer/counter interrupt	2	2
DIS TCNTI	Disable timer/counter interrupt	1	1
EN I	Enable external interrupt	1	1
DIS I	Disable external interrupt	1	1
SEL RB0	Select register bank 0	1	1
SEL RB1	Select register bank 1	1	1
SEL MB0	Select memory bank 0	1	1
SEL MB1	Select memory bank 1	1	1
ENT0 CLK	Enable clock output on TO	1	1
NOP	No operation	1	1

Mnemonic ©Intel	Description	Byte	Cycle
JZ addr	Jump on A zero	2	2
JNZ add,	Jump on A not zero	2	2
JT0 add,	Jump on TO = 1	2	2
JNT0 addr	Jump on TO = 0	2	2
JTl addr	Jump on Tl = 1	2	2
JNT1 addr	Jump on T1 = 0 - -	2	2
JF0 addr	Jump on FO = 1	2	2
JF1 addr	Jump on Fl = 1	2	2
JTF addr	Jump on timer flag	2	2
JNI addr	Jump on FN -T = 0	2	2
JBb addr	Jump on accumulator bif	2	2
CALL addr	Jump to subroutine	2	2.
RET	Return	1	1
RETR	Return and restore status	1	2
CLR C	Clear carry	1	1
CPL C	Complement carry	1	2
CLR FO	Clear flag 0	1	1
CPL FO	Complement flag 0	1	1
CLR F1	Clear flag 1 -	1	2
CPL F1	Complement flag 1	1	1
MOV A, R	Move register to A..,..	1	1
MOV A, @R	Move data memory to A	1	1
MOV A, #data	Move immediate to A	2	2
MOV R, A	Move A to register	1	1
MOV @R, A	Move A to data memory	1	1
MOV R, #data	Move immediate to register	2	2
MOV @R, #data	Move immediate to data memory	2	2
MOV A, PSW	Move PSW to A	1	1
MOV PSW. A	Move A to PSW	1	1
XCH A. R	Exchange A and register	1	1
XCHA, @R	Exchange A and data memory	1	˙1
XCHD A, @R	Exchange nibble of A and register	1	1
MOVX A, @R	Move external data memory to A	1	1
MOVX @R. A	Move A to external date memory	1	1
MOVP A, @A	Move to A from current page	1	1
MOVP3 A, @A	Move to A from page 3	1	2
MOV A. T	Read timer/counter	t	1
MOV T, A	Load timer/counter	1	1
START T	Start timer	1	1
STRT CNT	Start counter	1	1
STOP TCNT	Stop timer/counter	1	1
EN TCNTI	Enable timer/counter interrupt	2	2
DIS TCNTI	Disable timer/counter interrupt	1	1
EN I	Enable external interrupt	1	1
DIS I	Disable external interrupt	1	1
SEL RB0	Select register bank 0	1	1
SEL RB1	Select register bank 1	1	1
SEL MB0	Select memory bank 0	1	1
SEL MB1	Select memory bank 1	1	1
ENT0 CLK	Enable clock output on TO	1	1
NOP	No operation	1	1

INDEX

www.ingramcontent.com/pod-product-compliance
Lightning Source LLC
Chambersburg PA
CBHW081149250326
R18032300001B/R180323PG41598CBX00004B/7